THE REVELATION OF ST. JOHN THE DIVINE

THE REVELATION OF ST. JOHN THE DIVINE

COMMENTARY ON THE
ENGLISH TEXT
BY
AUSTIN FARRER

WIPF & STOCK · Eugene, Oregon

Wipf and Stock Publishers
199 W 8th Ave, Suite 3
Eugene, OR 97401

The Revelation of St. John Divine
Commentary on the English Text
By Farrer, Austin
Copyright©1964 Oxford University Press
ISBN: 1-59752-120-5
Publication date 3/10/2005
Previously published by Oxford University Press, 1964

PREFACE

FOURTEEN years ago I published a study in the Revelation of St. John, under the title *A Rebirth of Images*. The method and approach then set out I have continued ever since to follow in teaching and research upon the text; but I have been led bit by bit to alter the detail of the exposition greatly. I hope that the result is simpler and more unified. I have anyhow been able to dispense with a deal of hypothesis and of invisible machinery.

The form and scope of the present commentary are determined by the purpose for which it was originally designed. It was to have stood in a popular series of commentaries on Holy Scripture, and so I limited myself as far as I could to the essentials of interpretation. The work was still found too long, too difficult, and too speculative. How one is to write anything to the purpose about the Revelation on a level of greater facility, brevity, and common agreement, I cannot conceive; but in saying this I am also saying that I do not think that a school-book can be written on the subject at all. I am most grateful to the Delegates of the Press for their willingness to publish my work independently of the series for which it was intended; and I offer it as the plainest and most readable argument I can write, to establish the mere interpretation of the text.

The form in which the text is offered has no claims to merit, other than those of utility. I have simply made my own revision of the Authorised Version, with much reliance on the Revised Version. My sole object has been to have an English text which represents the Greek as closely as possible. You cannot modernize without paraphrasing a good deal, and without losing important distinctions; for example, between the second person singular and the second person plural. I cannot seriously believe that anyone who is prepared to use my commentary will be troubled by the antique phrases of our traditional English version.

I have commented on the text paragraph by paragraph. This does not mean, however, that the commentary can be dipped into here or there by those who have not read it from the beginning. The Revelation itself cannot be understood otherwise than as a whole, and neither can a commentary written with the express purpose of making that fact clear. Not only is the commentary to be taken as one; the Introduction is also integral to it.

A. F.

CONTENTS

INTRODUCTION

(I)	External Testimony	1
(II)	Place in the New Testament	3
(III)	The Period of the Half-Week	7
(IV)	Problems of the Half-Week Scheme	14
(V)	Continuity, or Recapitulation?	19
(VI)	Nature of St. John's Visionary Experience	23
(VII)	St. John's Written Authorities	30
(VIII)	Date of Composition	32
(IX)	Identity of the Seer	37
(X)	The Johannine Writings	41
(XI)	The Greek Original	50
(XII)	Proposed Method of Exposition	51

COMMENTARY

I. THE LORD'S DAY
(a) Exordium — 59
(b) Vision — 64
(c) Seven Messages — 70

II. THE LION OF JUDAH
(a) The Book — 87
(b) Seven Seals Broken — 96

III. WOES OF THE EAGLE
(a) First Woe — 116
(b) Second Woe — 120
(c) Third Woe — 137
(d) Evangel — 159

IV. THE HEAVENLY MAN
  (a) Seven Bowls   169
  (b) Babylon   180
  (c) The Last Things   196
  (d) Jerusalem   214

INDEX   229

INTRODUCTION

(I) EXTERNAL TESTIMONY

THE Revelation is first mentioned in Christian literature about the middle of the second century A.D. Our authority is St. Justin Martyr, an honest and clear-minded writer. The mention occurs in his *Dialogue with Trypho the Jew*, a book designed to prove the fulfilment of Old Testament promises in the Christian dispensation. More in particular, his Jew wishes to know whether Justin accepts the evidence of certain prophecies which predict a physical rebuilding of Jerusalem, and a gathering there of the elect, with Christ and the Patriarchs. Justin admits that some orthodox Christians hold a view of the blessed future which allows no place to such an expectation; but for his own part, he embraces the hope. There will be a millennium, a thousand years of earthly bliss, after Christ's Advent and before the General Resurrection. Justin establishes the doctrine from the Old Testament, and then proceeds: 'And further, there was a man with us called John, one of Christ's apostles. He prophesied, by a revelation accorded him, that believers in our Christ would fulfil a thousand years at Jerusalem; and that thereafter the general and everlasting resurrection would likewise come to pass, and the judgement of all men.'

The scene of Justin's Dialogue is set at Ephesus, and the Jew with whom he disputes is said lately to have escaped from the war in Palestine. The war referred to is one that ended in A.D. 135. However fictitious the circumstances of the dialogue, St. Justin will scarcely have gone out of his way to be unplausible. No doubt he really had been in Ephesus before A.D. 140, and talked there with learned Jews. Now Ephesus, with six sister-churches, had been the original recipient of St. John's Revelation. The fact gives St. Justin's testimony a special value. For it shows that in the very region of its origin the Revelation was honoured some forty years after we may suppose it to have been written; and accepted there as the work of John the Apostle.

St. Justin went subsequently to Rome, and was martyred there about A.D. 165. Some seven years later, the millennarianism he had innocently professed came into lurid prominence. The Phrygian Adventist Montanus proclaimed an earthly New Jerusalem. The reactions of the orthodox were so sharp that some were ready to throw over not only the Revelation of John, with its millennarian oracle, but even the Johannine Gospel into the bargain; Christ's promise of the Paraclete, as there recorded, being all too convenient to the Montanist propaganda. Such an extravagance of opposition could not last. There was certainly no need to reject a Gospel which teaches anything rather than hot-headed Adventism; all that was required was to interpret it correctly. It proved more difficult to restore the credit of the Revelation. Early in the third century we find the much-respected Roman presbyter Caius still attacking the book in violent terms, and attributing its authorship to St. John's traditional enemy, the heretic Cerinthus.

If we look at what Caius says, we can see that it is Justin's unlucky citation, rather than the Revelation itself, that draws his fire. For Justin had proved the millennarian application of an oracle in Isaiah, by the fact that it speaks of a renovated world where children are still to be begotten. This could not be after the great Resurrection, said Justin, for there would be then no more marrying, or giving in marriage; Christ himself had said it, when he answered the Sadducees. What else, then, could Isaiah's new age be, but St. John's millennium? And so it comes about that St. John (under the hated name of Cerinthus) is accused by Caius of bringing in a millennium, to satisfy unregenerate cravings for sensual delight. In fact St. John's millennarian vision contains not a syllable suggesting such ideas. Nevertheless the mud stuck. Though Irenaeus and Hippolytus defended both the Apocalypse, and its apostolic authorship; though Origen with his allegorizing methods could spiritualize the millennium; nevertheless, just after the middle of the third century, St. Denys of Alexandria, finding himself bothered by millennarians in his patriarchate, took no more than a middle position about the Revelation. The book could, and should, be read in an edifying sense. Still, its authority was in any case limited, for it could not, on critical grounds, be accepted as the work of St. John, the Apostle and Evangelist.

To sum up: there is no tradition reposing on historical memory about the origin of the Revelation, other than that which St. Justin presents. The objections came afterwards and were based either on dogmatic or on literary grounds. The literary question is one which we shall prefer to discuss for ourselves. As to the dogmatic difficulties, however real or unreal they may be, they can have no bearing on historical fact. It cannot be laid down as a principle that no apostle is to be deemed capable of making figurative statements at variance with what later passed for orthodoxy; not to mention the point that the scandal attaching to millennial expectations came from elsewhere, and not from any natural implication in St. John's text.

All positive tradition, then, goes back to a single root; and it affirms that St. John the Apostle saw the Revelation on Patmos. But the tradition, for all its straightforwardness, is not strong enough by itself to convince. The student of early patristic literature is sadly aware that the habit of verifying fact by particular inquiry was largely absent from the mind of the time. Let it be granted that St. Justin, and all the Christian Asia of his day, had a book, already venerable, from the hand of 'John'. Let it be granted that, as Irenaeus records, an older generation had talked to them of listening to 'John' in youth. Was it not an invitation to look up the oldest Christians surviving at Ephesus, and ask them carefully what they knew? Had Irenaeus, had Justin done so, he might have discovered whether their 'John' had been the Son of Zebedee, or some other. There is no reason to suppose, and every reason to doubt, that either Justin or Irenaeus ever took the trouble.

How far, then, will St. Justin's testimony take us? It may assure us that, before the book came under fire from dogmatic criticism, it was accepted in the country of its origin, as a work of apostolic authorship. We may fairly conclude that it was written some decades before A.D. 140; but then we can see that it was, merely by reading it. For any more precise decisions about authorship or date we must rely on such indications as the book itself may be found to contain.

(II) PLACE IN THE NEW TESTAMENT

It must be our first task, then, to get some general idea of the book; we cannot usefully consider date or authorship until we have done so. And if we are to form reasonable views, it will be just as essential for us as it was for third-century Christians to discount our prejudices. We are unlikely to be disturbed by the *millennium* passage (xx. 1–10)—it may puzzle us as an irrelevant curiosity; it will hardly alarm us as an invitation to heresy. Our causes of disquiet will be more general: the unabashed exultation over scenes of divine vengeance, the unhesitating physicality of symbols for heavenly things. No other New Testament writing presents such embarrassing pictures; and we may resent the judgement of the Church, which has included Revelation in the canon of Scripture. Yet to a large extent Revelation merely colours-in what was everywhere taken for granted. We have little reason indeed to suppose that the religious imagination of our other New Testament authors worked any differently from the Seer's. St. Paul suffered an ecstasy in which he was carried up, as it seemed, bodily, through three heavens into Paradise, and heard words too holy to repeat (2 Cor. xii. 2–4). And as for divine vengeance, no New Testament Christian felt any qualms about it. God's mercy was outpoured to save as many as would repent; but the triumph of his power over irreconcilable hostility was to have all the splendour of a victory.

We must not overstate our case—the Revelation is unique; no other New Testament author felt himself called to the same task; no other set himself to capture a visionary experience of the Last Things, by intense and systematic meditation on the whole prophetic tradition. The Seer meditated the scriptural matter into life, and his experience, like every great imaginative experience, was unique. But, like every great imaginative experience, it was also representative. By studying the book, we can learn to feel like primitive Christians about those secret things, which either the vault of heaven above, or the curtain of futurity before, conceals from our eyes. We cannot appropriate all St. John's visionary parables, as they stand, to our own use; it is vain to tell a man to imagine in a way that he finds unimaginable. But, suffering as our religion manifestly does from imaginative starvation, it can find much to feed upon in the Apocalypse, if we make the initial effort of sympathy, and yield ourselves to the movement of St. John's mind.

The Seer of the Revelation made a unique effort to clothe the scheme of Christian prophecy in the stuff of biblical images; the scheme itself was the common property of the Church. It

INTRODUCTION 5

is already to be found in the earliest Epistles, and in the earliest Gospel, that have come down to us.

Whereas St. Matthew gives us five great formal discourses of Christ, among which the Sermon on the Mount is at once the first and the most famous, St. Mark had given one only, the original of St. Matthew's fifth and (it is fair to conjecture) the model for his other four. It, too, is a Sermon on a Mount—the Mount of Olives. Christ is asked when and by what signs his disciples should look for that overthrow of the Temple which their Master has just predicted. He gives an answer which presumes that the violation of the Holy Place will be all one with the End of the Age. He warns his followers against false hopes or false fears. They have a time to face, characterized by natural disasters and desultory persecutions; these will be but 'the beginning-pains of the travail', not the crisis of the birth. The crisis itself will be introduced by the complete visible triumph of paganism, a triumph which Daniel has identified with the suppression of the true worship and the setting up of an idolatrous cult on Mount Zion; and Christ makes Daniel's language his own. The persecution will be frightful, but it will be short. For the salvation of his elect, God's predestining decree has limited the days. Once they have dawned and set, the Son of Man will come with clouds, to reap the harvest of his chosen.

If we put together the teaching of the two Thessalonian Epistles we get essentially the same picture. It is noticeable that St. Paul writes without any display of argumentative proof; he draws on the acknowledged stock of teaching about the Christian hope. The present time, he tells his converts, is one of persecution, but they are not yet to look for the end. Some mysterious condition has yet to be fulfilled before the enthronement of pagan blasphemy in the temple of God; and until this has happened, the Lord will not return. When he comes, he will annihilate the Wicked One, and gather his saints to meet him in the air. Such is the testimony borne by the earliest Christian writings of any kind which have come down to us

It is beside our purpose to examine the almost desperate barrage of argument that has been built up against the authenticity of Christ's discourse on the Mount of Olives. Suffice it to say, that the whole credit of St. Mark is pledged to the truth of his words. He gives the discourse a unique emphasis. Christ, who has proclaimed the coming Kingdom in general phrases, or in riddling parables, at last speaks plain. This is *the* teaching. It may well be that the very centrality of the discourse has led the Evangelist to rephrase it most radically. It is to be remarked that another evangelist, St. Luke, tends to be most drastic in rewriting his material where the passage is most important. It is perverse to refuse credence to the author, merely because he has taken special pains to be clear. St. Matthew has unquestionably systematized the Sermon on the Mount; we do not for that reason reject the teaching it contains. Why adopt a different attitude to St. Mark?

The difficulties felt by theologians on the subject of Christ's prophetical discourse are presented as difficulties of scientific history; they are at bottom difficulties of faith. It is taken as incompatible with Christ's divine authority that he should prophesy what did not literally come to pass. Jerusalem fell, the Temple was destroyed; but its destroyer proved no Antichrist, nor did the Son of Man come with clouds at the end of measured days. It is idle to deny that there is matter here for offence to simple minds. Was Christ's teaching erroneous? Then he was not Christ. But the thoughtful Christian will ask himself wherein he supposes the infallible truth of Christ's teaching to have lain. He must believe that the Son of God made a perfect use of the mental stock he inherited. But what is required, for the use to be perfect? We are not surprised he should have taken the picture of the past as it stood in the tradition; but what about the picture of the future? We do not expect Jesus to dissent from his contemporaries about the historicity of Genesis or the authorship of the Psalms. His view of past events was simply a biblical view. Why should not his view of the future be equally biblical? Is it not enough, if he made a perfect use of the biblical picture as a setting for the interpretation of things divinely happening through his own existence? There is nothing fresh in the prophecy on the Mount of Olives, in so far as it is historical prediction. What is new is the relating of the things predicted to Christ's person and to his disciples' action.

The prophecy was not new; but in its use of old materials it was inevitably selective. Since Christ identified himself with the mysterious figure of the Son of Man, it was natural that his predictive utterances should take form from associated images.

INTRODUCTION 7

The Son of Man is a Danielic emblem inseparable from its context. It stands for a divinely human kingship destined to supplant the brutalized empire of idolatrous power, when that empire shall have summed itself up in a supremely blasphemous and violent tyranny, both persecuting the saints of God and profaning his holy temple. If Christ had identified himself with Daniel's Son of Man, and yet made no allusion to the great sacrilege of Antichrist, it would have been indeed surprising.

(III) THE PERIOD OF THE HALF-WEEK

When Christ tells his disciples that God, out of mercy for his chosen elect, has cut short the days of their great tribulation, he is simply alluding in general terms to an emphatic and repeated prediction of Daniel. It will be no more than 'a time, times, and half a time', or, more explicitly, a half-week of years, from the setting up of the 'desolating abomination' to the hour of deliverance. Daniel also gives the time-count three times over in numbers of days.[1]

The half-week of years (three and a half years) finds its place and its meaning in Daniel ix. In that chapter the prophet meditates on Jeremiah's promise that seventy years would bring the restoration of Zion; seventy years, that is, from her destruction by Nebuchadnezzar. There had, of course, been some sort of restoration within the predicted period, but it had been a disappointing affair. What is now revealed to Daniel is that the fullness of restoration will be achieved in seventy *weeks* of years, the proverbial seventy times seven. Seven weeks of years bring us to the restoration of anointed rule, i.e. of the high priesthood; after which the temple-cult will continue for sixty-two weeks. In the sole remaining 'week' of the seventy-week period the true priestly line will be cut off. The invading tyrant will make a compact with a section—the Hellenizing party—of Israel for one week; for the half of the week he will cause the divine cult to cease; the desolating abomination will usurp its place until divine vengeance falls on the perpetrator.

The suggestion offered by Daniel's chronological scheme is exactly what Christ's saying expresses: Providence has cut short

[1] These counts do not exactly agree. They amount (roughly) to (a) three-and-a-quarter years of lunar months; (b) the same period, counting-in an intercalary month; (c) three-and-a-half years, without the intercalary month.

the days of the great tribulation—has cut them down to half a 'week', the sole fractional period in a series of events measured by whole 'weeks' or by multiples of them.

The most natural inference to draw from Daniel's system is that the terrible half-week is the *second* half of its week, and the end of the whole period. Daniel's text is, indeed, extremely obscure hereabouts, and if we are to take the Septuagint version as our indication of the understanding commonly achieved in New Testament times, we shall be wise to suppose that the thread was lost entirely. But quite apart from any sense they might or might not glean from Daniel ix, the earliest Christian minds had their own strong reason for thinking of the terrible half-week as the end of a week, rather than the beginning. The reason lay in a parallel between Christ's coming in flesh and his return in glory. The parallel was really inescapable and, wherever it may or may not be found, its influence on the Revelation is evident. If there was to be an apparent triumph of Antichrist before Christ's victorious Advent, there had been an apparent triumph of Antichrist also before his victorious Resurrection; and it had filled the end of a week, not the beginning. Christ was seized on a Thursday, suffered on a Friday, and lay in the tomb until the dawn of Sunday.

Christ's apparent eclipse occupied the end of an actual week, a week of days; the great oppression of his Church would occupy a half-week of years. The difference of scale is enormous, but the comparison is in no way forced. If you call forty-two months a *half-week* of years, you compare it with a half-week of days by the very language you use. The parallel did not need to be made; it lay ready to hand in Daniel's wording on the one side, and in the facts of Christ's passion on the other.

It may seem, then, that the fullest and most formal way for a primitive Christian writer to introduce the Danielic half-week of tribulation is to present us with a whole week, and then to mark off the second half of it as constituting that terrible period. And such is St. John's procedure in his Revelation. The pattern comes clearest in the trumpet-visions (chs. viii–xiv). Here a 'week' is introduced—a sevenfold series neither of days, nor of years, but of divine judgements following each upon the blast of one among seven trumpets. In the day of the fourth, that is, of the middle trumpet, an eagle appears flying in the zenith and screams out three woes on the inhabitants of earth from the blasts of the three angels yet to blow. So the last part of the 'week' receives a distinct and a sinister importance. The three last trumpet-judgements are the three woes, a fact emphasized by the marks of punctuation placed between them: 'The first woe has now passed, but there are still two more to come' and 'The second woe has now passed, but the third is soon to come.'

If one is to halve a series of seven, without actually splitting one of the items, one must make a choice between the division $4+3$ and the division $3+4$. Of these two divisions the $4+3$ has everything in its favour. For it emphasizes the Danielic suggestion that the last terrible days are cut short by mercy—they are not even the half of a week; and it squares with the traditional reckoning for Antichrist's apparent triumph in the time of Christ's former advent—Christ had risen 'after three days'.

As we have said, the second half of the week is most clearly and emphatically distinguished in the trumpet-visions of Revelation; and no wonder, seeing that the sacrilege of Antichrist, 'the abomination of desolation', is the principal subject of the trumpet series. But it is not here that the breaking of a 'week' into $4+3$ is first found. The seven trumpets have as their introduction the seven unsealings (chs. vi–vii) and here the division already appears, though in the opposite form. It is not the last three, but the first four that are here grouped together in a series counted separately from the rest. The first four unsealings release four horsemen, themselves matched against the four cherubim. And so we have seven unsealings, beginning with the judgements of the four horsemen; and seven trumpet-blasts, ending with the judgements of the three woes.

The numbered sevens we have mentioned are the middle two of four which give shape to the Revelation: seven messages to the churches (ii–iii), seven unsealings (vi–vii), seven trumpets (viii–xiv) and seven bowls (xvi ff.). It seems probable that the whole count of four sevens is to be viewed as 'a half-week of (halved) weeks'. Such 'squared' numbers were familiar to the Jewish mind. The harvest-season from Firstfruits to Pentecost was a week of weeks, forty-nine days. We have already noticed Daniel's 'seventy times seven'. The Revelation itself gives 'twelve times twelve thousand' as the number of the elect (vii. 4), and 'forty times forty' as the measure of sanguinary judgement (xiv. 20).

The way in which St. John makes a half-week in the trumpets is to take his stand in the fourth, and there to introduce the figure of the eagle, proclaiming three woes for fulfilment in the remaining three. The plan of the whole Apocalypse is not dissimilar. The apocalyptic drama occupies the last three sevens; the first seven, the messages (i–iii), introduce the figure of the Revealer, exhort the recipients, and promise a disclosure of the things that shall be hereafter. They also state the themes of the three sevens to follow. (See below, pp. 83–86.)

The formal scheme, if we have analysed it correctly, is not only elegant in itself; it squares well with the pattern of prophecy in Mark xiii or its Matthaean equivalent. First, there is the day outside the prediction—the day when Christ stands on the Mount of Olives exhorting his disciples and allaying their anxieties. Then there is the first 'day' within the prediction—the day of waiting, the 'beginning-pains of travail'. Next, there is the day of Antichrist, and finally, that of Christ. So in St. John's Revelation. In i–iii the Christ who once walked the earth returns in vision, and gives exhortations to his churches. Chapter iv transports us into the heaven of apocalyptic disclosure: the Lamb who had unsealed prophecy to his apostles unseals it again for the Seer. The first day of the disclosed apocalypse, that of the seven unsealings, finds its centre in the waiting of the saints. The four plagues of the Horsemen are but 'beginning-pains', the end is not yet; the martyr-souls cry 'How long?' and are told that they must wait for the completion of their number through the great Antichrist tribulation: a completion foreshadowed in the remaining visions of the series (vi–vii). The next day, that of the trumpets (viii ff.), brings in the great usurpation of Antichrist (xi, xii–xiii); the last day, that of the bowls, brings the great vision of the Advent Christ (xix. 11–16) and, in sequel to it, the end of the world. The half-week was found by St. John already embedded in the second stage of Christ's prophecy, where it defined the kingdom of Antichrist. While retaining it in that position, he has also (it would seem) made it a frame for the whole prophecy, from the day on the Mount of Olives to the day of Judgement.

We have called the whole Revelation 'a half-week of (halved) weeks', but of the four weeks, or sevens, it contains, we have only so far shown that the middle two are halved. What of the

INTRODUCTION

first week and the last, the seven messages and the seven bowls? There might not seem to be the same occasion for halving them. The 'week' of trumpets is halved, because the actual half-week of Antichrist belongs in the latter half of it; the 'week' of unsealings is halved, by way of introduction to it; for when we have seen a half-week taken out of the *beginning* of the unsealings, our minds are prepared for a compensatory balance in the sequel—a half-week taken out of the *end* of the trumpets. Such a stroke of art does not stand alone. We shall see that a great part of St. John's method is to emphasize the inevitability of each apocalyptic climax, by building up beforehand a pattern which calls for its occurrence. But before the apocalypse proper begins, while Christ is giving messages to his churches, it might not seem there is any call for the halving of the seven; nor again when the days of Antichrist are over, being brought to an end by a perfect sevenfold outpouring of judgement, and by the Advent of Christ.

What in fact do we find? The continuity of pattern over the whole book so far prevails, that a slightly marked halving does appear in the first and last sevens: but it is not nearly so emphatic as in the middle two. The messages fall into two cycles, the last three going back over the ground traversed by the first four: a repetition of themes which, though not in any way stressed, will be found of considerable importance in the development of St. John's vision (see below, pp. 83 ff.). While as for the bowls, they simply take over and maintain a division by four and three which has already played a secondary part in the trumpets. The trumpet-plagues were plagues on the several parts of nature taken in order: on land, on water, and on the starry sky. To get an initial four, St. John divided water into two, salt and fresh; by counting water as one, he had three elements for three final trumpet-plagues to smite. The pattern recurs in the bowls. The first four are poured on earth, sea, freshwaters, sun; the remaining three on the Beast's throne (i.e. on one of the kingdoms of earth), on the Great River, and on the air. Only in the bowls this halving by series of elements smitten is the sole principle of division; in the trumpets it coincides with other marks of bisection, far more obtrusive.

We need not hesitate, then, to affirm our previous conclusion: the whole Revelation has the form of a half-week of (halved) weeks: a greater half-week, embracing four lesser weeks, themselves also halved. But why should St. John use such a form? What way of viewing the Revelation is involved in the presentation of it as a greater half-week? The meaning of the greater half-week is determined by the meaning of the lesser half-week it contains within it; for the sense of the lesser half-week was fixed in the tradition already. It was a literal three-and-a-half years, a period of acute distress limited and cut short by the advent of him who promised that he would come quickly. The greater half-week cannot be a literal forty-two months; but it may be taken as stamping the same essential character on the whole period of waiting from now until the end. It is a time of suffering patience, measured and predestined.

Such a way of viewing the Revelation both accords with previous Christian tradition, and explains certain curious features in the book itself. St. John accepts the established pattern of rabbinic eschatology: the advent of Messiah, the great victory, the millennial reign, the rebellion of Gog, the last judgement, the descent of New Jerusalem, and eternal life in a renovated heaven and earth. But how paradoxical is the way in which he has squeezed these great matters into his book! They appear as short single scenes in the second part of the last act of the drama—in the second part, that is, of the bowls (xix ff.). The strangeness of the fact may be best appreciated by a moment's reflection on the millennial reign. The millennium is part and parcel of a rabbinic speculation on the ages of the world. God made the world in six days, and rested on the seventh, thereby impressing the pattern of the week on all future time. There is the recurrent little week of literal days, from sabbath to sabbath; and there is the one great 'week' of thousand-year epochs, spanning history from the first day to the last. As, then, there have been six working-'days' of a thousand years each, there will be a sabbath rest of the same duration. Only when that has passed, can there follow the dateless day of eternal life.

It must seem, then, that an apocalyptist who entertained the millennial idea at all could contemplate one way and only one for dividing a three-act apocalyptic drama: first, the final working-day age (or what remains of it); second, the millennial sabbath; and third, the age to come. The working-day age will be characterized by the enthronement of idolatrous power, and finally, of Antichrist; the millennium by the enthronement of Christ; the age to come by the descent of God's throne into the heart of a redeemed creation. For a three-act millennarian apocalypse, the scheme seems inevitable, and it is no objection to such a project that there is nothing much to be said about the millennial state. For there is plenty to say about the advent, the victory and the enthronement of Christ: of which the millennium is the simple perpetuation. Nor is such a scheme as this a mere construction of the modern commentator. The materials for it are actually in St. John's text. There is a formal series of enthronements—of Christ and the Saints, replacing the throne of the Beast; of God in the Great Assize and in the world to come. Dovetailing with the throne-series are the pairs of victories (over Antichrist, before the millennium; over Gog before the world to come), and of destructions (of Antichrist to make way for the millennium; of Satan to make way for the final state).

Yet all this cosmic architecture is cramped, as it were, into the bottom right-hand corner of St. John's visionary page. And why? Surely because he is controlled by the theme of the measured days—more narrowly, the half-week of the great tribulation; more widely, the half-week of weeks from now to the fulfilment of Antichrist's overthrow: so that everything which is subsequent to Christ's advent-victory must be squeezed into a sort of appendix. And the scheme of the measured days is no arbitrary imposition; it is only a formalized expression for the pattern of Christ's prophecy. St. John's Revelation is 'the Revelation of Jesus Christ', and the revelation Jesus gave on the Mount of Olives had concerned itself only with the period of endurance up to the advent. The Son of Man comes to gather his elect—that is the last recorded act of the drama; nothing is said about the Last Judgement, the resultant pains or rewards, the institution of a paradisal state, or eternal life. Christ spoke of these great themes in other parts of his teaching; he gave them no place in the prophecy on Olivet. Since the plan and purpose of St. John's Revelation is to colour Christ's outline and achieve fullness of vision, it is inevitable that the great final mysteries should obtain some expression. But they must be content to find their place in the amplification of Christ's advent; Christ's advent was the last act of the Christian Apocalypse.

(IV) PROBLEMS OF THE HALF-WEEK SCHEME

We have assumed that the Revelation essentially consists of four parts, characterized by the four counted sevens, the messages, unsealings, trumpets and bowls. It may be objected that the four sevens, though unquestionably prominent, are mere episodes; the most part of the book not being contained within them at all. There are twenty-two chapters, of which two are covered by the messages (ii–iii), two by the unsealings (vi–vii), four by the trumpets (viii–xi) and one by the bowls (xvi); a total of nine, leaving thirteen still unaccounted for.

But such a statement is more like a debater's case than a reasonable assessment. We must surely allow that the visions directly introductory to the Sevens belong to them. Chapter i presents the author of the messages; iv and v present the sealed book in the hand of Glory which the Lamb is to unseal; while xv simply introduces the bowls. With the addition of their introductory visions, the four sevens cover thirteen chapters, and the proportion above stated is exactly reversed—thirteen chapters covered, and nine so far unaccounted for.

What is more important than mere proportional balance is that the unaccounted-for passages reduce to two. We will describe them provisionally as the sequel to the trumpets (xii–xiv) and the sequel to the bowls (xvii–xxii). Our task is to determine whether these sequels are integral parts of the sections they respectively follow, or whether they are independent unities.

We will begin by a general consideration. The first eleven chapters build up a strong expectation in our minds that St. John will adhere to a scheme strictly contained in series of sevens. No sooner are the seven messages delivered, than he introduces the seven unsealings. No sooner is the last seal broken, than he introduces the seven trumpets. Shall we not naturally suppose that the trumpets will in some manner continue, until another seven is formally introduced? And that this further seven (of bowls, as it turns out) will carry on to the end —unless, of course, there is yet another act to the drama, and another series of seven?

Next let us take a more particular point. The immediate model for the series of trumpets is the series of unsealings which directly precedes. Now the unsealing visions have a progressively expanding form. The first four visions, those of the horsemen, are identical in length, character, and weight; they have two verses each. The fifth is of another form, and noticeably longer. The sixth begins with a vision half as long again, but does not stop there; it runs on through two more visions of steadily increasing length, to reach a total of twenty-three verses altogether. Our minds are prepared for a proportionally greater expansion in the seventh, nor are we disappointed; what the breaking of the last seal introduces is the whole new series of trumpets, which, by a minimum reckoning, runs to sixty-two verses (viii. 2–xi. 18).

The visions of the seventh seal are in length and weight what we were led to expect; their consisting of a new sevenfold series is, on the contrary, nothing but a surprise. The first seven, the messages, completed themselves with their own materials and so ended, before the unsealings were introduced at all. Why should the visions of the seventh seal turn out to be made up of the next succeeding seven, the trumpets? Not only is it a surprise this should be so, it is also a disappointment. We look for the seventh unsealing to open heaven and bring the Advent. But no, the seven trumpets have first to blow, and their blasts to lead us through a series of plagues and portents parallel with those of the horsemen, only a fraction more severe.

The trumpets copy the expanding pattern of the unsealings. Once more, the first four are short and equal, a verse or two each; the fifth runs to eleven verses; the sixth, after a vision matching the fifth in substance and length, runs on in the complex vision of the oath, the scroll and the reed, to a total of thirty-five verses. The seventh trumpet sounds; and there follows—if we reckon-in everything up to the introduction of the bowls at xvi—a series of visions amounting to sixty-one verses.

Hearing the blast of the seventh trumpet, we know that visions of some such weight and length will follow, because it is the whole meaning of the expanding series that they should. But we do not know, perhaps, whether the visions after the seventh trumpet are going to be allowed to be themselves, or whether they will cheat our hopes again by taking the form of another sevenfold series, retracing the old ground of plague, pestilence, and famine. Surely not again; if our hopes were dashed before, was it not that they might now be more joyfully and dramatically realized? Yes; on reflection we know they will be. For the vision directly preceding the seventh trumpet has assured us. In that vision a mighty angel swore by the Everliving God, 'There will be no more delay; but in the days of the seventh angel, when he sounds his trumpet, the hidden purpose of God is fulfilled, according to the evangel he gave to his servants the prophets.' The sort of delay which there might have been, but will not be, when the seventh trumpet sounds, is made clear by the verse directly preceding. Before the angel swears, he utters a great shout, wakening in echo the seven thunders of the sky. St. John is about to write what the seven thunders said—evidently a series of seven thunder-claps, each invoking a judgement, parallel to the series of seven trumpet-blasts, each with its accompanying judgement. A heavenly voice arrests his pen: 'Seal in silence what the seven thunders said; do not write it out.'[1] Why not? The reason follows immediately in the angel's oath. There will be no more delay: in the days of the seventh angel's blast the hidden purpose of God is fulfilled. The seventh trumpet will not be cheated of its evangel, by any sevenfold judgement-series treading over old ground.

The angel's oath, with its thunderous prelude, does more than prepare us for the omission of anything like a seven-thunders series after the blowing of the seventh trumpet. It gives us a positive indication of the matter which the 'days of the seventh trumpet' must include: 'In the days of the blast of the seventh angel, when he shall blow, is achieved the hidden purpose of God, according to the *evangel* he gave his servants the prophets.' If the 'days of the seventh angel' are to cover what is promised here, they must go farther than the descent of Satan, and consequent tyranny of Antichrist on earth (xii–xiii), because these events, taken by themselves, are no evangel. They must extend on as far as the *evangel* of the three angels in xiv. 6 ff., and the double harvest of the righteous and the wicked, which gives substance to it.

[1] By an arithmetical device, as simple as it is effective, St. John allows us to feel that a seven of thunders has actually been struck out from his row of consecutive Sevens. The seven unsealings, with their four horsemen-plagues, destroy a *fourth* of everything: the seven trumpets, with their *three* woes, destroy a *third*. If we are proceeding at this rate, there should be a seven which destroys a *half*, before total, or simple, destruction comes with the bowls. But there is, in fact, no such seven and no such half-destruction.

The great oath of chapter x, with its blessed word 'evangel', is of value in extending the days of the seventh trumpet over chapter xiv. So far as xii–xiii are concerned, we have more obvious and more compelling indications. The scream of the eagle at viii. 13 declares that the remaining three trumpet-blasts will bring three woes on the earth. The woes of the fifth and sixth trumpets take the form of demonic invasions; an army of demon-locusts bring sickness, an army of demon-cavalry bring death. The woe of the seventh trumpet ought to cap the series. But the scene immediately introduced by the seventh angel's blast does nothing of the sort; it is not a woe of any kind, but a short piece of liturgy in heaven (xi. 15–19). We are bound, then, to regard it as no more than introductory to what follows. And what does follow? The greatest demonic invasion of all. Satan, defeated in heaven, comes down to earth full of anger, and having chased the Church into the wilderness, sets up the kingdom of Antichrist, to make war on her children (xii–xiii). As Satan comes down, a voice from heaven in so many words pronounces *woe* upon the earth (xii. 12). If the day of the seventh trumpet is the day of the third woe, it extends at least as far as the end of xiii. The implications of the angel's oath, as we have seen, carry that day a chapter farther on.

We may conclude, then, that the trumpet section extends forward over the whole tract of vision from the blast of the seventh angel to the introduction of the seven bowls at xv. 1. It remains to attempt the same sort of demonstration with regard to xvii–xxii, annexing these chapters similarly to the bowls section which precedes them.

Not that the form is anything like the same. The progressive elongation of the trumpet-visions was a reaching forward, a building towards climax; a way of impressing upon us that the great events would come after the seventh trumpet had sounded. The significance of the bowls is exactly the reverse. The bowls pour final destruction; in them, says St. John, is completed the wrath of God. After all, it is the nature of a trumpet to be the signal of things to come; the pouring of drink-offerings from priestly bowls does not announce anything; it was, in Jewish usage, proverbially the crowning act, the completion of a sacrifice. So, in the pouring of the seven bowls, angelic hands complete the liturgy of judgement. The series goes straight through, without any notable variation of scale. 'It is done', cries a voice from the throne of God, when the seventh bowl is poured. The voice is echoed by a shaking which thunders in the sky and wrecks the cities on earth; Babylon the Great is not forgotten, but made to drink the wine of vengeance.

It is done, but what is done? The Revelation continues by way of comment, or of explanation. The change of form is perfectly expressed, when one of these same angels who have poured the bowls steps, as it were, out of the frame of the picture, and offers to show the judgement of the harlot city. He can scarcely be said to do so in the vision he directly shows and expounds, that is, in chapter xvii. He shows Babylon's royal state, and only touches on her overthrow. But the theme is fully and exultantly developed by further angels, and by heavenly voices, in xviii. 1–xix. 5. The joy is no mere cry of relief over a tyrant's fall; the fall of the harlot, Babylon, is the rise of Jerusalem, the bride, and we are led away by several transitions into visions of the last things; and indeed so far afield, that we might easily forget we are witnessing the fulfilment of divine vengeance, poured out in the seven bowls. The last vision (xxi. 9 ff.) brings us back. We, who saw Babylon destroyed, have just seen Jerusalem descend from heaven; and now a vision of the bride is shown to St. John, in careful parallelism with the vision of the harlot seen in xvii. Once again the interpretative part is undertaken by one of those angels who had poured from their bowls the seven last plagues. St. John could not have more emphatically assigned the end of his book to the section of the bowls.

The purpose of our argument has been to show that the whole Revelation is covered without remainder by the development of four sevens, the messages (i–iii), the unsealings (iv–xi), the trumpets (viii–xiv), and the bowls (xv–xxii). The introductory seven is outside the Apocalypse proper; the remaining three parts are roughly equal, once it has been understood that the unsealings and the trumpets overlap. As to this overlapping, St. John is perfectly conscious, and perfectly consistent. What is the revelatory power which causes the visions of unsealing to be manifested? It is the act of the Lamb in taking the heavenly book and breaking the seals. The breaking of the seventh seal causes the seven trumpeters to appear and to blow; the revelatory power of the seal-breaking will have effect as far as the seventh blast. What revelatory power will carry the Seer onwards after that? In chapter x a great angel descends to assure St. John, by a mighty oath, that after the blast of the seventh trumpet there will be no more delay. At the same time he brings him fresh resources of revealing power, to renew his prophesying and to keep it alive beyond that point. He brings him a book, no longer sealed, but open, and gives it him to feed upon and to digest.

Not only is the renewal of inspiration expressed in terms of the same imagery—the imagery of the book, or scroll—but the imagery is drawn from the same scriptural text, Ezekiel ii–iii. In Ezekiel the scroll is first spread before the prophet's eyes, then given him to eat. There is no question but that St. John develops the spreading in the Lamb's breaking of the seals, and holds over the eating for chapter x, when the Seer is empowered to prophesy on beyond the blast of the seventh trumpet; that blast in which the revelatory force of the spreading, or unsealing, has its last effect.

And it is in the blowing of the seventh trumpet, after all, that the unsealing *should* have its last effect. Christ had said that the first act in the drama of remaining history would be no more than preparatory—the beginning-pains of labour with the Age to Come, not yet the crisis of the birth. St. John has expressed this by associating the previsions of that time with the breaking of seals securing the scroll of prophecy. The document being rolled, and sealed with seven seals along the edge, the breaking of the first six will do no more than allow a little more of the margin to be turned back; the scroll is not open until the seventh is broken. There is the effective beginning of apocalypse —that is, of uncovering or unfolding. Then sounds the trumpet, the alarm-bell of history; and the agony of birth, the battle with Antichrist begins. As to the six previous trumpets, like the spaced warning-shots before the starting-gun, they are but preparatory: they belong to the days of unsealing, not to the hour when the scroll cracks open and history leaps forward.

(v) CONTINUITY, OR RECAPITULATION?

An exposition of the Revelation is at the same time an argument. And it is one of those arguments in which nothing short of the whole story proves the case. So far we have given the merest outline account of St. John's visions. Let us hope it is consistent with itself. It may (for all we have yet shown) be inconsistent with a dozen facts we have not so far troubled to mention. What can you not prove by picking, from an intricate complex, the pieces which suit your case? We cannot ask for more than a provisional acceptance of our construction until we have shown that every line of the book is consistent with it. But before we begin to interpret verse by verse there is one difficulty in the way of our interpretation so huge and so notorious that it demands some sort of previous discussion.

We have written as though the Revelation advanced steadily through three phases of approach to the end: the period of waiting, the days of Antichrist, and the day of the Son of Man; each phase being framed in a distinct sevenfold pattern of counted events. But, on the face of it, it simply is not so. None of the three sevens confines itself within the scope of the phase we have assigned it. As for the unsealings, the first five may deal with the period of waiting, but the sixth begins with the eve of Judgement Day, and ends with the saints' everlasting rest. It is no better with the trumpets. The visions of the seventh trumpet-blast are not concerned with the days of Antichrist alone. In the episode of the woman and the serpent (ch. xii) they go back to Eve in paradise, and touch on the birth of Jesus as well as on his ascension; while in the coming of the Son of Man on clouds (xiv) they anticipate the last act of the whole drama.

What are we to make of these facts? Ought we not to admit that the three sevens are three versions of the whole story, rather than three acts in a progressive drama? Does not each extend as far as the end? There is progress, of course, as we move on from one to another; but is it not progress in fullness of disclosure concerning the same events? Such is the nature of the movement from chapter to chapter in Daniel; and Daniel is not only the model of all apocalypses, it is a principal source of St. John's Revelation. The visions or dreams in Daniel ii, vii, viii, ix, and x–xii cover the same predicted history with certain variations of scope and emphasis; the advance is in explicitness of prediction.

But a second glance at St. John's book will assure us that a simple interpretation in terms of Daniel-style repetition is out of the question. St. John has set the unsealing-plagues, the trumpet-plagues, and the bowl-plagues in a series of progressive destructiveness. They smite the quarter, the third, and the whole respectively; while of the bowl-plagues he writes that they are the last, for in them is consummated the vengeance of God (xv. 1). However much St. John may hark back in reminiscence or forward in anticipation, he leaves unimpaired the systematic sequence of his three plague 'weeks'.

It will be prudent, then, to begin by establishing these plagues on the quarter, the third, and the whole as a genuine succession; and to proceed by attaching to these three fixed points as much of their context as is genuinely inseparable from them. Let us take them in order.

1. The waiting of the martyr-souls is inseparable from the plagues on the quarter. The sense of vi. 1–11 is that the four cherubim pray for the coming of Christ, and their prayers are answered in the riding of the four horsemen; yet still the martyr souls are left crying 'How long?'

2. The kingdom of Antichrist is inseparable from the plagues on the third. For these plagues have their issue and their climax in the three woes, of which the principal and last is a Satanic invasion establishing the throne of Antichrist on earth.

3. The fall of Babylon is inseparable from the plagues on the whole. For these plagues culminate in their seventh, which brings Babylon down.

Now a mere series of sevenfold plagues in order of increasing severity would give us virtually nothing: but the waiting of the saints, the kingdom of Antichrist, and the overthrow of heathendom give us the three essential stages of Christ's prophecy on Olivet. With these points fixed, we can look calmly at seeming irregularities of time in the accompanying material.

1. When the martyred saints are told they must wait for vindication against their oppressors, the delay imposed on them is to last until the martyrs' roll has been completed. The next vision shows us a picture of imminent doom, filling the hearts of their persecutors with terror. A further vision informs us that, if the doom is for the present held back, it is that all the predestined may be sealed with the mark of God. A last vision shows how the divine sealing and the merit of endurance under the great tribulation will have fitted an innumerable multitude for everlasting bliss. How fruitful, then, is the delay imposed on martyr-souls impatient to see the day of their vindication!

2. The kingdom of Antichrist can only be understood as the last violence of that usurpation, to terminate which is to establish the kingdom of Christ and of God. When the seventh trumpet blows we hear heavenly voices proclaim the establishment of the divine royalty, in spite of the rebellious rage of Messiah's enemies. The next vision shows us the picture of the great rebellion, from the temptation of Eve to the crucifixion of Christ. It goes on to show us how the triumph of Christ and of the Church in heaven drives the serpent to a last desperate throw: he raises the kingdom of the Beast on earth, the third and greatest woe, the seventh and last trumpet-plague. After describing the kingdom of the Beast, St. John in one short vision (xiv. 1–5) shows the spiritual kingdom of the Lamb to be unshaken. Then he lets us see and hear three angels, bringing evangel to the obedient and warning to the impenitent (xiv. 6–13). In a few final verses only (xiv. 14–20) prediction passes into vision; we see the figure of the Son of Man come to harvest his elect, while angel hands throw the vintage of wrath into the winepress.

3. The overthrow of Babylon is the immediate sign of Christ's advent. When the harlot Babylon falls, the bride Jerusalem arises, and her conquering bridegroom comes (xix. 11–16). We overtake at this point the advent-mystery so slightly sketched in the last verses of the previous series. The sketch was not only brief, it was allegorical besides. The overthrow of wickedness, whatever it will be, will not be a vintage. It will be more like a conquest; and we are now told in so many words that the warrior Christ is he who treads the vintage of the wrath of God. Moving steadily forward from the great battle, the last visions of the Revelation (and they alone) carry us in an orderly sequence through the destruction of the enemy, the millennial reign, the rebellion of Gog, the Last Judgement, the descent of New Jerusalem, and the glories of the world to come.

What we have just written is the barest summary; but it may suffice to clear St. John from the general charge of a senseless anarchy in the ordering of his episodes or (alternatively) of an unprogressive repetition in the presentation of his drama. The sequence is a sequence of topics—the patience of the saints, the reign of Antichrist, the victory of God. The three topics are each developed as topics, without strict adherence to a single or

INTRODUCTION 23

continous time-scheme. Yet the topics themselves attach to three periods which are in genuine historical sequence.

In following such an order of composition St. John gives us no just cause of complaint. There is not a line in the book which promises us (for example) a continuous exposition of predicted events in historical order. Our difficulties are of our own making; we are the victims of our own unjustified expectations. The secret of reading St. John is simply that of discovering what he is doing, and of being content to let him do it.

After all, what story does St. John undertake to tell us? Not (on the face of it) the story of the world's future destiny under the hand of Providence. If, on the other hand, we say 'The story of his own visionary experiences' we claim too little. For those experiences fall into a systematic pattern, and bear an objective meaning. What, then, is the pattern? Not a pattern of earthly history, but of celestial liturgy performed by Christ and the angels: the taking and unsealing of a book, the offering of incense, the blowing of trumpets; the opening of a heavenly temple, revealing the Ark of the Covenant and a series of other portents on high; the pouring of libations from angelic bowls. It is true that these heavenly actions spill over in earthly effects, and end with the total conquest of earth by heavenly grace. It would be indeed surprising if the sequence of earthly effects made no earthly sense, but we have little right to ask from it an unbroken chain of mundane history.

(VI) THE NATURE OF ST. JOHN'S VISIONARY EXPERIENCE

Now that we have taken a look at the structural complexity of the Revelation, we may usefully consider a question which it very naturally raises. What is the relation between so elaborate a form of composition and the author's claim to visionary experience? Can a book be at the same time the product of spiritual ecstasy and the construction of premeditated art?

The difficulty would vanish, if we could suppose that the angel made the poem and St. John suffered the ecstasy; that he passively received a verbal comment on the visions, as well as the visions themselves. The angel (in effect) dictated the book, St. John wrote it down. But if so, what a very late first-century, Asia-Minor, Greco-Semitic, apostolico-rabbinical angel! Perhaps when angels inspire prophets, they accommodate themselves to the minds of their human instruments so perfectly that you cannot get a knife's edge between the angel and the man. Perhaps they not only limit themselves to their man's stock of words and notions, but are careful to make no movement or transition of thought, other than the man might have made for himself. The whole revelation, then, will be true to the psychology of the recipient. But if so, the angel will have made psychologically correct the combination of visionary experience with hard constructive thinking; and we should be able to understand it as the work of St. John's own mind. The angel does not help us with our problem.

It seems more hopeful to try a more sophisticated formula, and one which has been found widely convenient. Spiritual experiences, we are accustomed to say, are very real to those who receive them, but private in their nature and, in their pristine form, incommunicable. If a man is not only touched by divine realities, but moved also to express them for his fellow-believers, he will be obliged to translate them into symbols of common currency. So let the imaginative and intellectual complexity be the work of St. John's mind; the 'seeings' and 'hearings' which they are employed to interpret may be none the less genuine.

The formula sounds well as a defence of St. John's sincerity; it breaks down completely as an exposition of his text. So far from reading like an attempt to communicate a previous visionary experience, the Revelation reads like a fresh and continuous scriptural meditation, conceived in the very words in which it is written down; as though, in fact, the author were thinking with his pen; a feat not at all out-of-the-way, for have not we all done it from time to time?—perhaps when we were writing a familar letter, and thinking no faster than we wrote.

Had St. John had his audience with him, he might have thought aloud to them with his tongue, as the Spirit moved him—that was the common form of Christian 'prophesying' in New Testament times, and St. John was a prophet. Being separated from his flock by the Roman police, he feels his way to them in addressing them with the pen. His adopting of the literary medium does not and cannot leave the form of his meditation unaffected. Thinking with a pen may be a substitute for thinking aloud; but a man who knows what to do with a pen does not extemporize in ink as he would extemporize in speech. Talking is like dancing—the figure, the product of the action, perishes in the creation of it. Writing is like modelling—the product remains. The writer has a sense of making, or of building, which inclines him to order and to articulate the structure of his work. Whether we talk or whether we write, we shall proceed by drawing out the suggestions contained in what we have already stated; but if we write, our own previous statement lies before us in physical fixity; we can cast our eye over it, we can make it the text of our further developments. No one can write longhand as fast as he might speak; the writer, however spontaneous, has time to ponder and to formulate. There is no reason why an inspired meditation, thought out in the writing of it, should be shapeless or incoherent.

If a visionary mind writes what he is moved to 'see' or to imagine, the words go down on the page, the pictures do not. If the purpose of his writing were to convey shapes and colours, the result might be what is called word-painting; the visions would remain in control of the words, even though words, not pigments, were the medium of expression. But if his purpose is to let the visions speak, to convey not so much the look as the meaning of them, then the words will surely wrest control from the pictures, for words are the very embodiments of meaning. The words go down on the page in a relentless chain, each linked by the sense to its predecessors and determining the choice of its successors. What can the mental pictures do but fall into line with the march of words? The result will be more like a story illustrated with appropriate drawings than a set of plates round which a story is somehow woven.

It is only under exceptional circumstances that the visual imagination takes us by surprise, or imposes on our waking life visionary objects we had neither the wish nor the expectation to see; and even when this does happen, psychological wisdom will find the causes in the action of wishes or of thoughts no less real in us because hidden from us. Imagining is not like seeing, where the picture is presented by an independent object; it is like painting in evanescent colours. As in day-dreaming, we imagine what we will and paint our changing picture over and over as our thought moves. We often do not know whether we are dreaming pictures or telling ourselves tales; the streams of vision and discourse melt into one another and direct one another in the smoothest, the most natural way.

What, then, is an inspired visionary experience? It is inspired; that is, the recipient falls under a supernatural control. He is convinced that he does not wilfully think or see what comes to him. He is led where he goes, shown what he perceives, and told what he formulates or understands. It may be that in such an experience compulsive vision holds a dominant part; the points at which divine communication is most strikingly imposed are points of sudden unexplained invasion by figures of a waking dream. But it need not be so, and more usually is not. A whole process of imaginative meditation, strung on a thread of words and clothed with various sensory phantasms, appears somehow to think itself in the mind; or rather, to be thought in the inspired heart by the Spirit of God. The man is not free to alter it, but he was not fettered in thinking it. The control of our Creator is not an alien control, preventing us from being ourselves. The more he directs us, the more we are what we have it in us to be.

St. John sees—he meditates into vision what he writes, and feels the presence of the mysteries he describes. But such vision can be achieved by a man working from words. The rabbis held that the most perilous technique of ecstasy was a meditation on the complicated text of Ezekiel's first chapter. St. John takes the risk; in the fourth chapter of his Revelation he sees his way into heaven by the use of Ezekiel's and of several overlapping scriptural texts. He claims to see, he claims equally to hear; both claims find their place under the claim to write by dictation.

We are inclined to carry away the impression that St. John is visited on Patmos by a visionary figure who commands him to write. But if we look at the text of his first chapter we shall discover that he is commanded to write, before he 'sees' anyone or anything. 'I find myself in the island called Patmos . . . I find myself caught up by the Spirit on the Lord's Day, and hear a loud voice behind me, like the sound of a trumpet: "Write down what you see on a scroll and send it to the seven churches. . . ." I turn to see whose voice it is that spoke to me, and turning, see seven standing lamps of gold. . . .'

The ancient author adopted the time-position of his readers

and referred to his present condition in the past tense. 'I wrote you this from Ostia; I was in excellent health. The purpose of my writing was to convey. . . .' St. John's past tenses are thoroughly ambiguous. He may be writing an account of visionary experiences after the event, or he may be writing his way through them, as the rendering I have just given suggests. How are we to decide which thing it is he means? Surely by the evidence of those passages where figures speak out of his vision and tell him to write this or that (i. 19–20; ii. 1, 8, 12, 18; iii. 1, 7, 14; x. 4; xiv. 13; xix. 9). It is very unnatural to suppose that the command is 'When you come to write up an account of your experiences, do not omit to mention . . .'. It has the urgency of an immediate dictation.

If we follow these indications in reading the passage we transcribed above, what will it tell us? Will it not be that the writer has fallen under the hand of the Spirit and must write a visionary meditation, as it is given him, for the benefit of the seven churches? He proceeds to 'turn himself' so that he may obtain a sight of the Divine Person under whose command he stands; and this he does (if we are to judge by the written evidence) through meditating into a new unity several old scriptures relevant to his purpose. Out of the vision spring the messages to the churches; just how, we will leave for the Commentary to explain.

When St. John looked to see the Jesus who had spoken to him, he looked for him in the candlestick-vision of Zechariah— and no wonder, for Jesus was there: Jesus the High Priest, of whom it was so mysteriously said, 'Behold the man, the branch his name.' Was not this as much as to say that the son of Josadek was a foreshadowing of the Son of God, the promised branch from David's stem? As St. John looked at the high-priestly figure, it clothed itself with the glory of angelic apparitions elsewhere described in scripture, and even with those features of divine majesty which no angel can do more than represent.

St. John had an authoritative matter for meditation in the scriptures: Zechariah, Ezekiel, and Daniel are, with Exodus and Isaiah, his favourite texts; but there is scarcely a canonical writing to which he does not somewhere probably allude.

The scriptures provide not only his sources, but his models; the sources of his meditation, and the models for the visionary drama in which that meditation takes shape. If we say that St. John's Revelation is a visionary work, we can mean either of two very different things. We can mean that it is the fruit of visionary experience, or we can mean that it adopts the form of a story about visions. As to the experience which gave rise to the book, we have said what we have to say, and decided that it was inspired and meditative, more verbal than strictly visionary. But a non-visionary inspiration need not stand in the way of the poet's telling a story about visions. Why should it? If a poet writes a heroical epic, the poem is the fruit of poetical experience; but no one expects that experience to take the form of banging about with obsolete weapons. No more need a poem about a vision spring from visionary experience. No one, indeed, would want to write about pure visionary experience if no one had ever had it; nor about heroic battle, if no one had ever fought with sword and spear. But Homer is not Achilles, nor need the author of Revelation be a simple visionary.

The prophets of Israel had seen visions, and recorded them. The visions, perhaps, had been simply seen. But they existed for St. John and his contemporaries in the form of written texts. St. John, taking example by the ancient prophets, might have done for himself what they did; he might have gone out into the street or into the field, he might have gazed about him with a divinatory eye, he might have felt some natural object or event stand out in bodeful prominence, and turn into the speaking sign of a divine message. But he did no such thing; he looked at the written records of these ancient visions until they fused into fresh shapes, expressive of a fuller truth. And since the scriptural images existed for him in written words, the fusion and new-minting of them in his mind would naturally be a literary process. It was equally natural that the process should issue in descriptions of vision, since vision was what the old prophets' written words depicted.

St. John's prophetic consciousness is undeniable. His book is 'this prophecy' (i. 3, xxii. 18), he is commanded to prophesy (x. 11), the angel of his inspiration is 'a fellowservant with him and with those who hold the testimony of Jesus—the testimony of Jesus being the spirit of prophecy' (xix. 10) or, as is more simply said in xxii. 9, 'a fellowservant with him and with his brethren the prophets'. Like an Isaiah or a Jeremiah, he loses his identity, as he speaks, in the person of the Lord (xvi. 15, xxii. 6–20).

It is commonly said that St. John's prophetic consciousness is unique in the New Testament world. The line of living prophecy had indeed revived in the Church, but the Christian prophet was an inspired preacher, or on occasion a soothsayer and walking oracle, like Agabus (Acts xi. 28, xxi. 10–11). No such man, to our knowledge, thought himself called upon, as St. John did, to add an inspired volume to the prophetic shelf. There is truth in this contention. Yet the singularity of St. John's commission need have risen out of nothing else but the singularity of his situation. Other Christian prophets were doubtless imprisoned; but in the common case the prisoner could be visited, and suffering confessors preached from behind their bars. But St. John had been transported. He was compelled to address his churches with the pen, and having fallen into the scriptural vein, found that he must write them a new Ezekiel.

However that may be, the claims St. John makes for the inspiration of his book are unmistakable. Blessed are those who read, hear, and obey it; it is what the Spirit says to the churches; it contains the very words of God. Christ assumes the person and the pen of the prophet to witness its truth; its words are sacrosanct, and any tampering with them is inexpiable sin.

The prophecies of Ezekiel or of Zechariah had been oracles or visions delivered at various times and, as every student knows to his pain, very imperfectly arranged on the pages in which we find them. St. John's comparatively artificial task of writing a new canonical prophecy enables him to do what no ancient prophet attempted—to make a whole prophetical collection a dramatic masterpiece. Modern taste may sometimes find his images stale or grotesque by comparison with their Old Testament models. His unique excellence, from a literary point of view, lies in the steady building of climax, and the movement of the whole to its inevitable end. There had been many apocalyptic books from Daniel onwards, some of which, and above all the Book of Enoch, were known to St. John. Yet none of them attempts the complex symbolical unity which he achieves. Neither does any of them claim to be a new prophecy in its own right, issuing from a living author. They all claim the dead authority of ancient names.

(VII) ST. JOHN'S WRITTEN AUTHORITIES

It belongs to St. John's character as a new prophet that he scarcely ever quotes a whole sentence from his predecessors. Everything he writes must be freshly phrased or at least freshly combined. No author cites so little and alludes so much. Such a principle of composition is no affectation; it is not that he studiously avoids a continuous quotation which would be natural and convenient. It is that, like the rabbinic preacher of his time, he seeks new inspiration by drawing old texts into fresh combinations. The procedure belongs to the very grain of his thought.

The ancient scriptures are authoritative with him, but their authority is that of starting-points, rather than limits. The unique status of what we now know as the canonical books is unaffected by such a manner of using them. He works from the Old Testament as he works from no other writings. His way of developing scriptural themes may often seem to be influenced by secondary works such as First Enoch. But Enoch is itself dependent on the Old Testament much as St. John is. It is a case of one preacher or expositor following another in his line of exposition. By so doing, he does not set his predecessor on a level with the scripture they both expound. There is much in the Revelation which presupposes a knowledge of scriptural texts and is scarcely meaningful without it. There is nothing which requires of St. John's reader an acquaintance with the Enochian visions. We may ask, however, into which category St. John put the Apocrypha, books acknowledged at Alexandria but excluded from canonical authority by the synagogues of Palestine and of Babylonia. We have little evidence on which to judge. Perhaps it would be proper to say that Wisdom xviii. 15–16 is one of the scriptures underlying Revelation xix. 11–15. Whether or not St. John used Wisdom as a text, he would seem to have used it as a guide in his interpretation of God's judgements, and especially of the Egyptian plagues.

But the supreme guide is Jesus Christ. As the Johannine Gospel says, he is the Way; that is, the *halacha*, the clue to the sense of the old Scriptures. He alone, in the imagery of Revelation v, is able to take, to open, or to scan the Book. The tradition of Christ's life and teaching has unique importance, not as standing beside the ancient scriptures, but as unlocking their treasures. And so we are brought to ask, in what written form (if it was in written form) the tradition of Christ lay before St. John.

We must hold over for the moment the very difficult question of the relation between the Johannine Apocalypse and the Johannine Gospel. We shall incline to judge that the Revelation is the older writing of the two. Even if the Gospel was the older, would the Seer take it as an authoritative source of tradition, or as being what the Revelation itself was to be—an inspired meditation on that tradition? Perhaps there was an older writing, standing behind our Fourth Gospel, somewhat as St. Mark stands behind our First; and perhaps this was a written authority for our Seer. Who can tell? The question can be asked; it cannot be answered. We could only hope to reconstruct a 'proto-John' from the Johannine Gospel as we have it; and if 'proto-John' contained an account of Christ's apocalyptic prophecy, our Johannine Gospel has in any case omitted or effaced it. It contains no detailed scheme of things to come, on which an Apocalypse could be constructed.

We may use the Fourth Gospel again and again to illuminate the development of the Seer's thought. It is the illumination cast by a parallel meditation. This was how men thought in Christian Ephesus about the turn of the century. In a lesser degree, we may derive the same sort of help from other New Testament writings— The Epistles to the Thessalonians and to the Romans, the First of St. Peter, and that to the Hebrews. Any of these St. John may, indeed, have read. But if he had read them, they did not so much supply him with data as suggest lines of development.

We have assumed, on the contrary, that something like the Synoptic account of Christ's prophecy on Olivet was a datum for St. John. Is it possible to guess in which form the synoptic story came to him? He would seem anyhow to have known Matthew's rewriting of Mark, to judge from a number of allusions; compare Revelation xii with Matthew i. 23–ii. 23 and Revelation i. 7 with Matthew xxiv. 30. That he knew or used Mark independently of Matthew may be difficult to prove; what Marcan features are there relevant to his purpose, other than those which Matthew reproduces? He would seem also to have known the Lucan writings; compare Revelation ii. 24 with Acts xv. 28, where not only the phrase but the context also corresponds. In the tradition of Christ's prophecy St. John follows the Marcan–Matthean form in the main, employing Luke in supplement to it whenever it suits him to do so. For example, St. John's setting of the fall of Jerusalem within the scheme of prophecy (Rev. xi. 2) appears to be exactly what is stated in Luke xxi. 24. On the other hand much that is basic for St. John has vanished from St. Luke entirely; notably, the false prophet and the Antichrist abomination. They must be looked for in Matthew xxiv. 15 and 24.

Beside our New Testament books, St. John will probably have known Christian writings since lost to the Church. We have no reason to suppose that, if he had such writings in his hands, he made a use of them different from the use he made of the books we know. It has frequently been held in recent years that he embodied whole passages from lost books, whether Christian or Jewish; or again, that his Revelation is essentially a re-editing of earlier work. No such hypothesis is tenable. The book, just as it is, grows and branches out of itself, like a tree. The incoherences formerly explained by the presence in the text of imperfectly digested older fragments were the products of scholarly misunderstanding. Only see what St. John is doing, and you have refuted every hypothesis of the kind.

Equally unhelpful and gratuitous is the supposition that the book was written in sections and at different dates; that the first three chapters were composed by themselves, and the rest by afterthought; or the last nineteen written first, and the first three later prefixed; or again, that the concluding visions were added to an apocalypse which went no further than the overthrow of Antichrist. There is no need to discuss such hypotheses separately. All that is required is to exhibit the unassailable unity of the book, and the continuity of its development. Naturally, no one can prove that St. John wrote the whole at a sitting. For all we know, he may have knocked off for several days or several weeks here or there in the process of composing it. All one can say is, that if he did, the cracks do not show.

(VIII) DATE OF COMPOSITION

In xvii. 10–11 St. John has inserted a note which promises a simple answer to the question of the book's date. It was written under the sixth of a series of emperors. Our sorrows

INTRODUCTION 33

begin when we try to decide who was the first. Was St. John counting the dynasty from its founder, or the persecuting princes from their original? Perhaps we can settle that question to our satisfaction; but when we have done so, our trouble is not at an end. It is still open to doubt which Caesars we should count in and which exclude. In the year after Nero fell three aspirants to the purple reigned for a few months each. Does St. John reckon them, or pass them over? Probable answers may be found to the questions which xvii. 10–11 raises; but not without the assistance of other texts in the book.

Great weight must fall on the fact that the coming of Antichrist is detached from the destruction or profanation of Jerusalem, and connected with the overthrow of 'Babylon'. In chapter xi the tradition connecting the violation of the holy city with Antichrist is rehandled, and virtually got rid of. The giving over of Jerusalem to the Gentiles is made to mark the beginning of a period still current, during which the dual prophetic witness continues unbroken, to the confusion of the Church's enemies. The period is to be terminated, not initiated, by 'the Beast who comes up from the abyss'. He kills the witnesses. The great usurpation of Antichrist is more fully described in chapter xiii. St. John so far departs from tradition as to direct his 'proud boasts and blasphemies' against no earthly Zion, but against 'the Name and Tabernacle of God in heaven'. His false prophet sets up a magical image of him; but not (for anything we are told) in the Temple of God. The association of the Antichrist abomination with the desolation of Zion is as fixed in Matthew and Mark, not to name 2 Thessalonians, as it was in Daniel. St. John's alterations are difficult to explain, except on the supposition that he was writing some time after the fall of the holy city, and even after the profound emotion stirred by the event had largely died down.

If this is so, St. John cannot be counting Caesars from the first Caesar; for if he were, Nero would be that sixth under whom he writes, and Jerusalem would be standing yet. Nor can he be counting a reigning house from its first emperor; for the Flavian House only produced three heads, not six; while to count from the next new beginning, in Nerva, will make St. John later than St. Justin Martyr. To lump together the Flavian family and Nerva's adoptive 'family' would be unreasonable, since Nerva came in through revolution and assassination, just as Vespasian did. And even if we commit such a violence against historical fact, it does us little good, for the sixth who reigns will then be Hadrian; and we cannot date the Revelation so late as c. A.D. 120.

St. John cannot, then, be counting the dynasty. He must be counting the Antichrists, that is, the persecutors, from their great original; and if so, Nero has the strongest claim to be the first; for the persecution of Christians remained an institution from his time, whether or not it was put into use. Caius (Caligula) had, it is true, planned an insult against the Temple of Jerusalem, but it was not carried into effect. The Judaised Sibylline Oracles, in a passage which seems to date from c. A.D. 125, give a sketch of the Roman Emperors from Julius to Hadrian (Bk. v, lines 1–50). The Sibyl mentions Caius without comment; she spreads herself on Nero's enormities. A Christian had even stronger reasons than a Jew for tipping the scales the same way.

If Nero is the 'first head' of Revelation xvii. 10–11, we still do not know for certain who the sixth is; because of the three pretenders to the purple who reigned a few months each after Nero fell, and whom St. John might either count in or count out. Nor can we say there is any superior probability on either side. If he wrote in A.D. 80 he would naturally count them in, because the drama of their battles was a recent memory; if he wrote in A.D. 100 he might as naturally count them out, since they had made no mark on imperial history. The Sibyl, writing (as we have said) c. A.D. 125, speaks, as usual, with an ambiguous voice. She mentions the three pretenders, but she lumps them in a phrase: 'Three monarchs who kill one another.' She does not identify them, as she does the other emperors, by ciphers on the initials of their names. So she can be quoted as authority either for leaving them out or for counting them in; but not for discriminating between them—a proceeding hard to justify in any case, Sibyl or no Sibyl.

It follows that 'the sixth now reigning' is either Titus or Trajan; the hardest name of all to get is Domitian, since it involves putting in two pretenders, and omitting one. (At a pinch, we might have one, Galba, the legitimate heir of a just revolution; we can scarcely have two, without the third.) Yet

INTRODUCTION   35

Domitian's is the name given by St. Irenaeus—'the Revelation was seen towards the end of his reign'—and all tradition has followed him, like a flock of sheep. Since the end of Domitian's reign (96) is nearer to the beginning of Trajan's (98) than to the end of Titus's (81) we must take St. Irenaeus as an inaccurate witness in favour of an early Trajanic date; which seems, indeed, the most probable on several grounds.

An indication which, like other indications, proves inconclusive, is the predicted return of Nero. Nero was killed in A.D. 68 at the age of thirty-one. His death was widely disbelieved and his return hoped for or dreaded; pretenders did not fail to exploit popular expectation. Now it is probable that St. John's identification of the coming Antichrist with an imperial head smitten to death and healed amounts to a prediction of Nero's return. The question remains, whether the Seer means that Nero was actually killed, or only seemed to be. If he only seemed to die, he must be expected to return with enough life and strength in hand to play his tremendous part. If he had in fact survived, Nero would have been forty-two when Titus succeeded, sixty-one when Trajan did. Since by St. John's reckoning there were still some years to pass before Antichrist was to come, we should not, on this hypothesis, want to date his book any later than Trajan's first years.

But the hypothesis may be wrong. Perhaps Nero really is taken to be dead: he is going to return either as a vampire, or (more prosaically) in the person of another tyrant. If that is what St. John means, then he is likely to be writing at a time when Nero's literal return has been given up; when Nero-haunted minds, unable to rid themselves of their obsession, recast it in a form not implying Nero's physical survival. According to this hypothesis any year in Trajan's reign is a natural enough time for St. John to write.

We have agitated an inconclusive discussion long enough to convince our readers that the Revelation cannot be dated with accuracy from its apparently precise dynastic references. The conclusion is disappointing, but by no means surprising. We want St. John to tell us under what emperor he writes, but that is the one thing he did not need to tell his original audience. Knowing that 'the Sixth who now reigns' is (let us say) Trajan, and finding Nero hinted at as one of a previous five, they knew that they had to discount the three pretenders of the year 69 if they were going to get Nero into the picture.

If we cannot securely date by St. John's emperor, still less can we do so by his persecution-situation. To begin with, it is not clear what that situation is. St. John knows on dogmatic grounds that Antichrist will come, and he sees the Antichrist-abomination as the ruthless development of an emperor-cult already in conflict with the Church. But what is the occasion of his writing? Is it to awaken churches, whose situation is deceptively easy, to a sense of their danger, or is it to comfort suffering confessors with the assurance of their victory? St. John mentions a past martyrdom at Pergamum, not (it would seem) very recent; and a threat of imprisonment overhanging the Smyrnaeans through Jewish delation. But the general theme of his messages is an attack on laxity and compromise with heathen ways. Are not the churches too comfortable in their heathen world?

We cannot, then, be sure what the persecution-situation is in St. John's seven churches. And if we could be sure, we should be little helped towards dating his book. Anyone who has explored the first hundred years of persecution-history, and observed the failure of learned historians to establish reliable landmarks along that featureless road, will be inclined to abandon the inquiry at sight. From Nero's time onwards Christian believers could always be delated by malicious neighbours on a capital charge, whether that charge was Christianity or something called by another name. We know, positively, that there were outbreaks of persecution in certain places and at certain times, involving the martyrdoms of certain persons. Negatively, we have not the evidence to date periods free from persecution in any given area which may happen to interest us. And if we are to speak, not of what happened, but of what might be feared, it becomes doubly preposterous to dogmatize. We cannot name a single year, say between A.D. 80 and 110, in which St. John could have had no grounds for supposing that persecution was about to be intensified in Roman Asia.

A more general indication of date might be sought in the development attained by certain theological ideas. We might dismiss this inquiry too, on the ground that there was no uniformity in the rate of theological development. Still, for what it is worth, we may remark that, alone among New Testament writers, St. John greets his friends from the Holy Trinity. It is true that neither the order nor the description of the Persons is in accordance with later usage; but the fact remains. Again, we may remark that St. John goes to every length in according Christ the names and attributes of deity. The description of him as the Ancient of Days (i. 14) is a visionary justification for the saying in the Johannine Gospel, 'He that hath seen me hath seen the Father.' It would be foolish to say that St. John's language could not have been used (even) in St. Paul's lifetime; but it can fairly be said that it finds a natural place about the turn of the century.

What, if anything, is the upshot of our discussion? On the count of emperors, Trajan is the likeliest ruler for the time of St. John's writing. The suggestion of xvii. 10–11 is, if anything, that imperial heads are falling fast. A date early in the reign is most natural, then. In fact Trajan reigned a score of years; but in his early days a visionary was not to know it would be so. No other indications are irreconcilable with a date about A.D. 100, except Irenaeus's statement dating by Domitian's reign, and the tradition subsequently built upon it.

The apparent position of the Revelation in the sequence of Christian writings points the same way. If the author knew St. Matthew and St. Luke's books he will not have been writing before A.D. 85 at the soonest; nor much after A.D. 100 if, as we are going to suggest, his work prepared the way for the Fourth Gospel. But the datings of all these books are like a line of tipsy revellers walking home arm-in-arm; each is kept in position by the others and none is firmly grounded. The whole series can lurch five years this way or that, and still not collide with a solid obstacle.

(IX) THE IDENTITY OF THE SEER

The writer calls himself 'John', a common Jewish name. A John at this date would be an Israelite. The name was not adopted by Gentile Christian families until later. And, from the character of the writing, we could scarcely doubt the nationality of the author. In Colossians we find a critical account of the tendencies of an Asianized Judaism, an influence which St. Paul resists. Whether this Judaism is half baptized, or not baptized at all, may be open to dispute. If we think of a baptized rabbi of the school who has fully digested St. Paul's lessons, we may have an author for Revelation. The Colossian teacher attacked by St. Paul is firm on Jewish food-rules (Rev. ii. 14 and 20), is deeply interested in angelology, and accused of angel-worship (in Rev. xix. 10 and xxii. 8 St. John is about to worship his angel); is strict about the calculation of days from the heavenly bodies, interesting himself in science, and the elements of the world, as well as in Jewish traditional lore; above all, he 'expatiates on the visions he has seen', a thing St. Paul declines to do in 2 Corinthians xii. In Revelation the visionary experiences, the calendrical schemes and symbolisms of the elements, the Jewish lore, the angelology, and the strictness of legal rule are brought into entire subjection to Christ; but they are all there nevertheless. The only element in the Colossian picture which finds no reflection in Revelation is the Hellenistic-Jewish propaganda-trick of passing off ritual tabu as philosophic asceticism (Col. ii. 23).

As we said above, our only positive tradition, and a tradition as old as St. Justin Martyr, identifies this Asianized Jewish visionary with the Lord's Apostle, son of Zebedee and brother of James. The tradition was early challenged, on two grounds, one of which is certainly irrelevant, the other probably so. The first ground was dogmatic prejudice; the second, a recognition of the stylistic difference between the Revelation and the Fourth Gospel. Such a difference only tells against the Apostle's authorship of the Revelation, if the Apostle wrote the Gospel. And we may well judge that, if he wrote either book, it is more likely to have been the Revelation.

In modern times it has been argued, on evidence so slender as to seem frivolous, that the Apostle can have written neither book, because he suffered an early martyrdom, like his brother James. If, on the other hand, we accept the much better supported tradition of his longevity, we may propose the following suppositions. The Apostle was a dozen years younger than the first Christian century. Though a Galilean fisherman by origin, he absorbed Asian rabbinism in the course of half a century's apostolate, exercised mainly (if we like to think so) in the Asian region. He saw the Revelation on Patmos in his middle eighties. It is a possible, but scarcely a likely tale. Would an active apostolate turn a fisherman like Peter into a rabbi like Paul? Did an amazing effort of imaginative creation take place in the mind of a man of eighty-five or more, who, so far as we know, had never before composed a literary work? One would be inclined to knock thirty years off the Seer's age.

If the Seer was not the Apostle, was he, in calling himself 'John', claiming to write in the Apostle's name? There is nothing either shocking or unlikely in the suggestion; to write in the name of a sainted predecessor was not a fraud, but a sign of humility and a source of inspiration; an extension of the principle which may bid a Christian preacher preach St. John or St. Paul, and not himself. The custom was anyhow widespread among Christians as well as Jews.

But the hypothesis allows of a very limited application to the case in hand. If St. John has died, and another writes in his name, it must be within a matter of months. Let St. John have died on Patmos (say) under Nerva, and a learned disciple at Ephesus be inspired in visions to reveal the Saint's mind to the churches, say after Trajan's accession. Then Trajan may be the seventh 'head', whose supposedly short reign St. John, imagined as writing under Nerva, had foreseen; and the white-hot exhortations and rebukes to the several churches, though supposedly launched some months previously, will still find their targets.

If we extend the time-interval between the Apostle's death and the visionary's writing, absurdity results. Suppose St. John died under Vespasian and is imagined to be prophesying in that reign, by a writer of Trajanic date. Then Vespasian is 'the sixth who now reigns', Titus the short-lived seventh, Domitian Antichrist, and the recipients of the Revelation are living after the end of the world. Moreover they are called upon to hear divine messages directed to particular occasions in the several churches, and all, according to the dramatic setting, thirty years out of date.

The hypothesis, even in its more possible form, seems hardly worth supporting. The high prophetic consciousness of the author does not read like a self-dramatization in the role of another man. Nor does the pretended apostle hint (as one would expect him to hint) at his own imminent death.

If the name 'John' is not that of the Apostle, either written with his own hand, or borrowed by another, is it the name of any other John known to history? There is only one candidate worth considering. St. Justin's contemporary Papias, an Asian bishop, left a book about the Christian tradition, now lost but for a few quotations. He distinguished the Apostle John from an Elder John, very likely to be understood as a venerable Asian bishop; and it seems quite possible that this Elder, and not the Apostle, was the 'John' who was quoted as a master of his youth by Polycarp, the long-lived bishop of Smyrna; even though our witness to his words, St. Irenaeus, writing in his later years, supposed Polycarp to have been talking about the Apostle. Polycarp was born about the year 70, and we may suppose that the John he quoted had been alive in Polycarp's twenties, i.e. from A.D. 90 to 100, when we conclude the Revelation to have been written.

If the Elder John was so great a figure, mentioned with awe and mistaken for his namesake the Apostle, on what was his greatness founded? It would have a solid foundation indeed, if he was a teacher able either to write or to inspire the Johannine Books.

We may pause at this point to remove a rank red herring drawn across the trail by Eusebius the Church Historian. Assuming that John the Apostle wrote the Gospel, and casting about for a different John on whom to father the Revelation, he pitched upon the figure of Papias's Elder. We need not make Eusebius's initial assumption. We may consider the Johannine writings as a group, and see, if we can, what hand the Elder may have had in any of them.

The Epistles of John do not contain his name. The First Epistle (so-called) is, indeed, a treatise or written homily, not an epistle: it has neither signature nor address; it tells us nothing about its author. The Second and Third are the letters of an anonymous 'Elder' of apostolic, or metropolitan, standing, with authority to call a local church-leader to book.

The Fourth Gospel is as anonymous as are the other Gospels. But it contains the figure of the Beloved Disciple, which (in spite of all that has been argued to the contrary) it seems proper to take as a portrait of St. John the Apostle. It ends with an enigmatical note about him: 'This is the disciple who bears witness of these things, and wrote these things; and we (i.e. the author and his fellows) know that his witness is true' (xxi. 24). Even if the critical opinion be accepted which assigns the last chapter of the Gospel to a second hand, it remains that it is written in character with the rest, and as though from the same pen; and it is quite illegitimate, therefore, to take the 'we' as standing for the writer of chapter xxi, who, with his group, confirms the veracity of the writer of i–xx. No; either 'And who wrote these things' means 'who left a written testimony, which we have used in this book' or the phrase is unauthentic, the gloss of an early copyist.

In conclusion: neither the Gospel nor any of the Epistles claims to be written by a man called John. The Gospel claims to rely on the authority of the Apostle John; who had not, after all, lived to see the Lord's return, but had outlived his fellow-apostles and handed down his tradition, perhaps written, more likely unwritten, for the use of a nameless Evangelist. Since, then, the other books are anonymous, while the Revelation is the personal prophecy of a John, its claim to be considered as the work of John the Elder is without a rival. The other Johannine books may be the Elder's, too; but only if they appear to come from the hand which wrote the Revelation.

Is it not rash, however, to assume that there can have been only one John in Roman Asia at the turn of the century? Why not allow two: John, a prophet, who saw the Revelation, and John the Elder, who instructed Polycarp? Why, because the author of the Revelation is not simply a prophet. His prophecy is contained in a pastoral letter to the seven churches. One cannot doubt that he was a figure of high pastoral authority. His name, John, is enough. He writes as if there were no other John. And it will be surprising if there was another, the great light of Asia, revered by Polycarp, and active in the same decade. Leaders with Jewish names, let alone the name 'John', were surely becoming less frequent in the Greek churches by A.D. 100.

(x) THE JOHANNINE WRITINGS

The identity of the Seer can be discussed without reference to the other Johannine books; but it would certainly be interesting to know whether he also wrote them; or, if he did not, then in what relation they do stand to him and to his work.

The only serious evidence (apart from tradition) which we

can consult is the character and contents of the books themselves. The Second and Third Epistles, it is true, show us an author exercising the same sort of influence over a local church as the Seer may be supposed to exercise over his seven churches; and if we knew that the province and the period of his pastoral activity were the same as the Seer's, we might argue to an identity of person from the identity of function. But as to time, there is nothing to prevent the one from being the other's successor; and as to place, there was plenty of room for the Epistle-writer to hold a sort of archbishopric in Christian Asia Minor, without touching the Seer's seven churches.

We turn, then, to the character and contents of the Epistles and the Gospel. Does any of them look as though it came from the author of the Revelation? The case best worth arguing is that of the Gospel. The Gospel may be thought to be a vision of the First Advent and, in its very different style, comparable with that vision of the Second which Revelation presents. In both works Christian tradition seems to be placed on its total Old Testament background, and the resultant picture re-meditated into life. It is commonly held that in the Johannine Gospel Christian eschatology is 'anticipated' or 'realized' as present experience; whereas in the Revelation the pattern of Gospel events is projected on the clouds of future expectation. Since we ourselves recognize both these movements of the mind as valid and necessary, we may be generous enough to allow that the same man might have wished to move in either direction at different times. If he did, we might expect to find that a common stock of images or ideas served both his purposes, though differently applied in each. On any showing there is a wealth of symbolism in the Gospel and it is worth seeing how it is related to the symbolism of the Apocalypse.

In the Johannine Epistles, by contrast, the scriptural symbolism is much effaced or, shall we say, buried beneath the surface. It is easy to show that the writer is familiar with certain of the Seer's characteristic ideas; it is hard to prove that they constitute the stuff of his mind. We have little to build upon and, even if we could throw a bridge from the Epistles to the Revelation, it would carry little traffic. The Revelation holds small promise of illuminating the Epistles, or vice versa. We shall, on the contrary, find frequent occasion in the course of our

INTRODUCTION 43

commentary to illustrate the symbolism of the Revelation from developments or parallels in the Gospel. We must content ourselves here with a few of the more striking points.

First, as to general structure. The most evident fact about the arrangement of Revelation is the dominance of the seven, or 'week'. Now the Johannine Gospel is alone among Gospels in fitting the events of the Passion to the scale of a whole week. St. Matthew and St. Mark do not begin counting the days until we reach the Wednesday, when the priests plot Christ's destruction and he dines at Bethany with Simon the Leper. Now while St. John begins his reckoning of days from the same events, he carries them back to the Sunday. The Passover, according to him, fell on the sixth of the week; when he says (xii. 1) that Jesus came to Bethany six days before Passover, he is simply reversing the count and indicating the first day. (There is really no doubt that New Testament writers say 'n days before' when they mean 'on the nth day before, by inclusive reckoning'. If we insist on going a day farther back, we shall make Jesus and his disciples travel from Ephraim to Bethany on a sabbath.) Next day, the Monday, Jesus enters Jerusalem; and discourses about the Greeks' request either on that day or the next. There follows a strongly marked break; Jesus withdraws from Israel as in Matthew xxiii. 39, and terminates his public ministry (xii. 36–50). The narrative recommences with a striking new introduction on Passover Eve, that is, Thursday, and runs continuously through the Supper into the Passion and Resurrection (xiii-xx). The division of days is like that of the trumpets in Revelation viii-xiv. A week is broken before the fifth day, and the remaining three are out of all proportion more weighty and more fully treated than the first four.

Equally striking is the fact that Christ's ministry, according to this Gospel, is arranged to the pattern of a week. The week here is not, of course, a week of days, but, like the apocalyptic weeks, a seven of mighty works. They are antithetical to the apocalyptic sevens; in the one case physical plagues, in the other, physical healings or bounties, show God's sovereignty over nature. The antithesis had been fully worked out already by the author of Wisdom (chs. xvi-xix).

There is, indeed, some uncertainty as to how we should count the great signs of blessing in the Gospel. The walking on the water is a wonder and a sign, but it does not fall into place beside acts of life-giving, that is, of healing or of nourishment. It is part of the story of the Feeding of Five Thousand, and interpreted as such in the great discourse of John vi. Discounting the walking on water, we have six signs of life-giving crowned by the Passion-and-Resurrection, which should count as the seventh. Then the literal week, Holy Week, will form the last item in a 'week' of mighty works; much as, in Revelation, the seven trumpets form the last item in the seven of unsealings. If, on the other hand, the walking-on-water is to be reckoned a distinct sign, we have an even simpler scheme. The first 'week' is complete before the second week begins, as in the sequence of the vials on the trumpets or of the unsealings on the messages.

It is plain that no such system as this (whichever way we reckon it) can be found in any of the other Gospels. In St. Mark there is a far less orderly grouping of the narrative round the healing of persons who, being thirteen, equal the number of Jesus and his company; St. Matthew shows some sort of breaking up into five or six 'books', by the intrusion of five great discourses; St. Luke a more flexible handling of the material altogether. We may say that John adjusts Matthaean-type discourses to a Marcan scheme of single healings, and cuts the whole to a heptadic pattern. As for that pattern itself, it seems more native to the Revelation than to the Gospel. The Revelation grows out of its sevens; the Gospel has them imposed upon it. One could scarcely doubt, if there is borrowing, which way the borrowing goes; or supposing identity of authorship, which book comes first in time.

A further general resemblance lies in the scheme of liturgy. The apocalyptic drama is set in a frame of divine service, offered in the temple of heaven by celestial beings. The effect of the liturgy is to fulfil the purpose of the temple, and bring it to an end, so that in the World to Come there is no sanctuary other than the presence of God and of the Lamb. So too the Johannine Gospel alone among Gospels sets the whole action of Christ's ministry in a frame of festal observances in the temple—in this case the earthly temple, 'the copy of the true'. Jesus, by his presence, fulfils the old ceremonial worship and brings it to an end; the time approaches when the true worshippers will no more worship on Zion than on Gerizim; the true and permanent temple is the person of the Lord.

INTRODUCTION 45

One last general similarity deserves a passing mention. Both books are sprinkled with numbers which probably carry a significance beyond their surface meaning. For the Revelation the fact will scarcely be denied. From the Gospel we may quote ii. 6, 20; v. 2, 5; vi. 7, 9, 13; viii. 57; xxi. 11. The Synoptic Gospels already contain elements of symbolical numerology, especially in the Feedings of Multitudes. The Johannine numbers seem more enigmatic and more widely distributed. It would take us too far to attempt the proof of a positive relation between certain of the numerical texts just listed, and the apocalyptic numerology.

We will turn now to more particular influences. The pages of a Gospel might most naturally reflect those visions in the Revelation which present the figure of Christ. We will list (*a*) Rev. i. 12–iii. 22, (*b*) v, (*c*) xii. 1–6, (*d*) xiv. 1–5, (*e*) xiv. 14–16, (*f*) xix. 7–16.

(*a*) and (*f*) both show the victorious Christ in human form. We may take them together. They tell us that he is Son of Man and Son of God; he has conquered death and the world; he calls on his disciples to share his conquest, that is, to be confessors and martyrs, to witness or testify (John xv. 27, xvi. 33). He is the First and the Last, the Beginning of the Creation of God; he bears the title, Word of God (John i. 1–3, 15). He is the searcher of hearts; he knows the deeds of men (John i. 47–48, ii. 24–25, iv. 17–18, 29). He gives, or is, the heavenly manna (John vi. 31). He warns his disciples against persecution and denounces a persecuting synagogue as no true Jewry, but a family of Satan (John viii. 37–44, xvi. 1–3). Those who know his voice open the door; conversely, he opens to them the door of everlasting life (John x. 1–9). They are bidden with him to a marriage-feast; he is the bridegroom of the heavenly bride (John ii. 1–11, iii. 29).

Now to take (*b*). Another John (the Baptist) testifies like John the Seer to what he has seen: how that the Only begotten who is in the bosom of the Father (= 'in the midst of the throne') has made the exposition of invisible God which Moses could not make (has opened the seven-sealed scripture: John i. 18). He is the Lamb of God, sacrificed for sins (John i. 29) on whom the Spirit rests (John i. 32–33). It is particularly worth noting that the Baptist's testimony in John i draws together the several features of the Christ-vision in Revelation v; and that in both texts the suddenness of the Lamb's manifestation recalls the sudden appearance of the ram which God provided to redeem Isaac (Genesis xxii). We may observe by the way that the Baptist who testifies to Gospel fact refuses the title either of Second Moses or Second Elias; and that these refusals accord with Revelation xi, which claims both roles for the prophetic Church.

Although the title 'Lamb of God' does not recur after John i, yet it is as the Paschal Lamb that Christ suffers his passion according to this Gospel. He is crucified in the afternoon while the lambs are being killed in the temple, and it is a special providence that, like a true paschal victim, he has not a bone in his body broken, when his fellow-sufferers are killed by the breaking of their legs (xix. 14-18, 31-36).

The Revelation hastens to press the paradox that the slaughtered Lamb is the Almighty Shepherd (Rev. vii. 14-17); and the Gospel tells us that the true shepherd is he who lays down his life for the sheep; no power can snatch them out of his hand.

(d) When the Jesus of the Gospel makes this last declaration, he stands in the temple under Solomon's Porch. We are reminded of this scene in Revelation xiv. 1-5, when in despite of all Antichrist can do, the Lamb-Shepherd stands on Mount Zion with the whole flock of his predestined elect, bearing *his name and his Father's name* stamped on their foreheads. It is the unity of the Father and the Son which secures the flock according to John x. 29-30, an assertion which calls down upon Jesus the charge of blaspheming the Name. When, in a later scene, Jesus prepares to depart, he prays the Father to keep his disciples by the Name he has bestowed on Jesus; the Name by which Jesus has kept them, while he has been with them (xvii. 11-12).

Those who stand with the Lamb on Mount Zion in Revelation xiv hear a voice as of thunder or of hymnody from the skies above, which none but they can 'learn'. In John xii. 28 Jesus stands on Zion again and hears a voice from the skies in articulate utterance; an unbelieving crowd says it has thundered, or that an angel has spoken. We are not told what the heavenly voices sang in Revelation xiv. 1-5; the significance of the voice in John xii as interpreted by Jesus is more like the heavenly voice of Revelation xii. 10-12—God's kingdom, or glory, is established by the casting forth of Satan.

(c) The Christ-vision of Revelation xii is bafflingly many-sided. It shows the Israel of God bringing forth Messiah in the childbearing of Mary, and, as we may almost say, in her person; and it is reasonably supposed, though scarcely proved, that the Fourth Evangelist likewise sees the Mother of Jesus as an embodiment of the Church, especially in xix. 26–27. The divine child of the Apocalypse, once born, escapes the lying-in-wait of the serpent by being caught into the throne of God; and it is a constant theme of the Evangelist that, whereas his enemies lie in wait for Jesus, and try to take him, they cannot; he departs to the Father and they cannot follow him (vii. 32–36, 44–46, viii. 21–23, xiii. 33, xiv. 30–31). His departure to heaven and becoming invisible on earth are the evidence of his vindication, and coupled with the condemnation of Satan (xvi. 10–11). So the snatching of the manchild to the throne of God procures the condemnation of Satan and vindication of the saints in the court of heaven: Satan, chased out by Michael, is flung down to earth.

In another aspect, the Eve who travails with the manchild is the people of God in the birthpangs of their messianic destiny. The travail of Mary at Bethlehem brought forth Jesus, the travail of the Church in the Great Tribulation brings forth the Messianic Advent. Similarly, according to the Gospel, the agony of Jesus's disciples in his Passion brought forth the Christ of the Resurrection but (says the Christ of John xvi. 19–22) the tribulation was to be blotted from memory by the joy to which it would give birth.

(e) Of the visions of Christ we listed above there remains only the harvester of Revelation xiv. 14, to whom is addressed the angelic voice 'Send forth thy sickle and reap, for the hour to reap is come, for the harvest of earth is dry'. John iv. 33 ff. makes an application of the theme to the days of Christ's ministry; but he might have it just as well from Mark iv. 29 as from Revelation xiv.

Beside the Christ-visions of the Revelation, the visions of final bliss might be expected to find an echo in the Gospel; for the Gospel promises in all things a present foretaste of future beatitude. In the heavenly city the Father and the Son come to take up their abode with the saints, as they do with the believer according to the Gospel (John xiv. 23). The Presence will *tabernacle* among the Blessed—it is the language of the Tabernacles Feast; and as in that Feast also, the Glory is manifested as light, and in the bestowal of living water. And so Christ speaks in the Gospel, when he comes to the Feast of Tabernacles (John vii. 37–38, viii. 12). The symbolism of light, and of living water, is not confined to Revelation xxi–xxii, still less to the Tabernacles Feast in the Gospel. It would be superfluous to enlarge on a theme so well known as the prevalence of light- and water-imagery in St. John.

The summary comparison we have drawn is not an argument, but the headings for an argument. The argument would need very full development before it came near to proving anything. It would have to be shown at every point, not only that the Gospel reflects the Seer's images, but that it reflects them more closely and more strikingly than it reflects any alternative sources known to us. If the case could be made out so far, it would prove that the Revelation exercised a real influence on the Gospel; it would not prove that this influence was predominant. For there is a vast deal of matter in St. John which lies outside the comparison we have so cursorily made.

Let us take the hypothesis that the case, on examination, appears as strong as the circumstances allow. Could we hope to advance to the conviction that the relation between the two books is not that of one mind influencing another, but of the same mind moving out into a new and broader field? It is at least not ridiculous to form such an opinion about the relation between the Gospel and the First Epistle; can we say the same of the relation between the Revelation and the Gospel?

In the case of the Epistle and the Gospel a directness of comparison is open to us which fails us in the other case. The Epistle is very much like one of the great discourses in the Gospel, especially the discourse in John xiii–xvii. There are, admittedly, important differences. The author of the Epistle speaks in his own voice, not through the person of Jesus. It is natural that he should be less tied to Semitic form, Gospel tradition, or Old Testament paraphrase; that he should use a more current rhetoric. But it is not absurd to claim that one can discount these differences and still hear an identical speech.

It is otherwise with the Gospel and the Revelation. Is there a single paragraph in the one, which performs the same sort of

INTRODUCTION 49

function as any single paragraph in the other? Revelation ii–iii and John xiii–xvi both record addresses of Christ to his disciples; but the short and flaming oracles from the mouth of Majesty are so different in *genre* from the humane and leisured style of a supper-discourse, that no comparison is possible. It is not that the same writer would be incapable of engaging in such different forms of composition; it is that we should have the greatest difficulty in detecting the identity of authorship if he did.

Not only is there difference of *genre*, there is the difference introduced by what we may fairly describe as 'writing in character'. A profane illustration may explain the distinction. Sonnet-writing and play-writing are very different *genres*, yet I suppose the critic might fairly claim to recognize the Shakespeare of the Sonnets in the Shakespeare of poetical speeches contained in the plays contemporary with them. He would scarcely claim to detect the author of the Sonnets in the hand that wrote the part of Falstaff, or the part of Juliet's Nurse. For these parts are written 'in character'. And it is very reasonable, on any showing, to suppose that the Revelation is written 'in character', as an old-style prophecy, a Christian Ezekiel or Zechariah. And we shall be compelled to make the supposition if we are going to entertain the possibility that the same writer wrote anything so differently expressed as the Gospel, some few years afterwards. But we cannot have it both ways; we cannot both have him write the Revelation 'in character', and argue from identity of personal style as between the Revelation and the Gospel.

'Never mind,' the traditionalist may say; 'let us cut our losses. We may not be able to prove identity of authorship on grounds of style. But neither can we disprove it. So let us follow tradition.' But we are not finished yet with linguistic difficulties. Even supposing that St. John writes the Revelation in character; that he is wilfully Scriptural, Semitic, antiquarian, and oracular; why should he so violate the first rules of Greek syntax as we see him to have done in this book? There is nothing like it in the Gospel. Suppose him a man whose native language is Semitic, writing in character as a biblical prophet, writing, moreover, in a high state of spiritual excitement. Such a man might under such conditions relapse completely and lose his acquired grip on Greek idiom. Even so, on reading over what he had written, why should he leave such gratuitous abominations uncorrected? We shall have to suppose, I fear, not only that he wrote the Revelation in character, but that he wrote it before he had half learnt to speak Greek; and that his Greek was of quite another order by the time he came to compose the Gospel.

Even if the traditionalist is prepared to make all the suppositions required to uphold unity of authorship, he has further yet to go before he can make the single author an Apostle. For how likely is it that so marked an improvement in Greek should have been achieved by so venerable a figure, between (say) his eighty-fifth and his ninetieth year?

Turning from the question of what we *can* believe to the question of what we *should*, we conclude as follows. The prophet John, who saw the Revelation, is probably the Elder John named by Papias, the John quoted by Polycarp as his master, and the reputed opponent of the heretic Cerinthus. The Gospel *according to* John deserves that title in a double sense: it claims the witness of John the Apostle to the saving events it records, and it follows the inspirations of John the Seer in interpreting the tradition it digests. The Epistles presuppose both Gospel and Revelation; and it is a case anyhow worth arguing that they come from the hand which wrote the Gospel.

(XI) THE GREEK ORIGINAL

We have assumed that the Revelation was written in Greek. Indeed, granting the conclusions we have reached about the date of the book, no other supposition makes sense. The Revelation takes the form of a pastoral circular to the seven churches of Asia; and it is absurd to imagine that these churches could be hopefully addressed in Aramaic or in Hebrew, by the turn of the century.

The Seer's Greek is uniquely bizarre, and if we were commenting on the Greek text we should need to go deeply into his linguistic peculiarities. But as it happens, we often have to wonder how he came to write what he wrote, but very seldom to wonder what he meant. The English rendering remains for the most part unaffected by our grammatical inquiries and we do not propose to trouble our readers with these nice points unless a serious difference in the English is involved.

As we have already said, we are driven to suppose two reasons for the author's bad Greek. He is writing in Old Testament style, and that means writing in the style of the Greek translations of the Hebrew books, as they existed and still do exist in the Septuagint version. These translations, in their anxiety to represent their original exactly, often do considerable violence to Greek idiom. But in addition to anything he either did or could borrow from the Septuagint, the Seer introduced solecisms of his own so inconsistent, so monstrous, so unhelpful and so unnecessary, that one can only conclude his sense for the language to have been very uncertain. It has been shown that the mistakes he makes are the sort of mistakes an Aramaic or Hebrew speaker might commit. It has not been, and cannot be shown that his solecisms are for the most part of any use in conveying Semitic *nuances* to Grecian ears.

In spite of his grammatical harshness and the obscurity it sometimes produces, the writer expresses himself with simple force and often with high poetical effect. Though often incorrect, he is neither careless nor vulgar; he writes in prophetic style and his Semitic cadences would awaken hallowed echoes in the ears of his Christian audiences.

It may be that the tremendous anathema with which he concludes his book has discouraged his early copyists from correcting his Greek or otherwise tampering with his text. The manuscripts in which it has come down to us exhibit the usual number of slight variations, a word more or less here or there, one or two inversions of order. It is surprising how seldom these divergences create any serious doubt about the sense intended, or affect the English rendering. Textual criticism is a subtle and ingenious art, and the Revelation is an interesting field in which to practise it. But we shall have little occasion to call the English reader's attention to its pro's and con's.

As to the antiquity of our evidence, we have part of a copy written on papyrus in the third century, containing nine chapters from the middle of the book; and an excellent copy on vellum from the century after, which is complete. There are any number of later copies.

(XII) PROPOSED METHOD OF EXPOSITION

Questions of language, date, and authorship, however intriguing in themselves, leave largely untouched our principal concern, the exposition of the book. Revelation sets the commentator a task of peculiar difficulty. It is not only that the text is sometimes hard to explain; it is just as much that we do not always know what sort of explanation it calls for.

How much more straightforward if one has to expound an historical book! We know exactly what our business is. We have to explain how such a thing as the author narrates came about, or how he came to suppose it did; what its place was in the contemporary texture of events, or what the author supposed it was. The answers to such questions may be hard to find; there is no doubt that they are the proper questions. For we know that the author put forward his episodes as events in a chain of events, and as events worth recording by virtue of their position in the chain.

With a visionary work like the Revelation the approach is by no means so simple. The author sets forth visionary episodes; but why? and as what? They are, in form, predictive. Yet they are little like history written in the future tense. They are not an attempt at hard-headed anticipation, showing how one coming event would lead on to another, or what either would look like when it happened. They are symbolical images, or mythic tales, casting a light of some kind (but of what kind?) on the expected future. Alternative images, different tales might have been put forward with the same general intent. So we are driven to ask, Why these tales, or these images particularly? They may be pregnant with futurity; but how did they get here, and what do they mean?

Here is a monster with seven heads (Rev. xiii. 1). What is it doing with so many? Well, standing as it does for Antichrist, it is a parody of Christ. Christ has already been seen as a Lamb, single-headed, but ringed with seven eyes and crowned with seven horns—he is one, but equipped with all the gifts of strength and vision. His parody has seven heads, for an earthly kingdom cannot survive in one royal head, like the heavenly. False Christ gives way to false Christ; a dynasty is many-headed.

Ah, but there are many ways in which Antichrist's parody of Christ might be symbolized equally well. Is it likely that a seven-headed monster was projected for the mere sake of the symbolical point? Must not St. John have somehow got a seven-headed monster on hand, and added the allegory by a subsequent stroke of wit? Let us suppose so. Then where had the seven-headed monster come from? Out of the sea, says St. John; and so, presumably, out of Daniel's seventh chapter. In that text the old prophet saw not one, but four beasts rise out of the sea, having seven heads among them; for one had four, the rest one apiece. St. John's beast, then, is the summary of all the bestiality they share. It combines their heads, as it combines their attributes—ten-horned like the fourth, leopard-bodied like the third, bear-footed like the second, lion-jawed like the first.

That St. John made such a play upon Daniel one can scarcely deny. Yet again, why such a play? To make up a sum of seven heads from three one-headed beasts and one four-headed is a gratuitous procedure. The Seer might as well have added up their feet and given his monster sixteen. Perhaps the seven-headed monster was a fixed type, and that is why St. John extracted such a figure out of his Daniel. After all, Daniel's own beasts from the sea are but allegorical applications of far older figures: the chaos-monsters of Mesopotamian mythology. Moreover we can find representations of the great chaos-dragon, Tiamat, a thousand years older than Daniel's book, and carrying seven heads. Tiamat, then, has come into her own; St. John's seven-headed beast is Tiamat.

We have written down a chain of questions and answers, one leading to another, and all quite naturally arising in a mind of commonplace learning, faced with Revelation xiii. But how many of the topics raised ought to concern the exposition of the book? To begin from the end. It is true, in a sense, that St. John's beast is Tiamat. The chaos-monster of Old Sumerian tradition did undergo a whole series of rehandlings in successive biblical strata and make its last scriptural appearance in Revelation. But the long history of the image, however interesting in itself, is largely irrelevant to the interpretation of St. John. It is with the provenance of images as it is with the etymologies of words. 'Lady' is the rubbed-down form of a word meaning 'mistress of the bread-bin', but it is no use telling me that I mean anything of the kind when I use the word. I am history-conscious, but not so history-conscious as that. When I say 'Lady', I do not simply mean 'Woman—and no offence intended'. The word carries overtones of aristocracy from previous usage—the historical background of my speech is a century or two old; it does not go back to Anglo-Saxondom and bread-bins.

So with St. John's images. They have an historical, which in this case is a scriptural, background in his mind. We have to appreciate in any given case how deep and how shallow that background is. He goes back to Daniel, and to other Old Testament texts, as they appeared to primitive Christian eyes. It is fantastic to suggest that he goes back to Babylonian epic.

No doubt, if we are to confine our attention within the range of St. John's conscious thoughts. But is not that too narrow a limitation? St. John did not know that he was rehashing Tiamat on a Christian dish. No; but perhaps the Tiamat-figure, by whatever name, had obtained a sort of independent power, and haunted the Semitic imagination. They could not help feeling there had to be a Tiamat—a monster of chaos, for God, or for God's champion to subdue. The figure took on various disguises, as the developing theology required; but in every disguise it stood for essentially the same interest, call it imaginative, psychological, or religious. So when Daniel had described idolatrous empires as beasts from the sea, the myth was no mere cartoon of political realities; it was the suggestion that demonic force, always in rebellion against divine order, had, in the centuries of Israel's oppression, taken the form of tyrant empires.

A claim of this sort is difficult to estimate and difficult to refute. Unquestionably Daniel's mythic language is something more than sapless political allegory. But what is that 'more', and how do we best appreciate it? Daniel and his contemporaries are under an appalling and an unexpected persecution; they are deeply concerned to justify it by relation to God's providence; the mythic colouring has something, surely, to do with such a justification. Is the implied justification that 'there has to be a Tiamat', and that for the present Tiamat takes the form of the Seleucid Kingdom?

It seems only fair to read Daniel's book forwards from the beginning and see what sense it places on the mythical figures. So far from suggesting that 'there has to be a Tiamat', he tells us that the first embodiment of 'bestial' power, Nebuchadnezzar, was given his kingdom by God, to punish Israel's sins; that in execution of this providential purpose he came up against the evident truth of Israel's religion, but wilfully persisted in idolatry and self-deification; that by so doing he lost the human image and became a brute; that he was restored by his subsequent penitence, a penitence which, however, his successors refused to follow. So, then, the 'bestial' character of Gentile empire is due to idolatrous perversity; it wilfully takes on the role of those monsters from the deep which old poetry had seen at issue with divine power.

Such is Daniel's doctrine; and if, after digesting it, we go on saying that his bestial figures are *really* Tiamat and her allies, all the same, then what can we mean? Are we claiming to psychologize the prophet? While we agree that the top of his mind worked as we have shown, do we allege that Tiamat haunted his subconscious and controlled his pen in spite of himself? It is difficult to see how we could know this to be the case. And even if we could, what would the alleged fact have to do with the interpretation of Daniel's text? He has written a sensible and connected story, in which the part played by dragon-imagery is simple and appropriate. If you tell us he had a dragon-haunted subconscious, you may be right. But the dragon-hauntings do not burst in or carry off the argument, as King Charles's head deflected the course of Mr. Dick's memorandum. Anything any of us says, however objective in its bearing, may provide evidence about our psychological type, or our emotional balance; but an expert estimate of these factors may be quite irrelevant to an understanding of what we say. If we are talking about the weather, we are talking about the weather. As with Daniel, so with St. John. He must be allowed to be his own interpreter and build up his symbolic background as he proceeds. We shall, of course, come across allusions to texts and images lying outside his book; and we must do our best to understand them. Many of his external allusions are unmistakable; and these will afford us a sound basis of analogy from which to judge the bearing of others less immediately clear.

St. John, we have said, must be allowed to build up his background as he proceeds. That is, we must read him forwards, not backwards. There is a sense, of course, in which the end of an apocalypse explains the beginning; for only in the end are those mysteries unveiled which have been in several stages prefigured. Yet at each point in the development of his vision the writer says as much as he means to say; and this much should be at least provisionally intelligible, without looking up the answer on the last page. A vintage of blood, not wine (Rev. xiv. 17–20) may be the figure of a battle presently to be won (Rev. xix. 15 ff.). But the figure is, in itself, provisionally acceptable; and the meanings of the words and images composing it are to be found by reference to the preceding context; or if not there, then in St. John's reference library, the Old Testament.

If we do find ourselves driven to interpret the very words and images employed, by the clue of their remoter sequels, then either St. John has failed as a writer, or we lack a key which was in the hands of his original audience. What do we do? We beat the whole field of his writing to see whether the idea obscurely expressed in one place may not have been clearly expressed in another. It may be a matter of accident, where the revealing passage comes; whether after, or before, or (if we have other writings from the same hand) in another book. It may even occur (but this is hazardous) in the work of another author, whom we presume to be operating with the same set of symbols.

By way of resistance to interpretations from remote mythology or from the subconscious, we may declare that our concern is with what St. John says. But we shall need to take 'says' in a liberal sense; it must include the movements he makes in passing from one said piece to another. For the significance of such moves, or transitions, is often integral to the intention of his book. We shall be driven to read between the lines; and for fear we should also run off the rails, we need constantly to ask ourselves, 'Would St. John admit that this is what he meant?'

Reading between the lines is most clearly legitimate when it is the interpretation of a formal procedure on St. John's part. St. John follows the convention of vision; his story is presented in 'stills', thrown one after another on the screen. Not absolute 'stills'—there is some simple movement within each visionary episode; but there is no continuous flow of movement from one to another. The gaps have to be filled by an appreciation of what the transition means.

In xii. 1 ff. the travailing woman is watched by the dragon. He means to devour her child, but the child, as soon as born, is snatched away to heaven, and the woman escapes. A fresh vision shows us battle in the sky, Michael and his angels rising to fight the dragon and his angels. They cast him down to earth, and there he rages. What is the connexion between the two conflicts thus depicted?

First, the storytale connexion. The child destined to destroy the dragon is attacked in infancy, when it seems easy to crush him. He miraculously escapes. The champion (Michael) intervenes, and drives the dragon off, thus covering the growth of the child to man's estate, that he may return and kill the dragon. Meanwhile the dragon, seeing that his days are numbered, has a last fling.

Second, there is the real connexion. The infancy of Christ (or rather, of his kingship) is in his earthly career, where Satan tried in vain to crush him. The prime of his kingship will be in his Second Advent, when he returns to conquer. The intervening champion is Michael, who has always been doing battle with Satan in the court of heaven for the souls of God's people; and who now, in virtue of the association of their merits with the merits of Christ, drives the accuser out—thereby covering the growth of Christ's kingdom in the body of his Church, until the day of visible triumph. The dragon's last desperate fling is the great persecution.

Some of what we have briefly drawn out is stated by St. John, some of it hinted, and some of it left to our wits; but we need have no doubt that he meant the whole of it, or that he would accept the substance of our exposition, could we put it to him.

Another of St. John's formal procedures is the exegetical. His whole apocalypse is a visualized meditation on sacred texts, and often enough the expository process is pressed on our notice and made the principle of unity in a passage of some length. The twelfth chapter will serve once more for our example. We need only take a step further back than last time. What is the connexion between the formal vision of the seventh trumpet, triumph in heaven (xi. 15–19), and the vision of the travailing woman, with its sequels (xii–xiv)? At least part of the answer lies in the exposition of Psalm ii. The text is stated by the voices of heavenly triumph: Though *the heathen have raged*, the kingdom is established of *the Lord and his Anointed*. The vision of the woman shows us how that *Son* is born, who is to *break the nations in pieces with a rod of iron*. Following visions show the rebellious rage of the heathen in some fullness (xii–xiii); then xiv. 1–5 reveals the fulfilment of the oracle, *Yet have I set my king upon my holy hill of Zion*. For we see the Lamb standing on Zion hill, and with him a hundred and forty-four thousands, marked with his name and with his Father's name. St. John has not told us that he is bringing alive in vision a Christian exposition of the Second Psalm. But he has done it, and surely meant us to see him doing it.

We will mention one more formal procedure of St. John's—the cyclic, or repetitive. We are not told that the bowl-plagues repeat the trumpets with significant variations; we are surely meant to observe it. We are not told that the rider on the white horse who opens heaven at last repeats the rider on the white horse in whom opened the first seal of revelation; but we are not intended to miss it.

We have cited clear and admitted examples. In such cases we can speak without hesitation of what St. John means by what he does, and not merely by what he says. It is not always as easy as this. St. John's images are not lifeless allegories clothing theorems which can be extracted from them. They live by their own life and claim for themselves all the meaning they can express; and how much meaning is that? Consider the Book which the Lamb opens in iv–vii. What book is it? The setting is a heavenly synagogue, where Christ alone is able to open the Divine Law. But at the same time the setting is that of Ezekiel's first vision; Christ's is that divine hand which spreads the book of prophecy before the eyes of his prophetic servant. Yet again, the setting is that of Daniel's seventh chapter. It is a heavenly court; the 'books are opened' that judgement may be pronounced in favour of the Saints of the Most High. What, then, does Christ open? Is it Torah? Is it prophecy? Is it judgement? And how can one book be all three? It is more; it is THE BOOK, it is all that a heavenly book can be, all that there is for Christ to unseal. It is what is meant when the Fourth Evangelist writes: 'No man has seen God at any time; the Only Begotten who is in the bosom of the Father, he has expounded.'

COMMENTARY

I. THE LORD'S DAY

(A) EXORDIUM

Revelation of Jesus Christ, which God gave him, to shew his 1
servants things which must shortly come to pass; and he sent and
signified it through his angel to his servant John; who bore witness 2
of the word of God and of the testimony of Jesus Christ in all that
he saw. Blessed is he that readeth, and they that hear the words of 3
the prophecy, and observe what is written therein; for the time is
at hand.

Since these verses refer to the book as an accomplished fact, they were presumably added to it by the author after he had written it. They are a sort of title: St. John writes down a descriptive phrase and proceeds to draw the meaning out of it, until he has a short paragraph. The closest model in the New Testament is the opening of St. Mark: 'BEGINNING OF THE JOYFUL MESSAGE OF JESUS CHRIST, as it is written . . ., Behold, I send my messenger. . .'. The subject which St. John announces is not simply a communication made to himself by Christ at Patmos on a certain Sunday. His theme is the revelation made by Jesus in his whole incarnate action, so far as it casts light on things to come; a revelation brought home to St. John with new clarity through the angel of his inspiration.

The original construction of the first sentence is arranged to express the development of the whole book, as we can see by numbering the clauses: (1) Revelation of Jesus Christ, (2) which God gave him, to show his servants what must shortly be, (3) and he sent and made it known through his angel to his servant John. In the sequel, i. 9 ff. discloses the person of Jesus Christ as revealer; iv ff. shows how he receives revelation from God in the form of a heavenly book; in x ff. the heavenly writing, brought down to John by the angel, is devoured by him and becomes the food of his remaining prophecies; the mediation of the angel in his continuing visions being emphasized at xix. 9–10 and xxii. 8–9. So the revelatory function of Christ, the Father's gift to him, and its angelic transmission to John, are set out in dramatic sequence; and the story of the Revelation reveals, among other things, the hierarchy of revealing powers. But even before the revealers have been severally disclosed, they must all have been in action. The whole revelation is the Father's gift to Christ, and the angel is active throughout in bringing it to John. For the most part the angel effaces himself; he 'preaches not himself, but Christ Jesus the Lord'. In xix. 9 ff. and xxii. 8 ff. his voice is heard as that of God, or of Christ. St. John may hold that, in the absence of Christ's actual person, all revelation is mediated by angels. But the angel no more stands between man and God than a telescope stands between the eye and the star.

In telling all that he saw, John 'bore witness' (verse 2). As explained above, these tenses are ambiguous (*supra*, pp. 26 f.). They refer to the time of writing, not to some previous time. The truth to which John witnesses is what God says and what Christ has witnessed to, by steadfast defence and by suffering; in witnessing, St. John is at one with Jesus; Jesus is THE witness (verse 5 below).

The blessing (verse 3) supposes that the book is to be read aloud to the congregation by one, and heard by many. The primary occasion will be the gathering of each church addressed, to hear the book on its arrival. But in view of the weight and depth of the message, its author can scarcely intend that it should receive one hearing only. On the significance of 'this prophecy', see the Introduction, pp. 28–29.

4 John to the seven churches in Asia: Grace be unto you and peace from him which is and which was and which is to come; and from
5 the seven Spirits before his throne; and from Jesus Christ, the faithful witness, and firstborn of the dead, and prince of the kings of the earth. Unto him that loveth us and loosed us from our sins
6 with his blood, and made us a kingdom of priests unto his God and Father, to him be glory and dominion for ever and ever.
7 Amen; behold, he cometh with the clouds; and every eye shall see him, and they also which pierced him; and all the tribes of the
8 earth make lamentation over him. Yea, Amen; I am the Alpha and the Omega, saith the Lord God, which is, and which was, and which is to come, the Almighty.

Verses 1–3 show that John, having finished his book, saw that what he had written was an apocalypse. 4–8 show us that what he sat down to write was a pastoral letter; for these verses were his starting-point. The common form of epistolary greeting in the New Testament is 'Grace to you and peace' (i.e. favour and prosperity) 'from God the Father and from the Lord Jesus Christ'. The form undergoes various elaborations. Galatians attaches participle-clauses to 'Lord Jesus Christ' describing his work of redemption, and concludes with a doxology. In 4–6 St. John does virtually the same, though his syntax is less continuous. But he also first elaborates 'From God the Father and from the Lord Jesus Christ'. 'God the Father' disappears in a haze of glory; he is indirectly named by his mastery of the three tenses of time, and by the seven Spirits annexed to his throne; while 'the Lord' is supplanted by three titles of which the last is more or less equivalent to it.

Exodus iii. 14–15 gives 'I am' or 'I am that (I) am' as the meaning of the mysterious name JHVH—so, at least, the Septuagint Greek translators rendered the text; a reader of the Hebrew might find the future tenses of the verb *to be* more natural expressions of the original. But why dispute the point? It became a rabbinic commonplace that God's being has all the tenses of the verb, and it is this thought that St. John throws into the most tortured piece of Greek his book contains. Guided by the Septuagint, he puts the *present* first, and then goes on to show that God's *present* embraces the *past* and the *future*. But for 'is, was, and shall be' he substitutes 'is, was, and comes'. St. John's vocabulary appears to lack the future participle of the verb 'to be'—'the about-to-be'; he writes 'the coming one'. The substitution may be a mere vulgarism, but if so, it is a happy fault. For it fits St. John's apocalyptic message; God's *coming* sovereignty can be seen in Messiah coming with clouds (verse 7).

The immediate motive for the mention of the seven Spirits lies in the magic of numbers. John sends to seven churches blessing from him on whose throne seven living blessings wait. The Spirit of God is the divine life revealed as communicable, single in nature and in source, multiple in distribution, and able to be described either as one or as many; cf. 1 Corinthians xiv. 32. The fluidity of the conception can be best appreciated in Revelation ii and iii. Because Christ has the seven Spirits of God, the message he inspires St. John to give each of seven churches in turn is 'what the Spirit says to the churches' (ii. 29–iii. 1; ii. 7, 11, 17; iii. 6, 13, 22). In the text before us the unqualified plural may seem to dissolve the Spirit into the gifts he bestows; but the fact that the Spirits are made, with the Father and the Son, givers of 'grace and peace', places them in the Godhead and adumbrates the trinitarianism of later orthodoxy. We must not, however, ask whether the seven Spirits are the Holy Ghost. 'Spirit of God' in the New Testament is a vaguer term, covering the being of the Holy Ghost, but also the graces he confers. Special warrant for calling the Spirit sevenfold could be found in the successive naming of seven Spirits according to Isaiah xi. 2, a text unquestionably alluded to in Revelation v. 5–6. Seven, being a 'perfect' or round number to the biblical mind, suggests a fullness or completeness of spiritual endowments. Similarly the seven churches on whom the seven blessings are invoked will appear as organically one, and typical of the perfect unity or wholeness which embraces all Christian congregations.

The three titles of Christ (verse 5ᵃ) begin with the idea of his witness, which is so relevant to St. John's situation, and so prominent in the context (verse 9, cf. 2). '*Faithful* witness' picks up a phrase from Psalm lxxxix. 37, and leads on to two messianic titles from verse 27 of the same psalm: 'firstborn' and 'higher than the kings of the earth'. 'Firstborn', being glossed as 'firstborn *from the dead*' (cf. Col. i. 18), brings the three titles into historical sequence: Christ is the faithful witness or martyr in his passion, firstborn in his resurrection, and sovereign in his session at God's right hand.

5ᵇ and 6ᵃ show that the whole act of redemption and glorification is conceived as a new deliverance from Egyptian bondage. Our being made a royal house in priesthood to God is a plain citation of Exodus xix. 6; and in such a connexion our being freed from our sins by Christ's blood carries the unmistakable suggestion that Jesus is the Lamb of Passover, and prepares us for his appearance as a Lamb from v. 6 onwards.

6ᵇ gives the doxology to Christ; the similarly placed doxology of Galatians i. 5 turns the praise to the glory of God the Father. St. John's formal doxology to the Son must reflect a development in Christian liturgical usage.

A biblical doxology carries an Amen as a matter of form. But in St. John's churches men cried 'Amen; come [Lord Jesus]' (xxii. 20, v. 14–vi. 1). If power and glory are given to God, or to Christ, *for ever*, it is appropriate enough to answer 'Even so: come (and reign)': such is the sequence of ideas in v. 14–vi. 1. But in the present context an asseveration is more proper than a prayer: instead of 'Amen, come' we have 'Amen: behold, he is coming!' 'Coming with the clouds' because to come in such a way is to take up the kingdom for ever and ever, as is made perfectly clear in the Daniel text to which the phrase always alludes (Dan. vii. 13–14).

In developing the picture of Advent, St. John makes the same connexion between Daniel vii. 13 and Zechariah xii. 10–14, as appears in Matthew xxiv. 30. The text of Zechariah is desperately obscure and it is irrelevant to St. John's application of it to decide what it originally meant. In Zechariah the families of the land of Israel look on whom they pierced, and, looking, lament. St. John (but not St. Matthew) extends the looking to '*every* eye', *including* Christ's countrymen who pierced him: and so we must suppose that he understands 'all the tribes of *the earth*', not 'of *the land* (of Israel)' as destined to wail; his Greek is ambiguous. That there had been a literal piercing, or stabbing, on the Cross, is emphasized in John xix. 37 by a citation of Zechariah's words. The 'lamentation' in Zechariah xii is a saving repentance. St. John knows that all men have opportunity to repent, but by the time Christ comes with clouds it is too late, and the lamentation is to be seen as unavailing remorse: cf. vi. 16 f.

The 'Amen' of the doxology having failed to bring the paragraph to a conclusion, St. John adds a second and strengthened Amen (Yea, Amen) to the advent promise; cf. xxii. 20. He supports this Amen with a further asseveration, but an asseveration which is finally conclusive. It is a paraphrasing expansion of 'Amen; I am the first and the last, saith JHVH Sabaoth'. For such confirmatory declarations cf. Isaiah xliv. 6, xlviii. 12, and parallels. The circle is complete—we return to the eternal being of God, from which we began (compare verse 8 with 4^b).

Now as to the paraphrases. 'Alpha and Omega' is the Greek equivalent of 'A and Z' in our alphabet, or of 'Aleph and Tau' in the Hebrew. Rabbinic speculation saw a figure of God's action through all from first to last, in the redundant Hebrew particle AT which appears in Genesis i. 1: 'In the beginning God created AT heaven and earth.' St. John may be simply translating this piece of rabbinism into Greek; but the fact that he makes A and Ω an actual title of God suggests that he is profiting from the change of language to find a more interesting verbal foundation for it than the particle AT. One of the vocalizations of the divine name JHVH was *Jahoh* and we know that this form, written in Greek as $IA\Omega$ (Iaō) was used in Roman times by magicians and others. A and Ω are not only the first and last letters, but the first and last vowels; and I is the middle vowel of the seven in the Greek alphabet. We do not know that $IA\Omega$ was related to A and Ω as 'first and last', but we do know that the name $AI\Omega$ [N], Eternity, a Greco-Oriental deity, was interpreted as extension from beginning to end. It seems likely enough then that $IA\Omega$ should be interpreted as AM, WAS, and SHALL BE, or alternatively as AM A and Ω; and the verse before us actually combines these two formulations in the same sentence. It is a reasonable conjecture, then, that St. John sees God's being the A and the Ω to be implied in the very fact that he is God the Lord (JHVH or $IA\Omega$), the IS, WAS, and COMES. He adds, 'the Almighty', i.e. 'the All-Sovereign'— *pantocrator*, a standing Greek equivalent of 'Sabaoth'; thus completing his paraphrased expansion of the sentence 'Amen; I am the first and the last, saith God the LORD Sabaoth'.

Implications drawn from accidents of spelling no longer impress us; they belong to the world of games, of puns and anagrams. But it was not so for St. John, as we shall have reason to see. To deduce

God's attributes from the letters of his Name was a way of saying that they are founded in his very nature.

(B) VISION

9 I, John, your brother, and partaker with you in the tribulation and kingdom and endurance in Jesus, was on the isle called Patmos, for 10 the word of God and for the testimony of Jesus. I was in the Spirit on the Lord's Day, and heard behind me a great voice as of 11 a trumpet, saying: What thou seest write in a book, and send to the seven churches; to Ephesus, Smyrna, Pergamum and Thyatira, 12 to Sardis, Philadelphia and Laodicea. I turned to see the voice that spake with me.

'For,' i.e. 'on account of, the word of God and the Jesus-testimony' leaves open the possibility that St. John had come to Patmos to preach. But in view of his self-description, 'partaker with you in the suffering, the sovereignty and the endurance' it is more natural to suppose that he had been deported to the island on account of his apostolic activity. Rocky islets were largely used for purposes of detention. 'The Jesus-testimony' is a perfectly ambiguous phrase: it can just as well mean 'the witness Jesus bears' as 'the witness borne to Jesus'. In view of verses 2 and 5 above, the former interpretation is preferable. Because God has spoken and Christ has witnessed, St. John is in prison—Christ's witness carries St. John's witness with it: his witness, like his suffering, his sovereignty, and his endurance, is 'in Jesus'. The 'in Christ' language so familiar to St. Paul is in general absent from the Revelation; but then it is bound to be, since the Revelation presents spiritual realities in visionary terms, and a vision of Christians 'in' Christ is scarcely conceivable. It is all the more notable that he can speak (outside the visionary picture) of Christians suffering, reigning, and enduring 'in Jesus'. According to xiv. 13, to die a Christian death is to die 'in the Lord'.

'On the Lord's Day', i.e. on Sunday. The alternative translation sometimes suggested, 'I found myself, through spiritual rapture, on the Day of the Lord', i.e. on Judgement Day, is false to the Greek and false to the context. St. John's being 'in the Spirit' does not define his experience any farther than to say that it was an experience of inspiration; the Greek is, however, a little more definite than the English: 'I *came to be* in spirit.' The first effect of his inspiration is verbal: it is borne in upon him that he is commanded to write down, and send to the seven churches, the things he 'sees'. The voice from *behind* expresses the surprise, the unsought-for character of the

THE LORD'S DAY

command. Being addressed, he turns to look, like St. Mary Magdalen in the garden (John xx. 16). The turning and looking are actions on St. John's part, and make room for that meditative exploration of scriptural memories which manifestly follows.

The trumpet-like sound of the voice, taken literally, conflicts with the description 'like the sound of many waters' in verse 13 below. But the conflict disappears if we turn from the images employed to the things they signify. St. John, not having yet attended to the person of the Speaker, experiences the voice as a peremptory summons to receive revelation, like the trumpet which called Moses up Sinai (Exod. xix. 13, 19). On turning to 'look', he appreciates the majesty of the Presence; the utterance comes home to him as the voice of the divine Person, and he so describes it.

The seven churches of verse 11 appear to be named in the order in which a messenger armed with St. John's letter would approach them if he made a circular tour from Ephesus and back.

And having turned I saw seven golden lampstands, and in the midst of the lampstands one like unto a son of man, clothed with a garment down to the foot, and girt about the breast with a golden girdle. His head and his hair were white as snow-white wool, and his eyes were as a flame of fire. His feet were like fine brass, fired in the furnace; and his voice as the voice of many waters. And he had in his right hand seven stars, and out of his mouth went a sharp two-edged sword; and his countenance was as the sun shineth in his strength. 13 14 15 16

The beginning of the vision takes up Zechariah iv. 1–2, as a comparison of St. John's Greek with the Greek of the LXX will show: 'And the angel *turned* who spake with me . . . and said to me, *What seest thou?* And I said, I have *beheld*, and lo, a *lampstand all of gold . . . and seven lamps.*' Cf. '*What thou seest*, write . . . and I *turned* . . . and having turned *beheld seven lampstands of gold.*' Zechariah's vision was familiar to Israelites as a prophetic lesson for the Feast of Lamps, Dedication, the Jewish Christmas; and familiar to Christians as occurring in a series of visions which give a messianic significance to the High Priest Jesus, making him typical (it must seem) of Jesus Christ. The seven lamps of Zechariah stand for the temple worship of Israel, and lend themselves naturally enough to symbolize that worship of the Christian churches which is their whole existence. Zechariah's lamps rest on a single seven-branched stand, the one 'candlestick' of the temple at Jerusalem. St. John's lamps stand each on its own base at Ephesus, Smyrna, Pergamum, or wherever it may be. Moreover their relation to their High Priest Jesus is quite different. In the Jewish scheme the 'candlestick' of Israel's worship holds the centre; on either hand are planted oil-trees, symbolizing the two anointed stocks, the princely house of Zerubbabel and the priestly house of Jesus, to feed the wicks with the oil of their anointing. In St. John's picture the single figure of Jesus, both priestly and royal, takes the centre; the churches burn as candles round him, but his own radiance is greater—he holds the seven stars in his hand, his face shines as the sun. We recall that in the thought of St. John's Gospel everyone who 'witnesses' is a burning lamp, yet there is only one witness who is the light of the world (John i. 4–9, v. 33–35, viii. 12–14).

In developing the figure of Jesus St. John passes to other texts. Jesus is that 'as it were a Son of Man' who comes with clouds (Dan. vii. 13, already touched upon in verse 7 above). The LXX translators allow us to think, if we like, that the Son of Man shares the form of the Ancient of Days himself. 'Lo on the clouds of heaven', they write, 'came as it were a Son of Man and as it were an Ancient of Days appeared'; where, on mere grammatical evidence, 'appeared *he*' is as natural an interpretation as any; especially if we recall that the Almighty appears 'as the semblance of a man' in Ezekiel's great theophany (Ezek. i. 26). Following these indications St. John gives to Christ the head of hair white as wool, which is the characterizing mark of the Ancient of Days in Daniel vii. 9. For the rest, St. John gathers the features of glory from the composite figure of divine majesty in the Ezekiel text first cited and in the parallel (Ezek. xliii); or from the great angel, presumably Gabriel, described in Daniel x.

Rabbinic thought wrestled with the relation between the spirituality of a God everywhere present, and the localized physical traits of that 'glory' in which God appeared to Moses or to Isaiah; a 'glory' in which, perhaps, he will likewise manifest himself to the blessed in the world to come. Justin Martyr and other early Christian writers were happy to escape the embarrassment: Jesus was the Glory; it was through the Son that the Father had visited patriarchs and prophets. It is not likely that St. John held this as a systematic belief—in other visions he places Jesus at the right hand of Glory—but he is able to see the Glory in Jesus. The Jesus of the Resurrection whom he sets before us here is not seen as the Man of Nazareth transfigured, but as the Divine Glory personified.

The figure of Daniel's angel can add traits to the person of Glory, because in the Old Testament angels who come on God's errands are commonly indistinguishable from God—they present him, not themselves; the messenger is as he who sent him. But St. John may mean more than that the glory of Gabriel is an evidence for the Glory of God. He may mean that the figure he sees is the angel of Christ's presence, as Christ himself is the 'angel' of God's. Has he not told us in the title of his book that Jesus makes the revelation of God by sending John his angel? It is only in representing God that his messengers are as himself; when seen as the adjuncts of his majesty they appear in a different guise. Even Christ is not seen in heaven as Ancient of Days, but as a sacrificial Lamb, next beside the throne.

The description in verses 14–15 follows the order of features in Daniel x. 5–6, with omissions and additions; the actual phrasing is often substituted from Ezekiel. Verse 16 is outside the Danielic model. St. John pulls the whole together into his own pattern; the sequence is not determined by a systematic procession over the parts of the body, but by words and ideas. A painfully literal translation is required, to show how it goes:

(a) And I *turned* to see the voice that spoke with me
and *turning* beheld seven candlesticks *of gold*
(b) And among the candlesticks as it had been a Son of Man
clad in an alb and girt about the breast with a girdle *of gold*.
(c) His head and his hair *white*
like wool as *white* as snow
(d) And his eyes as flame of *fire*
and his feet like fine brass, as in a furnace *fired*
(e) And his voice as the voice of *waters many*
and holding in his right hand *stars seven*
(f) And from his mouth a sharp two edged sword issuing
and his look as the *sun* shines in his strength.

From (a) to (d) we have simple refrain-words. In (e) the *waters many* and *stars seven* are parallel in connecting divine majesty with the great elements of the world. As between (d) and (e) there is a structural parallel, each couplet pairing characteristic limbs (feet, hand) with organs or powers of the head (eyes, speech). The theme of (e) is continued in (f); the utterance of the voice is given a second symbolization and coupled with a sunlike characteristic, an inevitable counterpart for the stars in (e) line 2. Moreover (f) draws together (e) and (d), voice and look.

(d) contains a paradox. Christ's eyes, alight with the terror of fire, are organs of judgement (cf. ii. 18 and 23); his feet are as though they had been through fire—he has undergone the judgement of which he is the master. For the feet of the Son of God treading the furnace of fire which is martyrdom cf. Daniel iii. 25. The Jesus of Zechariah iii. 2 is also 'a brand plucked from the burning'. The assay of fire refines the metal: cf. iii. 18. It is commonly gold that is said to be refined by fire, but the feet of brass were established in the tradition

(Dan. x. 6, Ezek. i. 7) and St. John will go no farther than to name a special and doubtless precious mixture of brass, not otherwise known (*chalcolibanus*). To talk of the refining of common brass as though it were an exquisite process would doubtless have sounded absurd.

(*f*) presents the striking-force of word and look, so leading on directly to St. John's falling as dead in the presence. The sword of the lips may represent Isaiah xi. 4 expressed in the language of Psalm lix. 7; or perhaps of Wisdom xviii. 18. In any case there is no mystery about the meaning.

The seven stars require more explanation. As to which seven are meant we ought to accept the obvious identification. Just as the twelve stars (xii. 1) are the constellations marking the months of the year, so the seven stars are the seven planets naming the days of the week, Sun, Moon, Mars, Mercury, Jupiter, Venus, and Saturn. Christ embraces them in the span of his hand, because Sunday is his. Christ rose on the octave-day of Holy Week; he spans the week from Sunday to Sunday. And since the pattern of the week is printed upon all created time, and history itself is a week of ages (see above, p. 12), the Christ of Sunday is the First and the Last, the beginning and end of God's creation (i. 17, ii. 8, iii. 14). It is of the highest significance in this connexion that the vision before us is a Sunday vision (i. 10). And in parallel with his mention of the seven stars St. John places the statement that Christ's countenance shines like the sun.

To our symbolical convention, it is an offence that Christ should both be identified with the sun, and hold the sun among seven planets in his hand. It was no offence to St. John. The Virgin crowned with the Zodiac in xii is herself one of the twelve signs; the parody of Christ in xiii and xvii is a monster personally identical with one of the seven heads he carries, and in each of which he successively reigns. The mystical Christ of St. Paul is both the whole body composed of several members, and one of those members (the head).

Christ, as Lord of Sunday, is established in possession of the seven stars. In the sequel (iv ff.) his mastery over the 'weeks' of human history will be abundantly displayed. But for the moment that aspect of the matter is in abeyance. Here the stars are, and St. John is moved to interpret them not as nature's calendar (Gen. i. 14) but as what they are in themselves—heavenly bodies. Stars were gods to the heathen, and angels to the Jews; cf. ix. 1 and xii. 4^a = xii. 9^b. The interpretation is fixed in verses 19–20 below.

17 And when I saw him I fell at his feet as dead. And he laid his right
18 hand upon me, saying, Fear not; I am the first and last, he that

liveth and was dead, and, behold, am alive for ever more, and have
the keys of death and Hades. Write therefore the things thou hast 19
seen, the things which are, and the things which shall be hereafter.
The mystery of the seven stars which thou sawest in my right 20
hand, and the seven lampstands—the seven stars are the angels of
the seven churches, and the seven lampstands are the seven
churches.

The dead faint in the presence of Glory, and the reviving touch,
both belong to Daniel's picture (Dan. x. 8–10, cf. viii. 17–18). But
they are out of all proportion enhanced by being seen as a mystical
death and resurrection through contact with the Christ of Good
Friday and Easter Sunday. Christ's self-description may be taken as
an exposition of the Sunday idea: he is the first and the last; he is the
resurrection and the life. 'The Living' (God) is a title of the God of
Israel (cf. iv. 9, x. 6, xv. 7). In holding the keys Christ is the Father's
steward or vizir (Isa. xxii. 22, cited below, iii. 7) having control over
the door between death and life and over the 'treasury of souls'
(Sheol or Hades). Because of Christ's saving mastery St. John need
not be afraid; he can calmly write the overwhelming realities of the
present and the future.

In the interpretation of the stars and lamps, the lamps really take
control. As we have seen, they are a natural symbol for the churches
and have doubtless been so understood by St. John from the beginning of his vision. But now seven stars have (from quite different
symbolical motives) appeared in Christ's hand, and stars are the
lamps of heaven. How are they related to the earthly lamps, which
are the churches? Surely as their heavenly counterparts. But why
should the churches be accorded a dual existence? To make possible
the symbolism which follows. Praise and blame are to be awarded
for the constancy and brightness (or the reverse) of the lamps' burning. But a lamp does not feed or trim itself; in Christ's parable of
wise and foolish virgins, it is not the lamps that come under judgement, but the children in charge of them. So if the churches are
lamps, it is in the aspect of their performance—the witness offered
to men, or the worship offered to God. The soul or will of each
church is its angel; stars are the doubles of lamps in being lights, but
being also angels, they differ from them in being alive. So it is the
angels that are admonished in the messages to the churches; yet
what Christ says to the angels is, in more literal terms, what 'the
Spirit' (St. John's inspired utterance) declares to *the churches* (ii. 7,
11, 17, &c.).

But the twofold representation of the churches' existence, forced upon St. John by the demands of allegory, allows him to express a great mystery. Though the saints have their sphere of action on earth, they are 'in Jesus' (i. 9, xiv. 13), they are in heaven (xii. 1) or tabernacle there (xii. 12, xiii. 6); the 'dwellers upon earth' are the enemies of God (vi. 10; viii. 13; xiii. 8, 12, 14; xiv. 6). The churches, as we have seen, are not a seven-branched lampstand, but seven distinct stands. The only single bearer of seven lights in St. John's picture is the Christ who holds the seven stars. It is by their heavenly being in him alone that the churches scattered through the land have their unity as one Israel of God.

(c) SEVEN MESSAGES

II To the angel of the church in Ephesus write: These things saith he that holdeth the seven stars in his right hand, who walketh in the
2 midst of the seven golden lampstands: I know thy works, thy weariness and thy endurance, and that thou canst not bear evil men, and hast tried them that say they are apostles and are not, and
3 hast found them false; and thou hast endurance, and hast borne
4 for my name's sake, and not wearied. But I have it against thee
5 that thou hast let go thy first love. Remember therefore whence thou art fallen, and repent and do the first works; or else I will
6 come to thee and will remove thy lampstand out of its place,
7 except thou repent. But this thou hast, that thou hatest the works of the Nicolaitans, which I also hate. He that hath an ear, let him hear what the Spirit saith to the churches: To him that overcometh will I give to eat of the tree of life, which is in the paradise of God.

The stars and lamps have just been taken in an order which reverses their positions in the preceding vision (verse 12 lamps, 16 stars). Such a reversal is very natural; one names first what one has mentioned last and has most immediately in mind. Following the same principle, St. John seeks inspiration for messages to the churches by going back over the text of the vision he has just written down. (For another unmistakable example of the same procedure see xiii. 1–2). So he takes in order Christ's command (i. 19–20) for the first message, Christ's self-description (i. 17–18) for the second, Christ's attributes (i. 16) for the third, and Christ's person (i. 13–15) for the fourth. If he takes another step back for the fifth, he comes to the golden lampstands which are the subject of Christ's command in i. 20 and which he has already used in the first message; so he finds himself again at his starting-point. Not at all dismayed by the repetition, St. John goes on with it: having re-used the matter of the first message in the fifth, he re-uses the second in the sixth and the third in the seventh. There are thus four types in all, the first three types being used twice; and there are two unequal cycles of messages, the four in chapter ii and the three in chapter iii.

The description of Christ as holding the churches' 'angels' in his hand, and walking among their golden lamps, leads on naturally to the claim, 'I know thy works.' 'Works' tends to have the meaning 'level of performance, merit'; 'thy', the singular of the second person, keeps up the convention that the person addressed is the angel, not the congregation; throughout the messages the convention is maintained. Since the message is constructed by way of drawing out verbal suggestions, we proceed to offer a paraphrase which allows them to be seen.

'Work(s)' suggests *weariness* and *endurance*. But not all things should be endured: it is a merit that the Ephesian angel *cannot bear* bad Christians, but has unflinchingly put false apostles to the test and found them out. In face of this trial he holds fast his *endurance* and has *borne* it for Christ's sake and (in spite of his *weariness*) not *wearied*. Yet Christ has it against him that he has lost his first love. He is admonished, as a star, to remember the heaven from which he has fallen (for falling stars, cf. vi. 13, viii. 10, ix. 1, xii. 4) and as the guardian of a lamp, to fear that Christ may remove it from its place. But while Christ *has it* against the angel that he has forgotten his first *love*, the angel *has it* in his favour that he *hates* the works of the *Nico*laitans which are hateful to Christ. To the *nicōn*—the Christian conqueror—Christ will give fruit from the tree of life in the Paradise of God—a rich compensation for the forbidden food offered by Nicolaitanism to its followers, as the apple in Paradise was offered by the serpent to Eve (cf. below, verses 14 and 20).

To see how St. John is carried forward by verbal suggestion is surely to learn a good deal about the way in which his inspiration comes to him. The divine word, once planted, is a seed which continually grows and branches out.

There is no reason to distinguish the false apostles from Nicolaus and his partisans; nor to infer from the description that true apostles were still current. False apostolic claims are even more odious after true apostles have ceased. We know nothing of any value about Nicolaus or his sect beyond what this chapter tells us. They stand for compromise with heathenism in matters of sex and of idolatrous custom. There is a possible hint of dark esoteric doctrine in ii. 24, but we are in no position to interpret it with confidence.

The exhortation to use what ears one has, and hear what the Spirit says to the churches, refers specially to the promise for him who is victorious; and so also in the conclusions of the other messages. For the authority of the Spirit in confirmation of a divine promise cf. xiv. 13.

8 And to the angel of the church in Smyrna write: these things saith
9 the first and the last, which was dead and lived: I know thy tribulation and thy poverty—but thou art rich—and the slander on the part of them which say they are Jews and are not, but are the
10 synagogue of Satan. Fear not the things which thou art about to suffer. Behold, the devil is about to cast some of you into prison, that ye may be tested, and ye shall have tribulation ten days. Be thou faithful unto death, and I will give thee the crown of life.
11 He that hath an ear, let him hear what the Spirit saith to the churches: He that overcometh shall not be hurt by the second death.

In passing to a second message, St. John has not only his vision-text, i. 18, to apply; he has also the model provided by the first message to imitate. He takes from it the following points of form: 'These things saith the ... who ... I know thy [works] ... Those who say they are ... and are not ... He that hath an ear, let him hear what the Spirit saith to the churches! He that overcometh ...

Whereas the Ephesian angel is troubled by self-styled apostles, the Smyrnaean is troubled by self-styled Israelites. The phrase, natural in its first context where it spontaneously grew, is forced in being transplanted to fresh ground. The 'apostles' of verse 2 were not apostles, but the Jews of 9 are Judaeans in every ordinary sense; only they are no true spiritual members of Messiah's tribe (cf. v. 5, vii. 5). For they slander his people, and this is serious. By repudiating the Christians they deny them the legal protection extended to the synagogue, and expose them to Roman persecution as an unlawful society or 'religion'; even if their 'slander' does not go the length of denunciation to the Roman authority. Indeed they are a synagogue of Satan, for 'Satan' means 'adversary' or 'legal accuser'; a point which becomes clearer for St. John's Greek audience when he translates the name in the next verse. 'The *Slanderer* (Diabolos, Devil) will throw some of you into prison', through the action, no doubt, of his Jewish disciples. What of it? They need not fear; the Christ who laid his hand on St. John, raised him as from death, and told him not to fear, holds the keys of the only prison worth fearing: 'I have the keys of death and Hades' he says. Hence the exhortation: 'Be faithful to the death, and I will give thee the (victor's) crown of life'; and the promise, 'He that overcometh shall not be hurt by the second death'—in Rabbinic phrase, 'He may die to this world, but he shall not die for the world to come.' It had happened to Daniel and his companions, under very different circumstances, to be put to the test for ten days (Dan. i. 12, 14); the testing led to their high promotion. Even if the Smyrnaeans' imprisonment ends in martyrdom, they will have but a short time to wait before the keys of Christ bring them forth to enjoy everlasting glory. Cf. vi. 10–11, and, for 'second death', xx. 6, 14; xxi. 8.

And to the angel of the church in Pergamum write: These things saith he that hath the sharp two-edged sword: I know where thou dwellest, even where Satan's throne is; and thou holdest fast my name, and didst not deny my faith even in the days of Antipas my faithful witness, who was slain among you, where Satan dwelleth. But I have a few things against thee, because thou hast there some that hold the teaching of Balaam, who taught Balak to cast a stumbling block before the children of Israel, to eat things sacrificed unto idols and to commit fornication. So thou hast some that hold the teaching of the Nicolaitans in like manner. Repent therefore, else I come to thee quickly, and will fight against them with the sword of my mouth. He that hath an ear, let him hear what the Spirit saith unto the churches: To him that overcometh will I give of the hidden manna, and will give him a white stone, and on the stone a new name written, which no man knoweth but he that receiveth it.

The third message adopts all the elements of standing form which the second took over from the first, except that 'those who say they are... and are not' is dropped; the comment '[but are a synagogue of] Satan' is taken up instead. Satan, as slanderous accuser, was the moving spirit of Jewish hostility at Smyrna; Satan, as the god of pagans, is enthroned at Pergamum, for it is the seat of Roman provincial administration, and consequently a centre of the organized emperor-cult. It is reasonable to suppose that Antipas's martyrdom had been due to conflict with the demands of this cult; a cult which became the formal ground of persecution throughout the empire (cf. xiii. 12–15).

Among the attributes of Christ in i. 15^b–16 St. John takes for his title the two-edged sword. The immediate suggestion for such a choice lies in the last words of the preceding message, 'Shall not be hurt by the second death'. No sooner is this said than Christ is shown as the sole possessor of the ultimate power of the sword; cf. xix. 21.

Nicolaitanism has taken root at Pergamum, as at Ephesus, and in rebuking it, St. John returns to the form of the Ephesian message: 'I have it against thee, that . . .', 'Repent . . . or I come to thee and . . .'. As there, so here, the threat is borrowed from the title of Christ which heads the message: he who walks among the golden lamps will remove the Ephesian's lamp from its place; he who has the sharp two-edged sword will make war on the Pergamene with the sword of his mouth. In the message to Ephesus St. John produced a play on the name Nicolaus, 'victor of the people'; the Christian confessor is the true victor, the true Israel, victorious with God (Gen. xxxii. 28). Now St. John produces a second play on the name: this 'victor of the people' is a Balaam (= 'master of the people'), and so a false prophet. No wonder that Nicolaitanism calls for the judgement of Christ's sword; for did not the Lord's angel confront Balaam with a sword drawn in his hand? He would have perished, had not his ass been wiser than he. Even so, his reprieve was short; he died by the sword in the holy war against Midian waged in revenge for the seduction of Israel by the Midianites at Baalpeor (Num. xxxi. 8). The interpretation followed by St. John supposes that Balaam, defeated by the Spirit of the Lord in his attempt to curse Israel on Balak's behalf (Num. xxii–xxiv), had inspired the subsequent attempt of the Moabite women to seduce Israel into idolatry (Num. xxv). The parallel fits; for the Nicolaitans encourage their disciples to eat sacrificial victims at pagan feasts and to break the biblical rules of chastity. 'Fornication', *porneia*, is a word widely used by Hellenistic-Jewish writers for incorrect sexual behaviour of all kinds. We do not know how far the Nicolaitans felt free to go. For 'things sacrificed to idols' and 'fornication' as burning questions in the primitive Church, see 1 Corinthians v–x. We have no means of judging whether St. John was any more rigorous than St. Paul.

The mention of Balak might seem superfluous here; Nicolaus's bad counsel did not, like Balaam's, attain currency through being offered to a heathen prince. But the pairing of false prophet and godless king is of the highest importance for St. John's subsequent symbolism; see chapter xiii. It is not necessary to suppose that St. John foresees such developments in writing chapter ii; he may just as well be moved by the 'false anointeds and false prophets' of Mark xiii. 22 (= Matt. xxiv. 24).

Those who ate idolatrous meats at Baalpeor were turning their backs upon the divine provision of the manna; it is appropriate that it should be promised those who resist the wiles of the new Balaam. It is 'the *hidden* manna' because, once Israel had entered Canaan, it was hidden away among the secrets of God for revelation in the last times. That St. John attaches a mystical sense to it can scarcely be doubted; perhaps John vi. 30–63 is the proper comment. The manna was a small round white thing of unknown name, scattered on the ground (Exod. xvi. 14, 15, 31). St. John doubles the promise of it with the promise of a white pebble marked with an unknown name. The white pebble, being the ballot used by Greek jurors in voting an acquittal, suggests the forensic victory, or justification, of 'him who is victorious': but this divine ballot is presented to the victor as a passport or talisman inscribed with his name. Not with his earthly name, but with a new name given him in heaven. For the 'victor with God' is an Israel, that is, a Jacob renamed by God in being brought into a new relation with himself. Abram had been similarly renamed, and Isaiah (lxii. 1–2, lxv. 15) promises that in the age to come God will rename the people he redeems.

And to the angel of the church in Thyatira write: These things saith the Son of God, who hath his eyes like a flame of fire, and his feet are like fine brass: I know thy works, thy love and faith, thy service and endurance, and that thy last works are more than the first. But I have it against thee that thou sufferest the woman Jezebel which calleth herself a prophetess, and teacheth and seduceth my servants to commit fornication, and to eat things sacrificed unto idols. And I gave her space to repent, and she is unwilling to repent her fornication. Behold, I fling her upon a bed, and those that commit adultery with her into great tribulation, except they repent of her works. And I will kill her children with the death; and all the churches shall know that I am he which searcheth the reins and hearts; and I will give unto every one of you according to your works. But to you I say, the rest that are in Thyatira, as many as have not this teaching, which have not had knowledge of the deeps of Satan, as they say; I lay upon you none other burden. Only hold fast what ye have, until I come. And he that overcometh and keepeth my works unto the end, to him will I give authority over the nations, and he shall rule them with a rod of iron, as a potter's vessels are broken to shivers; as I also have received of my Father. And I will give him the morning star. He that hath an ear, let him hear what the Spirit saith unto the churches.

When St. John comes to take up the first piece of his vision (i. 13–15) by way of title for his fourth message, he changes 'As it were a Son of Man . . . his eyes as flame of fire, his feet like fine brass, as though fired in a furnace' to 'the Son of God, whose eyes', &c. There are two reasons for the change. First, he who appears in vision under the human form (as a son of man) intrinsically is the Son of God; and it is as such that he addresses the churches. Second, 'his feet of brass, as though fired in the furnace', recall the mysterious fourth figure, 'like a Son of God', whom Nebuchadnezzar saw walking free in the furnace and leading the 'three holy children' safely through the fire of their martyrdom (Dan. iii. 25). His eyes are a flame of fire, and so the judgement he will execute on sinners at Thyatira (unless they repent) will show that he is 'the searcher of men's hearts and thoughts'. He is the Son of God, whose feet are as *brass*, whether to walk through fire or to tread down enmity; to him belongs the blessing of Psalm ii: 'The Lord saith unto me Thou art my Son... I will give thee the nations for thine inheritance... thou shalt shepherd them with a rod of *iron*, as potter's ware is smashed to pieces.' Such is the kingly power Jesus shares with his faithful disciple (26–27). It is noteworthy that the divine name *Father* appears here in connexion with Christ's title of *Son*; and that it has not appeared since the exordium (i. 5–6) when the context is similar—Christ extends to his followers the kingship he holds from his Father.

Psalm ii is Davidic; it equips Messiah with the rod or sceptre. Now Balaam, so lately mentioned, when he prophesied in his own despite foresaw the Davidic kingdom under the two emblems of sceptre and star (Num. xxiv. 17). Having mentioned the sceptre, St. John adds the star—this also Christ shares with his faithful. It is the morning star, because Balaam's 'star issuing from Jacob, and sceptre arising from Israel' cannot but recall the rod or shoot from Jesse or from David in Isaiah xi. 1 and, more relevantly, in Jeremiah xxiii. 5, xxxiii. 15, Zechariah iii. 8, vi. 12. For in Jeremiah and Zechariah a word is used which can just as well mean 'dayspring' as 'shoot', and is taken as the former in (for example) Luke i. 78. The ambiguity appears to cover both sides of Balaam's double oracle; the shoot, rod, or sceptre is the star—so long, anyhow, as the star may be taken to be the star *of morning*. To understand how a kingly power can be a star we must have recourse to astrological lore. Stars rise and 'reign' in the heavens: kings reign on earth by the influence of their stars. In making us parties to his dominion Christ gives us the star of his empire. For such ideas, compare the story of the Magi in Matthew ii.

To turn now to the body of the message. Verse 19 is a conscious reversal of 4–5 above: the Ephesian angel had lost his first zeal, the Thyatirean's latter merits are greater than his former. The 'I have it against thee...' passage closely follows that in the message to Pergamum, both in form and in substance. Thyatira, too, tolerates Nicolaitans. The 'woman Jezebel' must be taken as a real figure, like 'Balaam'; with the difference that 'Balaam's' real name, Nicolaus, is given, 'Jezebel's' is not. The Jezebel of history was not a prophetess, but she was the royal patroness of idolatrous prophecy. She was accused of 'many whoredoms' (2 Kings ix. 22), though whether in the literal sense, or in the transferred sense of spiritual infidelities, one cannot tell. It seems probable that she is accused of supporting a licentious Baal-cult, and of thereby 'committing adultery' against the God of Israel; and we may take St. John's accusations in the same double sense. His 'Jezebel' sponsors some kind of sexual laxity; her 'adulterous lovers' however are not those who share her bed, but those who sin against Christ by flirting with her doctrine. It is difficult to see what is meant by the distinction drawn between her 'lovers' and her 'children'. Probably the difference is one of time. Those who associate with her are threatened with present punishment; her whole issue, or sect, is to be ultimately exterminated by 'the death' or pestilence, as Jezebel's posterity was extirpated by Jehu. In view of the parallel 'great tribulation', the bed on to which Jezebel is flung must be a bed of sickness or pain; we may compare the bed from which Jezebel's son never came down alive (2 Kings i. 4). But the punishment fits the crime—she who profaned the bed of love is pinned to the bed of sickness.

Verse 24: Those who have not (in Nicolaitan phrase) got to the bottom of Satan. The Nicolaitans call Satan's bluff by accepting the temptation which ruined Eve. Redeemed from physical bondage through the new Adam, they can, and should, exert a liberty denied to the old; they may venture to share in idolatrous feasts or (perhaps) to let flesh have its way. St. Paul would almost allow the principle (Col. ii. 20-23); he would emphatically deny the application (1 Cor. v-x). Such is the likeliest interpretation we can offer for an obscure phrase. It has been suggested that St. John is parodying a claim to sound the deeps of *God*, but if so he has written both misleadingly and uncharacteristically. It is scarcely conceivable that the Nicolaitans, like certain really lunatic sects of later Gnostic breed, were Satan-worshippers; for surely, if this had been so, St. John would have had more to say about it than a passing allusion.

'I lay on you no other burden', i.e. 'make no further requirement of you': the accepted rule suffices. Cf. Matthew xxiii. 4 and Acts xv. 10, 28. The phrasing is so close to that of Acts, and the occasion so similar, that it is difficult not to suppose a direct reference. Does not St. John make the rule laid down in Acts his own? The Christian, even if he is of Gentile race, should abstain from idol-victims, blood, non-kosher meat, and 'fornication'. There are other grounds for attributing to St. John an acquaintance with the Lucan writings.

And to the angel of the church in Sardis write: These things saith he that hath the seven Spirits of God and the seven stars: I know III

2 thy works, that thou hast the name of being alive, and art dead. Be watchful, and stablish the remaining things that were ready to die; for I have found no works of thine fulfilled before my God.
3 Remember, therefore, how thou hast received and heard; observe and repent. If therefore thou watchest not, I will come as a thief,
4 and thou wilt not know what hour I come upon thee. But thou hast a few names in Sardis which have not defiled their garments;
5 and they shall walk with me in white; for they are worthy. He that overcometh, shall be thus arrayed in white garments, and I will not blot out his name out of the book of life, but will confess his
6 name before my Father and before his angels. He that hath an ear, let him hear what the Spirit saith unto the churches.

'The Seven Spirits of God *and* the seven stars'. 'And' can, of course, express an identity, as in 'Our Lord and our God' (iv. 11), where the sense of the words makes the relation plain. But in a case like the present all analogy is against the supposition (cf. v. 6), which in any case introduces such confusion into St. John's whole symbolism that we beg leave not to discuss it, though it has influential advocates.

St. John places the seven stars (which are the 'angels' of churches) in two relations: in relation with the seven lamps which they tend, and in relation with the seven 'breaths' of divine utterance by which they are admonished to tend them. The first of these two relations is expressed in the title of the Ephesian message, the second in this message to Sardis—for at this point, as we explained above (pp. 70 f.) St. John begins a second series of messages, repeating the first series in order, with, of course, significant differences. That the seven Spirits are to be found in the seven 'breaths' of the divine word to the angels or churches is made abundantly clear by the way in which St. John had contrived the sequence in ii. 26–iii. 1. Departing from the form of the first three messages, he has moved the exhortation 'He that hath an ear...' from its position before the promise for the victorious Christian to a position after it. The result is as follows: 'And I will give him the morning *star*. Hear, you that have ears to hear, what the *Spirit* says to the *churches*. And to the angel of the *church* at Sardis write: These are the words of him who holds the seven *Spirits* of God, and the seven *stars*.' We have the familiar pattern of reversed order: star, Spirit, churches; church, Spirits, stars. He who offers the morning star, and sends the voice of the Spirit to the churches, calls on another church to obey his word, since he has all seven Spirits, and all seven planets (not only the morning star). If this is not what St. John meant, he has certainly taken great pains to make himself misunderstood. For other examples of the sense running over from the end of one message to the beginning of the next cf. ii. 11–12 and iii. 12–14.

The stars are visible parts of the visionary picture in i. 12–16; the Spirits may seem not to be. Not visible, certainly, but audible (cf. John iii. 8); the *phenomena* of the Spirit(s) are the 'breaths' of Christ's speech to the churches. In fact, not all the traits of the visionary description in i. 12–16 were visible phenomena. The couplet 'His voice as the voice of many waters, and having in his right hand seven stars' is a fair enough archetype for 'Thus saith he that has the seven "breaths" of God, and the seven stars'. When he comes to the heavenly vision of iv, St. John squares the introductions of his first and fifth messages with one another, by symbolizing the seven Spirits themselves as seven lamps; in these terms, 'seven stars and seven lamps' are equivalent to 'seven Spirits of God and seven stars' (iv. 5). But that stroke of symbolical balancing is an afterthought, and requires the heavenly setting to make sense of it; it will not fit into the picture exhibited by i. 9–iii. 22.

In the body of the message St. John develops the relation of the (star-)angel of Sardis to the lifegiving breath or Spirit. 'Thou hast the name of being alive, but thou art dead.' He goes on to gloss death and life with sleep and waking, an obvious comparison: 'Wake up and live!' If the angel does not wake, or watch, Christ comes as a thief—a familiar Gospel image for those surprised by the Advent. The next move is to develop *name*. 'You have the *name* of a real live person, but are dead. . . . Still, you have a few *names*' (on your roll) 'at Sardis who have not defiled their garments. . . . He who is victorious, . . . his *name* I will not blot from the Book of Life, but will acknowledge his *name* before my Father.'

The introduction of the image 'defiled garments' as a gloss on death or sleep shows that the torpor of Sardis has taken the same practical form as the Nicolaitanism of Ephesus, Pergamum and Thyatira—a compromise with heathen ways. The promise of white robes recurs in iii. 18, vi. 11, vii. 13, xix. 8, 14. The parallel with the name kept in the Book of Life (cf. Daniel xi. 35 and xii. 1) strongly suggests that the white robes signify justification. In xix. 8 they are said to be the 'righteous deeds of saints'; and if the saints are given them to wear as a badge it means that they are justified on the ground of them.

We may observe that several fresh elements of form are taken over by the Sardian message from its predecessor: 'But [the faithful remainder] in [name of city]'; the sacred name 'Father' in the concluding promise; and the exhortation 'He that hath an ear' in the final position to which the preceding message removed it.

7 And to the angel of the church in Philadelphia write: These things saith the Holy, the True, that hath the key of David, that openeth
8 and none shutteth, and that shutteth and none openeth: I know thy works. Behold, I have set before thee an open door, which none can shut. For thou hast a little power, and hast kept my word
9 and not denied my name. Behold, I set them of the synagogue of Satan, which say they are Jews and are not, but do lie—behold, I will make them to come and worship before thy feet, and to
10 know that I have loved thee. Because thou hast kept the word of my endurance, I also will keep thee from the hour of trial, which
11 is to come on all the world, to try the dwellers upon earth. I come quickly. Hold fast that which thou hast, that no man take thy
12 crown. Him that overcometh will I make a pillar in the temple of my God, and he shall go out thence no more; and I will write upon him the name of my God, and the name of the city of my God, the new Jerusalem which cometh down out of heaven from my God,
13 and mine own new name. He that hath an ear, let him hear what the Spirit saith to the churches.

The message to Philadelphia is worked from the stuff of the message to Smyrna, with which it corresponds in serial order, being the second message in the new cycle. The title of the Smyrnean message was taken from the self-description of Christ in i. 17–18, 'Fear not; I am the first and the last, the living who died, and lo, am alive for ever.' The Philadelphian title continues just where the Smyrnean ended: 'And hold the keys of death and hades'—only that St. John glosses it from Isaiah xxii. 22, a text already quoted in connexion with the gates of hades at Matthew xvi. 19: 'The gates of hades shall not close over it, and I will give thee the keys of the kingdom of heaven.' St. John is closer to Isaiah in saying, 'The key of [the house of] David', but he follows Matthew in seeing it as the key of life and death, which excludes from or admits to the Messianic Kingdom, or the New Jerusalem. In Isaiah's text an unfaithful key-bearer is deposed and a worthy minister put in his place; so Christ here names himself the holy, the true, in contrast to the elders of the synagogue, who are false pretenders to the authority of David's house (Judah). They shut the door, no doubt, in the face of the Christians, but Christ opens them a door which none can shut (cf. John ix. 34–x. 9). The 'Jews who say they are such, and are not but a synogogue of Satan' come straight from the message to Smyrna; so do the reference to the limited time of trial and the mention of 'the crown of life'. Only the Smyrnean is simply promised the crown; the Phila-

THE LORD'S DAY

delphian is warned, 'Hold fast what you have, and let no one rob you of your crown.' The change is appropriate to the use of Isaiah xxii, where the worthless Shebna, in forfeiting the keys, loses his crown (so the LXX) to faithful Eliakim. Eliakim also receives the promise that the Lord will fix him as a nail in a sure place; Christ's promise to the victorious Philadelphian is, 'I will make him a pillar in the temple of my God, and he shall never go out of it.'

The body of the message is constructed as follows. The key-bearer of the house of David opens the Philadelphian a door which none has *power* to shut. He continues, 'BECAUSE (*a*) thou hast but little *power* and yet (*b*) hast *kept* my word and (*c*) not denied my *name*, THEREFORE (*a*) I make the men of Satan's synagogue fall before thy feet and acknowledge thee as my beloved and (*b*) since thou hast *kept* my command to endure, I will *keep* thee from the hour of trial ... and (*c*) him that is victorious I will make a temple-pillar and write on him the *name* of my God and the *name* of New Jerusalem and my own new *name*.' So (*a*) there is a reversal of power and (*b*) a reversal or reciprocation of keeping and (*c*) of naming or of acknowledgement; those who acknowledged Christ's name in this word are acknowledged as his by being marked with divine names in the World to Come.

The two ideas, 'I will fix him in a sure place' and 'I will honour him with my name', are drawn together by the recollection that the twin pillars in Solomon's temple had 'personal' names (1 Kings vii. 21); and, of course, inscribed pillars were universally familiar. So the victorious Philadelphian is to bear the name of the God whose servant he is, of the *New* Jerusalem in which he is a pillar, and the *new* name of Christ, in whom his life is renewed. The name of New Jerusalem, according to the last verse of Ezekiel, itself contains the name of God; it is Jehoshannah, 'The Lord is there'. The prophecy in Isaiah lxv. 15, which we have already quoted for the promise that God's servants shall be called by a new name (ii. 17 above), also tells us that the Lord will rename himself. St. John will not doubt that if the changeless God reveals himself in a new name it must be in the person of his newly revealed embodiment, the Christ. For saints marked with the Name, and therefore everlastingly in God's temple, see vii. 3–8, 15.

And to the angel of the church in Laodicea write: These things saith the Amen, the faithful and true witness, the beginning of the creation of God: I know thy works, that thou art neither cold nor hot. I would that thou wert cold or hot. So then, because thou art lukewarm and neither hot nor cold, I will spew thee out of my mouth. Because thou sayest, I am rich and increased with goods

and have need of nothing, and knowest not that thou art the
18 wretched and pitiable, the poor and blind and naked; I counsel
thee to buy of me gold fired in the flames, that thou mayest be
rich; and white garments that thou mayest clothe thyself, and the
19 shame of thy nakedness appear not; and eyesalve to anoint thine
20 eyes that thou mayest see. As many as I love, I rebuke and chasten.
Be zealous therefore, and repent. Behold, I stand at the door and
knock. If any man hear my voice and open the door, I will come
21 in to him and sup with him, and he with me. To him that overcometh will I grant to sit with me in my throne, as I also overcame
22 and sat down with my Father in his throne. He that hath an ear,
let him hear what the Spirit saith to the churches.

The message to Philadelphia ended abruptly with 'my own new name', leaving a question in our minds. The beginning of the message to Laodicea answers it. The proof text for the new divine name (Isa. lxv. 15) implies that it will be 'the God Amen', i.e. the God of truth. For a similar case of an open question answered by the title to a new speech of Christ compare John vii. 52 f. (omitting, of course, the interpolation of the adulteress). 'Search and see that out of Galilee there arises no prophet.' Again Jesus spoke to them and said: 'I am the light of the world' (referring to Isa. ix. 1–2 as cited in Matt. iv. 15–16). The name Amen is appropriate here for the further reason that Amen is a liturgical conclusion and the message to Laodicea is the final message of the seven. Christ, who is the Amen to all the words of God, attests his sevenfold message to the churches. At the same time the name offers the opportunity of a link with the corresponding message in the first cycle, i.e. that to Pergamum. Antipas had been Christ's witness, Christ's faithful one (ii. 13), but the Amen himself is *the* witness faithful and true, according to Psalm lxxxix. 37, already cited in i. 5 above. In the world of messianic proof-texts Psalm lxxxix. 37, associating Messiah with the witness of the sun and moon, is inseparable from Psalm lxxii. 17 which, as read by the rabbis, was the basis of the dogma that Messiah's name was older than the world: it holds a cardinal position in 1 Enoch (xlviii. 2–3). So it is easy for St. John to pass from 'faithful witness' to 'beginning of the creation of God' (Prov. viii. 22 and Gen. i. 1), and in so doing to balance the Amen with which he started: Christ's name is not only the Amen to God's work, but also the prelude to it; he is the first and the last (i. 17).

The astonishing figure of speech in verses 15–16 must surely owe its place to the Pergamene theme, Christ making war with (the sword of) his mouth. Half-heartedness, or lack of zeal, has been rebuked in most of the messages; here it is described as presenting the divine Christ with a lukewarm offering which he will spit from his mouth. The Old Testament had spoken of God's disgust at his people's offerings, or his rejection of them; and had even described the people themselves as food not fit to eat (Mic. vii. 1–2, Jer. xxiv). But the boldness of St. John's figure is unique.

The transition from 'You are lukewarm' to 'You say, I am rich and in need of nothing' is perfectly natural; complacency leads to loss of fervour. The sweeping condemnation of verses 15–18 is most kindly compensated in the offer of 19–22. The image of the door, introduced in the previous message, is here reversed. Christ opens his door to the Philadelphian; he asks the Laodicean to open his door to Christ. If he is admitted to sup with the disciple now, the disciple will be admitted to sup with him in the messianic feast. The shift from sitting at a common table to sharing a throne (20–21) is scarcely felt in such a context; cf. Luke xxii. 29–30.

Looking back over the messages as a whole, we are prompted to make the following observations. First, the ingenuity of commentators racking the text to establish the difference of spiritual type as between the seven churches is largely misplaced. There is some difference in degree of merit or demerit, but the virtues praised or vices rebuked in all are much the same. The variety of treatment is mainly due to the variety in symbolical approach.

Second, a more positive remark. We have seen that, in virtue of their starting-points, the seven fall into a four and a three, the three doubling the first three of the four. So we may speak of four types, of which the first three do double duty. Now if we look at the four types in the only complete cycle (i.e. the first) we see that the forces of evil are presented systematically in four forms: as false apostles in the first, as a false synagogue in the second (and also in the sixth, its double), as a false prophet and godless king in the third, and as a royal harlot in the fourth. We recall that St. John is going to give his whole Revelation a four-part form, characterized by the seven messages themselves, the seven unsealings, the seven trumpets, and the seven bowls; and we observe that the bowls show the great vision of the royal harlot, the trumpets that of the antichrist king and false prophet; while the unsealings show the Church as the true synagogue of heaven or Israel of twelve tribes, and (to complete the list) the messages show the churches as a field for the activity of her own homebred misleaders, the false apostles of Christ.

There is, then, a prima facie case for supposing that St. John used the four message-types as texts for exposition in the four parts of his book, much as he used the four parts of the Christ vision in chapter i as texts for the messages in ii–iii. The most striking fact about the whole parallel so far noticed is, of course, the position of the Jezebel-figure. It is surely a curiosity deserving explanation that the two last parts of the Revelation should present the kingdom of evil first as a royal monster, then as a harlot-city. To find a corresponding sequence of figures in the last two of the four message-types is a discovery deserving further investigation. Only a complete commentary can test the case; we must be content here with the merest sketch of the evidence. We take the four message-types in turn, with the corresponding 'sevens'.

1. The messages to Ephesus and to Sardis present the Christ who has the seven breaths of Spirit to admonish the seven angel-stars on the tending of their seven church-lamps: who moreover threatens the Ephesian with the removal of his lamp from its place. All this imagery attaches most closely to the setting of the seven messages themselves; and so, as we have already observed, does the *literal* description of the misleaders as false apostles (rather than as Balaams or Jezebels.)

2. The messages to Smyrna and to Philadelphia present the dead yet living Christ as alone empowered to open. The second part of the whole Revelation (iv–viii) manifests the Lamb 'standing as slaughtered', and alone empowered to open the Book. The book, not any mere door; for heaven is *the Synagogue of God*, where the Almighty sits at the head of the elders, and where the great act is the taking and 'opening' of the divine Law. So the saints, repelled on earth from the *synagogue of Satan*, have access to the congregation of heaven. Christ set before the Philadelphians an open door; he shows St. John an open door in the sky, and summons him to ascend into the heavenly congregation. Israel according to the flesh show themselves to be false Judaeans; the Lamb is revealed as the Lion of the tribe of Judah, his faithful are the new people of God (v. 9–10). When they are brigaded as a new people of Twelve Tribes, Judah is set at the head (vii. 4–8). The Smyrneans are threatened with a 'ten days'' test in prison, which probably foreshadows the martyrs' short time of waiting until Advent. The heart of the unsealing-visions is the fifth, in which martyr-souls, confined under the altar, ask 'How long?' and are assured that they have but a little while to wait. The Philadelphian is promised protection from the testing which comes on the whole earth. In the sixth unsealing the impending judgement is held back from the whole earth until the saints have been sealed for protection from its ravages. This is done by the imprinting of a divine mark, afterwards revealed to be a combination of divine names (xiv. 1). The result of the marking is that the saints serve God day and night in his temple (vii. 15). And the Philadelphians

had been promised that they should be pillars in the temple of God, marked with divine names, and never to go out from thence.

3. The Pergamene message contains the figure of Antipas, the martyr, 'the faithful witness'. The first five trumpet-visions are mere descriptions of portents; the sixth introduces the figures of the two witnesses, the ideal embodiments of martyrdom (xi). Proceeding to the seventh trumpet, we have the beast-visions, which present the attack launched against the Saints by the Antichrist (Balak) and his persuasive ally the false prophet (Balaam). We are shown by the way how the throne of Satan, set up at Pergamum, comes to be established over the earth (xiii. 2).

4. No sooner are the formal plagues of the bowls finished than the angel shows St. John the judgement of the great whore, Babylon. Like Jezebel, she is a queen, drunk with the blood of God's servants, and the seductress of multitudes. The message to Thyatira scarcely adds another feature to the visions of bowls beside the Jezebel figure, but the part she plays is enormous. The visions of her overthrow (xvii–xix. 5) and of her replacement by her counterpart, the bride (xix. 6–8, xxi–xxii. 5) give form to the whole *finale* of the Apocalypse.

In view of the way in which our experiment has worked out we may venture to add another point, which would scarcely stand on its own. The seventh message derives its title from the third; but at the same time it is developed in a way which strongly marks the character of the seventh as the last ('Thus saith the Amen . . .'). If, then, we are doubling back the second cycle of messages on the former, to make one set of four, we might hesitate whether to use the seventh in reinforcement of the third, or of the fourth (since that is the last and where the Amen belongs). In the subsequent sevens of his book St. John comes down firmly on the side of pairing the seventh with the fourth—a tuck being taken in the sixth. When, therefore, he comes to write his extended antitypes to the third and fourth messages in the trumpets and bowls respectively, we may expect the seventh message to be taken with the fourth, and so used as material for the bowls. And so in fact we find. The ill-founded boast of present possession made by the Laodicean angel in iii.17 is echoed by the boast of the Jezebel-city in xviii. 7 ff. And St. John has no sooner done with Jezebel in xix. 3 than he provides the saints with pure raiment (xix. 8, iii. 18) invites them to the supper of the Lamb (xix. 9, iii. 20) and opening the doors of heaven, reveals Christ as the Amen, the Faithful and True (xix. 9–13, iii. 14).

Looking at the results we have tabulated, we see that the farther St. John gets from the text in ii–iii, the less detailed his applications become; and that is surely what we should expect. In the unsealings, it is his immediate model and he exploits it in much detail. Many other influences intervene before he composes the trumpets, and more still before the bowls. Yet the later applications of the model, though in the main simpler and bolder, are by no means of less significance than the earlier.

The relationships which we have outlined, and will hope to verify, cast much light on the manner in which St. John's vision developed. They cast a light no less clear or precious on the meaning of the related parts. How did St. John conceive of the evils besetting the churches, and of the churches' struggle against them? And how were the apocalyptic visions proper intended to enforce the exhortation in the messages? Were they nothing but an underlining of the promise and the threat, 'Lo, I come quickly'? No, that was not all. The Christians were to be strengthened against Judaic pretensions by the revelation of their membership in God's heavenly congregation. They were to be shown that Nicolaitanism within the gates was the very tool and spirit of the pagan Antichrist; and they were to be made to see what Antichrist essentially was. They were to understand that the tolerant laxity of a complacent Church was the inebriating cup of the great harlot, the degenerate city-culture destined to destruction. And they were to know that their faithful but helpless resistance to imperial power was a 'conquest' sealed by the victorious overthrow of all God's enemies at the hands of Christ and his elect.

II. THE LION OF JUDAH

(A) THE BOOK

After these things I saw, and behold, a door opened in heaven, and IV the first voice which I had heard, as of a trumpet, speaking with me, and saying, Come up hither, and I will show thee what things must come to pass hereafter. Straightway I was in the Spirit; and 2 behold, there was a throne set in heaven, and one sitting upon the throne; and he that sat was like a jasper and a sardius to look upon; 3 and there was a rainbow round about the throne in look like unto an emerald. And round about the throne were four and twenty 4 thrones, and upon the thrones four and twenty elders sitting clothed in white raiment, and on their heads crowns of gold. And 5 out of the throne proceeded lightnings and voices and thunderings. And there were seven lights of fire burning before the throne, which are the seven Spirits of God; and before the throne as it 6 were a sea made of glass, like crystal.

'After these things I saw' is a rubric introducing a fresh vision in parallel with the long oracular vision (i. 12–iii. 22). St. John's existing state of inspiration enables him to see a door set open in the firmament above, and to hear a second address from the trumpet-like voice which had introduced his first vision. The trumpet-voice now summons him (as it had summoned Moses in Exod. xix) to come up. An ascent on to the heavenly plane requires a fresh gust of inspiration; this being granted him, St. John finds himself in a visionary heaven, and sees the throne.

In spite of the impressive new beginning, there is no break in the continuity of ideas. The end of the message to Laodicea sets open the door between man and God, speaks of the Father's throne, on which the Son has a place, and proclaims the Spirit's present influence. The new vision brings a fresh rapture of Spirit, reveals the Father's throne, that the Son may presently find a place in it through his victory (v. 5–6, vii. 17), and opens the door of heaven. It is true that the opening is reversed; Christ opens to the disciple, not the disciple to Christ. But this reversal of the image merely turns it right side up again; for the door-opening in the message to Laodicea is itself a reversal of the door-opening in the Philadelphian and in the corresponding earlier Smyrnean message, where it is Christ that opens to us. So the end of the Laodicean message acts as a sort of bridge, carrying the Smyrnean–Philadelphian themes over into chapters iv–vii where, as we have said above, they are to play a dominant role.

The great new vision in iv ff. is required to complete the programme of the former vision. The Christ figure of i. 19 commands John to write what he has seen—both what is now, and what will be hereafter. He proceeds immediately to tell John the meaning of something he has seen which is now—the existence of the churches as displayed in the stars and lamps; a meaning which he draws out in the seven messages by relating the stars and lamps to the other parts of the Christ-vision which St. John has seen. So much for 'what is now'. The voice of the new vision calls St. John up to a height, where he may be shown what must be hereafter; for the glories that shall be are already present on high. The trumpet-like voice is still the voice of Christ or of his angel—it is all one; see above, pp. 66 f.

The heavenly glory described in verses 2 ff. is, like the divine Christ seen on earth, the reflection of several Old Testament texts; Ezekiel i. 4–28, Daniel vii. 9–14, Isaiah vi. 1–3 and xxiv. 23 are the most important of these. But St. John's vision develops according to its own logic; he uses the Old Testament originals rather as quarries than as models.

His starting-point is the Father's throne, as open to be shared by Christ and, through him, by Christians (iii. 21). So he begins with the throne, not with its occupant; he mentions, but scarcely describes him, and hastens to show the honour of heavenly enthronement as something that is shared by other enthroned figures. A full description of the divine person here may be all the better spared because it has been given in i. 13–16. The Father, invisible in himself, is made visible in the Son. Cf. John i. 18, iii. 12–13, xiv. 7–9. Such a hint of description as St. John does give here, in deference to the conventions of pictorial vision, is little more than a formalizing of Ezekiel i. 26–28. In Ezekiel the firmament and the throne are described by precious stones, as crystal and sapphire; the divine person is 'as the colour of amber (*electron*), as the appearance of fire'; the nimbus round him is like a rainbow. We may suppose that St. John relates the iridescent nimbus to the sapphire of the throne, and thinks of the rainbow-colours in some stone such as a diamond. He proceeds to translate the rest into terms of precious stones. We must suppose that his 'emerald' is pale and iridescent, while his jasper and his sard, or cornelian, have the colours of amber and flame. Having so described the divine glory, St. John will be able in due course to describe Jerusalem adorned with her bridal jewels as having the glory of God, her light like a stone most precious, a jasper crystal-clear (xxi. 11).

Warrant for beginning a description of Glory with a plurality of thrones may be found in Daniel vii. 'Thrones were set, and an Ancient of Days' [the prototype of all elders] 'took his seat. . . . The court was seated and the books were opened.' A court of elders, sitting with their president in an assembly of Israelites, was either a synagogue for reading the Law or a sanhedrin for pronouncing it. St. John profits by the ambiguity. With their thoughts fixed on 'the things which must happen hereafter' his readers will see in his vision a setting of the scene for the Last Judgement; the book, presently to be revealed, will be the scroll of written evidence. But otherwise viewed, this will be the 'synagogue of God', set against the 'synagogue of Satan' which excludes the Christians. They have access to the heavenly congregation through the incense of their prayers (v. 8, 9). And here the book of the Law, the living will, a sealed book to Jewry, is opened by Christ.

The picture of this heavenly court as a court of judgement is supported by Isaiah xxiv. 21–23. 'The Lord shall bring his hand down upon the *cosmos* of heaven and the kings of earth. They shall gather and lock them in stronghold and prison; after many generations their case shall be tried. . . . The Lord shall reign in Zion . . . and before his elders shall he be glorious' (LXX). This text must surely be St. Paul's warrant for claiming in 1 Corinthians vi. 2–3 that the saints are to judge the *cosmos*, i.e. angels. For Isaiah speaks of the cosmos *of heaven*; and, of course, stars are angels. It must also be St. John's warrant for calling those who sit on thrones with the Lord *elders*, and for seeing their session as kingly, not merely judicial: they have crowns of gold on their heads. An order of angels called 'thrones' was known to Judaism, and is the highest named in Colossians i. 16: 'thrones, lordships, dignities, powers'.

The number of elders, twenty-four, is best derived from the twenty-four elders of priesthood—'princes of fathers' houses, princes of the holy things, *princes of God*' according to 1 Chronicles xxiv. 4–6. The Jewish eldership was not limited to the priesthood, but the elders of priesthood had a privileged place in the Jerusalem Sanhedrin, and ideally the offices should coincide. It was the duty of the priesthood to declare the law; and Ezra the priest was the prototypic scribal elder.

In verse 5 we have translated as 'lights' a word whose original sense is 'torches'. Torches of flaming pine were carried to light travellers; they were scarcely used as fixed lights in St. John's day. The Greek word could carry other senses beside 'torch'; the oil lamps of the little girls in Matthew xxv. 1–13 are so named. Nevertheless it is proper to mark the *lights* here as differently named from the *lamps* in the previous vision. What would seem to have happened is this: Ezekiel says of the four cherubim, whom St. John is just about to describe: 'They went each straight before him; where the Spirit was going, they went and turned not aside. And in the midst of the cherubim [was there] an appearance as of coals of fire burning, as a likeness of lights [or torches] clustering amid the cherubim, and brightness of flame, and from the flame issued lightning' (Ezek. i. 12–13, LXX). St. John sees the fire and lights among the cherubim as the phenomena of that Spirit which guides them; and this becomes his warrant for the attaching of a cluster of lights to the divine glory, revealing the presence of the Spirit and offering an archetype above for the seven lamps ranged on the temple lampstand below. So they too must be seven; the seven lights of heaven supply the spiritual fire to the seven lamps of the churches on earth. St. John therefore writes: 'And from the throne issued *lightnings* and voices and thunders' (amplifying Ezekiel from Exod. xix. 16), 'and before the Throne were seven lights of fire burning, which are the seven Spirits of God.' St. John has already set the seven Spirits before the throne in i. 4, but not, of course, as burning lights.

St. John proceeds: Before the throne also [was] as it were a sea made of glass, like crystal. Since 'crystal-clear glass' was an ordinary description of a commodity, we have no need to think of ice—the alternative meaning of *crystallon*. Compare the 'jasper clear as crystal' and 'transparent glass' of xxi. 11 and 21 below. To determine what St. John means we must observe the careful divisions of his description. He gives us first the throne and the thrones surrounding it (2–4). Then, returning to the throne itself, three things issuing from it (5ᵃ) and two things placed before it (5ᵇ and 6ᵃ). He then goes on to the four cherubim, who are attached to the throne, encircling it (6ᵇ ff.). One of the things placed before the throne is a cluster of seven lights; the other is 'a sort of sea, made of crystal-clear glass'. Since the cluster of lights is the heavenly archetype of a piece of temple-furniture, the 'sea made of glass' might be expected to be the same sort of thing: something that could also stand before the presence. Now Solomon's temple contained a celebrated piece of furniture, the sea of brass, a water-tank; cf. 2 Chronicles iv. 6–7, 'The sea was for the priests to wash in. And he made the ten lampstands of gold.' Its heavenly archetype is made of glass, not brass; but then even the gold of New Jerusalem has to be 'like transparent glass' (xxi. 18, 21). A great glass tank is a vulgar object to us; it would be a miracle to St. John's age. It is *made* of glass; it *contains* water; what else?

The question still to be asked is why in a scene which mentions so little temple furniture the great laver, or 'sea', should be mentioned at all. The answer must be that the fires of the Spirit carry with them the waters of regeneration, in virtue of the constant Christian

THE LION OF JUDAH

association of water and spirit. The conclusion of the great heavenly vision is the redemption of the Saints; bought with the blood of the Lamb, they are priests to God (v. 10). The sea was for the ministering priests to wash in. God's new people of priests, who have their ministry in heaven, have their washing there too. The vision which at length translates the saints to heaven (xv) places them by, or over, the glass sea.

And on the throne round about it were four living creatures full of eyes before and behind. And the first creature was like a lion 7 and the second creature like a bullock, and the third creature had a face as a man, and the fourth creature like a flying eagle. And 8 the four creatures having each of them six wings, are full of eyes round about and within; and they rest not day or night from saying: Holy, holy, holy is the Lord God Almighty, which was and is and is to come. And when the living creatures give glory and honour 9 and thanks to him that sitteth on the throne, who liveth for ever and ever, the four and twenty elders will fall down before him that 10 sitteth on the throne and worship him that liveth for ever and ever, and cast their crowns before the throne, saying, Thou art worthy, 11 our Lord and our God, to receive glory and honour and power, for thou hast created all things, and at thy will they are, and were created.

The four animal figures (man is an animal) form in Ezekiel's vision a four-faced living winged Chariot, on which the throne rests. For St. John they have no such function, but are still the immediate guardians of the throne; rather as though the carved figures round the base of an earthly throne should come alive. St. John describes their position as 'within [the fabric of] the throne, encircling it'. The word for 'within' means literally 'amidst'. St. John uses it, however, in a weakened sense. He has it seven times in all; it never need, and often cannot, mean 'in the middle of'. The common meaning appears to be 'in the area of' either one thing, or several.

The four faces according to Ezekiel i have the order Man, Lion, Bull, Eagle; and have, in that order, been traditionally assigned to the Four Evangelists. We know that current Jewish symbolism associated them with the four quarters of the heaven; St. John identifies them with the middle signs in the four quarters of the Zodiac, and is going presently to associate them with the four winds blowing from the four quarters (chs. vi and vii). The Eagle, indeed, is not a Zodiacal sign, but is also a constellation; and does duty for the Scorpion, a sign of ill-omen; for their heliacal risings were equivalent.

That is to say, when the sun rose in the Scorpion, and so the Scorpion rose too, the Eagle came over the horizon at the same moment. St. John makes the minimum change in Ezekiel's order which will allow the four signs to be read straight round the Zodiacal ring. Lion (summer), Bull (spring), Man, the Waterer (winter) and Eagle, for Scorpion (autumn).

In St. John's order the Lion comes first: and in the visions of unsealings Christ himself is revealed as the victorious Lion of Judah, for which a slaughtered Lamb is the paradoxical visionary equivalent. It is the victory of the Lion of Judah which opens the Book, and so the visions of unsealing (iv–vii) are specially dominated by the lion-figure. St. John proceeds in the direct order of the seasons, advancing from summer to autumn, when he goes on from the Lion to the Eagle, making the Eagle similarly introduce the cardinal visions of trumpets, the three woes (viii. 13); the visions of bowls are introduced by one of the cherubim, and doubtless the winter sign, the water-pourer; for he hands seven angels seven bowls of plagues to pour down upon the earth (xv. 7). So the four cherubim, like the four message-types, are no sooner written down, than they become a text for exposition in the sequel. The fourth, the Bull, does not get a whole quarter of the Apocalypse to himself; for while it is true that there are four cherubim, and four parts to the Revelation, the first part is already finished before the cherubim appear. There is nevertheless a sense in which the Bull can be seen retrospectively to belong to the seven messages; we shall mention the point in a more suitable place (see below, p. 117).

The four cherub-faces of Ezekiel take on in verse 8 the character of Isaiah's six-winged[1] seraphs, whose hymn they continually sing. In sympathy with the unbroken succession of time which their singing covers (they rest not day or night) their hymn rearranges the three tenses of divine being in historical sequence, WAS, IS, COMETH: contrast i. 4, 8, xi. 17, xvi 5. The three 'Holy's of Isaiah's seraphim fittingly support St. John's threefold exposition of the divine existence. The many eyes of Ezekiel's cherub-chariot come in equally well to express or guarantee a sleepless watch, as in the Greek fable of Argus. In Ezekiel's picture the eyes are in the wheels, a feature for which St. John has no use. Since his cherubim form a fence round the base of the throne, they can be described as full of eyes around (i.e. outside) and within, towards God and towards his creation.

St. John transfers the second half of Isaiah's seraphic hymn from the cherubim to the elders. 'Heaven and earth are full of his glory'

[1] So we have the formal pattern: the One on his four-sided throne; its four supporters fringed with twenty-four wings; and twenty-four thrones encircling them.

THE LION OF JUDAH

becomes 'Thou art worthy to receive the glory . . . for thou createdst all things . . .'. The elders seem only to have their royalty that they may cast it down before the feet of God.

And I saw in the right hand of him that sat on the throne a book V written within and on the back, sealed up with seven seals. And 2 I saw a strong angel proclaiming with a loud voice, Who is worthy to open the book, and to loose the seals thereof? And no one in 3 heaven nor in earth, neither under the earth, was able to open the book or to look thereon. And I wept much, because no one was 4 found worthy to open the book or to look thereon. And one of the 5 elders said unto me, Weep not; behold, the Lion of the tribe of Judah, the root from David, hath overcome; he can open the book, and the seven seals thereof.

The divine Glory whom Ezekiel saw showed a scroll in his hand, written within and without (Ezek. ii. 9–10). He spread it before the prophet's eyes and gave it him to devour. Although Ezekiel makes little of the 'spreading', St. John may well reflect that it is no small matter. Does not Isaiah declare that all vision is become as the words of a sealed scroll, which men deliver to one that is learned, saying, 'Read' . . . and he says, 'I cannot, for it is sealed'; and the scroll is delivered to one unlearned . . . and he says, 'I am not learned'? Such, says the prophet, is the present position in Israel (Isa. xxix. 11–12). In due course the scroll will be given the prophet to devour (below x. 8–11). But for the present the business is to open it. The emotion of the scene, the public proclamation in vain search for one capable of opening the oracles, may recall similar narratives in Daniel (ii. 1–24, iv. 4–8, v. 5–17). In the last of the three passages cited it is actually a question of deciphering divine writing. In the second Daniel passage the mystery to be explained is a loud proclamation made by 'a watcher and a holy one' according to our Bibles (Dan. iv. 13–14), but according to LXX 'an angel of strength', *angelos en ischyi*. The title is reflected in the 'strong angel' who makes loud proclamation here. There is another 'strong angelic' herald in Revelation x. 1, a strong-*voiced* angel in xviii. 1–2, and in parallel with him a strong angel at xviii. 21. St. John virtually creates an angelic order of *Ischyri* or strong ones, with the function of heralds. Their strength appears to lie in their vocal powers.

If the angelic elders are the archetypes of the human, whether Jewish or Christian, then teachers or expositors should be found among their number (1 Tim. v. 17); so an elder comforts St. John by pointing to the fulfilment of two scriptures. Jacob's blessing in Genesis xlix. 9–10 presents a figure of conquest, the Lion of Judah:

this is the royal heir of David, the springing again of Jesse's root, endowed (says the oracle in Isa. xi. 1-2) sevenfold with the Spirit of the Lord. The combination of conquest (in the Lion) with inspired power to interpret (in the Scion) is expressed by the strange phrase, 'The Lion ... has *prevailed* (conquered) to open the scroll.' Hebrew idiom transfers 'to win' from battles to lawsuits; and by extension of usage, since to win acquittal or vindication is to merit it, 'win' can be used for 'deserve'. Since the question here is 'Who is worthy to open ...?', 'The Lion has deserved to open' is a direct reply, and might be an adequate translation if St. John were writing Hebrew. But as he is writing Greek, however much influenced by Hebrew, his strange phrase forces the 'conquest' idea on our attention, an idea further emphasized by the title 'Lion'. 'Has won the right to open' is still too flat: 'has won the battle; he can open' is nearer the mark.

By interpreting the two prophecies the elder in fact designates the reader and expounder of the sacred scriptures; and this again is a function which belongs to the elders of the congregation. Since the 'Lion' pointed out by this elder turns out to be the Lamb, we cannot but compare his action with that of John Baptist in designating Christ according to John i. 29 and 36. The Baptist, like the elder, speaks on the basis of scriptural interpretation; like the elder's, his interpretation goes no farther than to designate the sole true interpreter. As suggested in the Introduction (p. 45 above) it is reasonable to see an influence of the Revelation on the Gospel at this point.

6 And I saw between the throne with its four living creatures, and the elders, a Lamb standing as it had been slain, having seven horns and seven eyes, which are the seven Spirits of God sent
7 forth into all the earth. And he came and took it out of the right hand of him that sat on the throne.

The manner in which the Lion has conquered and won his right is revealed when he paradoxically appears in the guise of a Lamb slaughtered (that is, with his throat cut) yet standing on his feet. This sudden appearance of the saving lamb in the hour of need cannot fail to recall the sudden appearance of the ram which redeemed Isaac (Gen. xxii. 13). The Christian revelation has shown that the lamb provided by God to redeem the beloved and only son whom Abraham spared not to give is a type of the beloved Son whom God spares not to give: Abraham received Isaac back from the dead 'in a figure of speech', God received Christ back from the dead in literal fact (Rom. viii. 32 citing Gen. xxii. 16, Heb. xi. 19). He is the Lamb with his throat cut, standing on his feet: the victim who lives, yet who, unlike Isaac, was really offered, bound to the wood.

That the Lamb is Isaiah's 'shoot from Jesse' is shown by his sevenfold spiritual endowment. We are probably to understand that the seven horns of his conquering strength, as well as the seven eyes of his visual discernment, are manifestations of the seven Spirits of God; even though the expository phrase 'which are the seven', &c., is directly applicable to the eyes alone. By his sevenfold strength he can open the book, by his sevenfold vision he can look it over; none other in heaven or in earth could do either (verse 3 above).

The expository phrase about the eyes rests upon a very interesting interpretation of prophecy. Isaiah equips the shoot from Jesse with sevenfold Spirit; Zechariah (iii. 8–10) presents the branch (a synonymous title) with a cluster of seven eyes. 'Hear, O Jesus', he writes. . . . 'Lo I bring my servant the Branch' [that Jesus is himself the Branch is stated on the next page, Zech. vi. 12]. 'For the stone that I set before Jesus—there are seven eyes on the one stone.' It seems that the seven-eyed (i.e. faceted) stone authenticates Jesus as the branch; and why should it do so, unless the seven eyes signify his endowment with the sevenfold spirit of Isaiah's branch, or shoot? Zechariah's next vision adds confirmation. It is the vision of the seven golden lamps. 'What are these?' asks the prophet; and receives the answer: 'This is the Lord's word to Zorobabel: Not by great power or might, but by my Spirit, saith the Lord of Hosts.' [Evidently, then, the seven lamps express the grace of the Spirit in some fashion.] . . . 'These are the seven eyes of the Lord that range over all the earth' (Zech. iv. 4–10). St. John is free to deduce from these texts (*a*) that seven lamps express the Spirit, (*b*) that they are God's seven eyes, ranging the earth, (*c*) that, as eyes, they are given to Jesus, (*d*) that Jesus, as the branch or shoot, is equipped with sevenfold spiritual power. So St. John gives the seven lamp-spirits to the Father in iv. 5, and in v. 6 confers them upon the shoot from David to be his seven eyes; God's sevenfold spiritual beam, sent to radiate from Messiah's countenance throughout the earth.

Where does the Lamb appear? Our traditional English translators allowed themselves to be governed by vii. 17, where the Lamb is 'in the midst of the throne'. But he is not there yet; he has still to *go and take* the scroll from the hand of the enthroned Glory (verse 7). St. John is following Dan. vii. 13, where, at the book-opening in heaven, the Son of Man appears, and *comes to* the Ancient of Days. What St. John writes is 'I saw in the midst of the throne and four living creatures, and in the midst of the elders. . .'. 'In the midst of A, and in the midst of B' is a translators' phrase employed by the LXX in the sense 'between A and B'. The Lamb appears between the throne and its cherub-supporters on the one hand, and the ring of seated elders on the other, i.e. next outside the throne, the cherubim being taken as all one with the throne.

8 And when he took the book, the four creatures and the four and twenty elders fell down before the Lamb, having every one of them harps and golden bowls full of incense, which are the prayers
9 of saints. And they sing a new song, saying, Worthy art thou to take the book and to open the seals thereof; for thou wast slain and hast purchased unto God with thy blood men of every kindred and
10 tongue and people and nation, and made them unto our God
11 a kingdom and priests, and they shall reign on the earth. And I saw, and heard the voice of many angels round about the throne and the living creatures and elders; and the number of them was ten thousand times ten thousand and thousands of thousands;
12 saying with a loud voice: Worthy is the Lamb that was slain to receive power and riches and wisdom and might and honour and
13 glory and blessing. And every creature which is in heaven and on earth and beneath the earth and in the sea, even all that are in them, heard I saying, Blessing and honour and glory and power be unto him that sitteth upon the throne and to the Lamb for ever and
14 ever. And the four living creatures said Amen, and the elders fell down and worshipped.

The taking of the scroll signifies that both judgement and revelation are put into the hands of the Son. The cherubim and elders greet the event by giving him divine praise; in substance, their hymn repeats the doxology to Christ in i. 5–6. The Lamb cannot be worshipped but as the redeemer of men; they present along with their praises the incense of human prayers, and celebrate the saving purchase of the precious blood. For prayers as incense, see Psalm cxli. 2; for the 'new song' see Psalms xxxiii. 3, cxliv. 9. The song is as new as the mercy it extols—as new as the redemption of the gentiles. The saints are to reign *on earth*, not only in the millennium (xx. 4–6). The Future State is in a new-created earth, into which New Jerusalem comes down from heaven (xxi. 1–2, xxii. 5).

The whole infinity of angel hosts join in the worship of the Lamb, with a doxology echoing 1 Chronicles xxix. 11. Then a wider circle still—every created being in any part of God's universe—takes up the theme, uniting the praise of the Lamb with that of the Almighty Father.

(B) SEVEN SEALS BROKEN

VI And I saw when the Lamb opened one of the seven seals, and heard one of the four living creatures say as with a voice of thunder,
2 Come. And I saw, and behold, a white horse, and he that sat thereon

had a bow; and there was given unto him a crown; and he went forth conquering, and to conquer.

And when he opened the second seal, I heard the second living 3 creature say, Come. And another horse came forth, red; and to 4 him that sat thereon it was given to take peace from the earth, and that men should slay one another; and there was given unto him a great sword.

And when he opened the third seal, I heard the third living 5 creature say, Come. And I saw, and lo, a black horse, and he that sat thereon had a balance in his hand. And I heard as it were 6 a voice in the midst of the four living creatures, saying: A measure of wheat for a florin, and three measures of barley for a florin; but hurt not the wine or the oil.

And when he opened the fourth seal, I heard the voice of the 7 fourth living creature say, Come. And I saw, and behold a pale 8 horse, and his name that sat thereon was Death, and Hades followed with him. And power was given unto them over the fourth part of the earth, to kill with sword and with famine, by the death and by the wild beasts of the earth.

The opening of the scroll by the successive breaking of its seven seals is to provide a new seven of visions in parallel with the seven messages. It is worth observing how closely the new design is patterned on the stencil of the old. In v. 1, just as in i. 16, the Person of Glory has a cluster of seven in his right hand; there it was stars, here it is seals. The messages arose through the Revealer's attending one by one to the stars, the unsealing-visions through his attending one by one to the seals. The messages were concerned with the seven lamps at the feet of Glory, interpreted first as the seven churches, but reinterpreted since as those seven Spirits through which the Revealer addressed them. And the unsealings are performed in the power of these same seven Spirits, first manifested as lights before the feet of Glory, but afterwards as the 'horns' and 'eyes' of the Revealer, through which he is empowered to unseal. We remarked that successive addresses to seven stars (the planets) contained the implicit scheme of a week; but because the messages dealt with 'the things that are now' there was no room for temporal or historical movement; the 'week' was purely formal. The repetition of the pattern is to take up the second part of the programme—'the things that must be hereafter'; here the week comes into its own, and historical movement sets in.

In the messages, a mere scheme of seven angel-stars to be

addressed did not supply the suggestions necessary to get the addresses moving; the seer cast back over his previous vision, and found starting-points in four descriptions of Christ contained in the four parts of it. The bare idea of seven seals to be broken is equally unfertile; once again St. John casts back, and finds the positive suggestion he requires in four figures of the vision directly preceding —the four faces of the cherubim.

The development is perfectly continuous. *When the Lamb took the book* the cherubim and elders started a doxology which echoed through the universe; the four cherubim closed it with their united 'Amen'. *When the Lamb opened the first seal* (and each of the next three) one of the cherubim cried 'Come' (= Maranatha). We have already inferred in comment on i. 6–7, that 'Amen; come [Lord]' was a customary response to a doxology giving Christ the kingdom and the glory. The 'Amen' asseverates that the kingdom is his indeed; the 'Come' prays that it may prevail on earth, as it is in heaven. Now since true prayer does not go unanswered, and since the Lamb is actually breaking the seals, we may expect to see some movement of his coming.

The first cherub cries with a voice like thunder, for he is the lion; cf. x. 3 where an angel's voice, being like the roar of a lion, awakes seven echoes of thunder. The lion's roar fitly evokes the figure of conquest, following the elder's words in v. 5, 'The Lion has conquered.' The conqueror is no other than the Lion of Judah, the Word of God; cf. xix. 11–16, where he is unambiguously presented in the same guise. He comes victorious from his resurrection, to subdue the earth. But had not he said himself 'Think not that I came to bring peace on the earth; I came not to bring peace, but a sword'? (Matt. x. 34). And had not he also said, that the first phase of the church's history would combine wars and tumults, persecutions and natural disasters, with the preaching of the gospel to all nations? (Matt. xxiv. 6–14). So when the Maranatha of the lion is followed in due order by that of the bull, a beast of slaughter, there appears the bearer of the sword, to take peace from the earth, that they may slaughter one another.

At this point St. John falls visibly into the lines of a preconceived design. 'Sword' is the first of a traditional list, the Lord's three grievous plagues, sword, famine, and pestilence (Ezek. vi. 11, and parallels). Can these be squared with the last three cherubic figures? The bull for sword, or knife (the Greek word is perfectly ambiguous). The Man should come next; but the constellation of the scales, the sign of scarcity, is in the very claws of the Eagle's zodiacal equivalent, the Scorpion; while the Man (Aquarius) presides over the death of the year, a season marked by the memory of death in the Jewish calendar;

so let him stand for *the* death (the pestilence)[1]. An alternative version of Ezekiel's list (Ezek. xiv. 21) adds 'wild beasts'; and when St. John comes to summarize in verse 8, he feels the appropriateness of four plagues to four cherubim, even though the first cherub evoked no plague by his recorded cry. So in listing the plagues he goes one place farther, and takes the lion again; he has no difficulty in interpreting him as a sign of marauding beasts from the wilds.

St. John's pattern, already complicated enough, is still incomplete. The cherubim cry in heaven; their cries are suitably answered by supernatural figures intervening on earth. Where shall St. John look for the four figures he requires? He need not look far. He has already drawn heavily on the fourth and fifth visions of Zechariah (Zech. iii–iv). He has only to turn back to the first (Zech. i. 7–17) and there he has the figures of four horsemen scouring the world. And they are exactly what he needs. If the four cherubim, that is, the four aspects of the sky, cry aloud, who shall be the executive ministers of their voices? Who but the four winds of heaven, which blow from the four quarters? The four riders of Zechariah i are not actually said to be the four winds; but Zechariah vi presents four chariots, explicitly so named, and drawn by horses of the same four colours as those on which the riders of Zechariah i are mounted. One can scarcely hesitate to make an identification. St. John, in fact, follows Zechariah fairly closely. For he, too, begins with a vision of horsemen not explicitly revealed as winds; and follows it presently with an explicit vision of four winds at the four corners of the earth (vii. 1 below). In Zechariah the second vision of horses shows the winds as ministers of destruction; the first shows them as scouts. In St. John both visions reveal ministers of destruction.

The horsemen of Zechariah are distinguished from one another by the colour of their mounts, and by nothing else. Zechariah's text is, however, confused. Red, black, and white are mentioned; so is dapple-grey. St. John rearranges them to suit his scheme. White for victory, red for slaughter; black must do for famine (we read of blackened faces, where famine coincides with a scorching drought). To get a colour for pestilence, St. John gives the forced description 'livid' in place of dapple-grey.

So much for the general lines of the symbolism. We turn to the detail of the several episodes. Sword and bow (verses 2 and 4) are the two proverbial weapons of war. Since the word for sword means equally 'butcher's knife', sword may stand for slaughter, leaving bow for the other symbol St. John requires—victory. The best positive warrant we can find in older scripture for a special association of 'bow' with 'conquest' is 2 Kings xiii. 15–17. But St. John relies on

[1] Ezek. i. 10 (cf. x. 14) gives the sense of St. John's order: front, two sides, back.

no such out-of-the-way association to make his point. He does not draw bow and sword into direct comparison, but garland and sword. The first rider, a bow-bearer, is *given* a garland of victory; the second, a minister of discord and slaughter, is *given* a sword.

Scales (verse 5) are a sign of famine, since Ezekiel makes the starving Jerusalemites 'eat their bread by weight' (Ezek. iv. 10). Not content with this reference, St. John puts in a cruel reversal of the promise of plenty in 2 Kings vii. 1. A *dinar*, that is, a day labourer's wage (Matt. xx. 2), is to buy one person's allowance of wheat—the measure St. John names is variously estimated at $1\frac{1}{2}$ pints, or a quart. So a man will be hard put to it to feed his family, even if he buys barley, which is three times cheaper. Libra spanned September and October. Perhaps if the corn-harvest failed in April and May, men might begin to tighten their belts in October. They would then be just finishing the fruit-gathering, and might observe the irony of nature, that grapes and olives had gone unscathed; of the traditional triad corn, wine, and oil, corn, at a pinch, will keep you alive without the other two, but not they without the corn.

But in the context of St. John's serial judgements, the suggestion cannot fail, that the fruit-trees will have their day of visitation. In Exodus ix–x the plague of hail smites the barley and spares the wheat; but only that the plague of locusts may eat up whatever the hail had left. The trees spared in Revelation vi. 6 are duly smitten in viii. 7; but merely to prepare for a more sinister climax. When St. John's locusts come at last, it is to spare vegetation of all sorts, and strike at mankind (ix. 4).

The first three horsemen have their distinguishing attributes, bow or garland, sword, scales. It is enough to say of the fourth, that his name is '[the] death'. Such is the awful name pestilence bears in the Greek Old Testament. St. John drives it home by adding, 'And Hell was at his heels'. The equivocation on the meaning of death enables St. John to treat this plague as not one form of death only (i.e. pestilence) but as all the four forms, whether sword, famine, pestilence, or wild beasts. By thus epitomizing the four in the last of them, St. John shews his sensitiveness to the prophecy he is rehandling, Ezekiel xiv. 12–23: 'If I send famine. . . . If I cause noisome beasts to roam the land. . . . If I bring a sword. . . . If I send pestilence. . . . How much more, then, when I send my four grievous judgements [all together], sword, famine, noisome beasts and pestilence. . . .' The warning accompanying Ezekiel's four 'if's and his 'how much more' is that in each case the righteous should save their own souls alive, no one else's. If St. John's reader recalls his Ezekiel, he will be well prepared to see, at the next seal-opening, the souls of the righteous, saved or treasured up in these days of the four grievous plagues.

The *four*fold death, with his assistant, Hades, is given power over a *fourth* part of the earth. The sequel (viii. 7 ff.) may convince us that a fourth-part destruction has been widely scattered over the inhabited earth, rather than that one quarter of it has been totally depopulated.

And when he opened the fifth seal I saw under the altar the souls of them that had been slain for the word of God and for the testimony which they held; and they cried with a loud voice, saying, How long, O Master holy and true, dost thou not judge nor avenge our blood on them that dwell on the earth? And white robes were given to every one of them; and it was said unto them that they should rest yet a little while, until their fellow-servants and brethren, which should be killed as they were, fulfilled their number.

The first four unsealings have given occasion for all four cherubim to say their *maranathas*. The fifth finds new intercessors, and a new prayer; the souls of martyrs cry 'How long, O Lord . . .', a set phrase for invoking God's intervention, familar from the Psalms (vi. 3, lxxiv. 9, 10, lxxix. 5, lxxx. 4) and, even more relevantly, from Zechariah i. For when the four riders have scouted the earth, and given their report, 'How long, O Lord of Hosts,' asks the angel, 'wilt thou not have mercy on Jerusalem?' The cry in Zechariah is motived by the horsemen's discovery that all the earth is quiet; the cry in St. John, by their having lighted a false dawn of hope. The white rider's triumph is not the final victory; the plagues brought by his successors are but 'the beginning-pains of travail'; as Christ had hinted in his prophecy, the saints need to be fortified against a loss of patience.

The cherubim have cried, and now the martyrs cry. The cherubim are native to the throne; the martyr-souls are denizens of the altar. The throne has spoken; now the altar speaks. In the earthly Zion the two great components of the Holy Place were temple and altar, the presence-chamber of God, and the place of his people's offerings. Of these two features, the temple symbolized heaven, and itself contained an incense-altar symbolizing the heavenly altar. It logically follows that the temple of Heaven above has no altar standing before its doors, only the altar within it; no animal-sacrifice, only the offering of incense, and that within the very shrine, in God's immediate presence; the veil, which on earth hid the Mercy Seat from even the interior altar, having in heaven no place. In iv the throne-room of Glory has been manifested rather as a synagogue than as a temple. Yet it has some temple features, the seven lights, the 'sea', the cherubim; and when the sole qualified reader of the scroll is found to be the sacrificial Lamb, synagogue and temple come into that equipoise which they have in the Christian cult. So the Presence may be seen as a temple, and we may look to find throne and altar both there, and cries from the altar in sequel to voices from the throne. Cherubim belong to the throne; what vocal beings are there in the altar? The blood of victims ran down into the hollows under the altar of sacrifice, making propitiation, 'because the blood is the soul'. Shall not the blood-souls of the martyrs come up upon the altar of heaven, seeing that the Lamb himself, slaughtered like them on earth, is a living sacrifice above? So there they are treasured, in the ground beneath the altar; and from the ground they cry. For the blood of righteous Abel cries from the ground, calling down vengeance on the head of Cain (Gen. iv. 10). As a whole catena of texts from different strata of i Enoch shows, the cry of Abel's blood had been built up into a dogma; martyr-souls beneath the ground invoke judgement on their murderers until it is fulfilled.

The dogma had received Christian expression in Matthew xxiii. 29–36, a text specially suggestive to St. John's present concerns, since it traces martyrdom from Abel to Zacharias slain between the temple and the altar. In saying 'Fill ye up, then, the measure of your fathers ... that on you may come all the righteous blood spilt upon the ground from the blood of Abel ...' the Gospel may be thought to touch upon another current dogma—that a predestined number of martyrs must be 'made full' before the end comes; a dogma anyhow presupposed in the answer here given to the martyr-souls, that they must wait a little, for the filling up of the number destined to die as they have died.

The gift of white robes is an assurance of justification, and foretaste of glory. It is certainly not the resurrection body, for which they must wait until the millennium (xx. 4). As we have seen, justification is victory (above, p. 94). The first rider came on a white horse, and was given a victor's garland; the martyrs are given white robes. Compare the promise 'to him that overcometh' at Sardis (iii. 5).

The matching of the white robes in the fifth unsealing against the white horse in the first is part of a whole system by which the second half of the seven is brought into parallel with the former half; St. John works over the four in the three, just as he had done in the messages.

1. White horse for victory.
2. Red horse for bloodshed. ⎫
3. Black horse for famine. ⎭
4. Livid (lit. 'green') horse for pestilence; four plagues on a fourth of earth.

5. White robes for victory.
6. Earthquake; sun black as haircloth, moon as blood.
7. Seven new plagues, the first on a third of earth and on all green grass.

The meaning of the parallel is a lesson already plain in Christ's prophecy on the Mount of Olives. Christ's victorious passion may bring 'the beginning-pains of travail'; only the addition of the Church's passion to his, will bring the new world to a birth; and not even the Church's passion, until it has been made full in the 'great tribulation' of Antichrist. So the plea of the altar, where the saints are sacrificed, must be added to the plea of the throne, in which Christ is already glorified; and the plea of the altar must be made full—the full number of martyrs must be offered.

And I saw when he opened the sixth seal, and there was a great 12 earthquake; and the sun became black as sackcloth of hair, and all the moon became as blood; and the stars of heaven fell to earth, 13 as a fig tree casteth her unripe figs under the shaking of a strong wind. And the heaven removed as a scroll rolled together, and 14 every mountain and island moved from their places. And the kings 15 of the earth, the nobles and captains, the rich and the mighty, every man bond or free, hid themselves in the dens and rocks of the mountains. And they say to the mountains and rocks, Fall on 16 us, and hide us from the face of him that sitteth on the throne and from the wrath of the Lamb; for the great day of their wrath is 17 come, and who is able to stand?

The 'beginning-pains' of the Synoptic apocalypse are war, earthquake, and famine and (according to St. Luke alone) pestilence. Famine and pestilence belong with war, as its natural consequences. They are among the horsemen, and ride after the sword. Earthquake is another thing entirely, an 'act of God', a direct answer to the martyrs' prayer. It requires no secondary agent; the Lamb's breaking of the sixth seal rocks the universe. It looks like what they pray for, the end of the world. The pillars of the earth are shaken; the sky seems to reel. St. John develops the description with time-honoured strokes of hyperbole. Two of his own improvements are worth noticing. According to Joel ii. 31 the sun is turned to darkness when the moon is turned to blood; he puts on black sackcloth, according to St. John, now the saints have put on festal white. When the sky rolls together like a scroll according to Isaiah xxxiv. 4, the stars fall as leaves from a vine or a fig. They fall according to St. John like unripe fruit cast by a fig in a high wind; a formula which keeps alive the idea of destruction by gales implicit in the horsemen-image, and about to be taken up in vii. 1. The guilty terror of the heathen is as though the heavenly firmament had folded up indeed, leaving them under the naked threat of almighty vengeance. The language derives from Isaiah ii. 10, &c., and Hosea x. 8. It is typical of St. John's combination of images that the Lamb's having all but completely *opened* the scroll of judgement should cause the sky to *roll up* like a scroll.

VII After this I saw four angels standing at the four corners of the earth, holding back the four winds of the earth, that no wind might 2 blow on the earth or on the sea or on any tree. And I saw another angel ascend from the sunrising, having the seal of the living God; and he cried with a loud voice to the four angels to whom it was 3 given to hurt the earth and the sea, saying: Hurt not the earth, neither the sea, nor the trees, till we have sealed the servants of our 4 God on their foreheads. And I heard the number of the sealed: a hundred and forty and four thousands sealed out of every tribe 5 of the children of Israel. Of the tribe of Judah were sealed twelve thousand, of the tribe of Reuben were sealed twelve thousand, of 6 the tribe of Gad were sealed twelve thousand. Of the tribe of Asher were sealed twelve thousand, of the tribe of Naphtali were sealed twelve thousand, of the tribe of Manasseh were sealed 7 twelve thousand. Of the tribe of Simeon were sealed twelve thousand, of the tribe of Levi were sealed twelve thousand, of the 8 tribe of Issachar were sealed twelve thousand. Of the tribe of Zebulun were sealed twelve thousand, of the tribe of Joseph were sealed twelve thousand, of the tribe of Benjamin were sealed twelve thousand.

The insertion of a chapter-division between vi. 17 and vii. 1 is particularly unfortunate, since it disguises the continuity between the three visions under the sixth seal (vi. 12–17, vii. 1–8, vii. 9–17). The theme is perfectly unbroken; it deals with the fulfilment of the martyrs' prayer and of the promise made to them in the previous unsealing. The great earthquake of vi. 12–17 shows the figure of the vindication against their enemies for which they prayed; but wrath is manifested only that it may be held back until the saints have been sealed against its effects. A last vision (vii. 9–17) will show how the sealing, and the endurance of the great persecution under Antichrist, give God the multitude of saints he desires. The unexpected prolongation of the sixth unsealing gives almost physical expression to the delay which the impatience of the saints must learn to stomach. We expect the breaking of the seventh seal at vii. 1, but we do not witness it until viii. 1.

Of the pictorial elements in the previous vision St. John picks out

THE LION OF JUDAH

the cosmic hurricane which shook the stars from the branches of the sky; he puts it in charge of the angels of the four winds, who correspond, as we have explained, to the four horsemen; and they are made to hold destruction back. There is nothing much like this in canonical scripture; it seems likely that St. John has accepted a hint from 1 Enoch lxvi, where 'the angels of punishment prepared to come and let loose all the powers of the waters' are commanded to hold them in check, while the Ark is built to save Noah's righteous family. We may remark that, in the prophecy on the four grievous judgements (see above, p. 100), it had been the burden of Ezekiel's oracle that the righteousness of even *Noah*, Daniel, and Job should save their souls alive, and theirs alone, in the terrible day. St. John changes the waters to winds, in harmony with his context; and he turns from Ezekiel's oracle of the four grievous judgements to his description of the divine justice taking visible effect. In Ezekiel ix an angel-scribe puts an ink-mark on the foreheads of the righteous, before the destroying angels (symbolizing Nebuchadnezzar's troops) are let loose on Jerusalem. In conformity with his own images, St. John substitutes the divine seal for the ink-mark. God's stamp must be inviolable; none but the Lion from the tribe of Judah could touch, or look upon, the seven seals of God's book; no created power will dare to defy God's seal on the elect foreheads from the tribe of Judah, and from the other tribes brigaded with it.

Can we look behind the imagery, and ask what reality St. John is describing? Several texts in the messages suggest that the device on the seal is the name of God or of Christ; and especially the promise to the Philadelphian (iii. 12) of which we have explained the special relevance to this passage (above, p. 81). The suggestion is strongly confirmed by xiv. 1 below. Sealing with the Name is surely the imparting of Christian status in baptism. Circumcision had been the *seal* of the old covenant according to Romans iv. 11, while of Christians the same apostle says: 'He who makes firm our standing in the Anointed, and who has anointed us, is God; who has sealed us also, and set the earnest of the Spirit in our hearts' (2 Cor. i. 21-22). St. John's way of saying that Antichrist cannot be manifested, nor the end come, until the Gospel has been preached to all nations (Matt. xxiv. 14) will be to say that the predestined number of the elect must be stamped with the Name, before the persecution of Antichrist gives them the opportunity to merit their eternal reward. St. Paul reminded the Thessalonians that a caretaker power, or person, delaying the accession of Antichrist, was a part of the Christian scheme (2 Thess. ii. 6-7); Antichrist cannot come 'until this power is out of the way'. In spite of all that has been written to the contrary, the most natural interpretation of St. Paul is that which follows the lines of Revelation vii. An angel of God, or a commandment of God (it is all one) restraining the appearance of Antichrist, holds sway until the apostolic mission has run its course; then 'the obstacle will be removed'.

St. John hears the result of the census when it is reported: cf. 2 Samuel xxiv. 8–9. The ideal 'squareness' of the number, twelve thousands in each of twelve tribes, requires no comment; it fitly symbolizes a perfect Israel of God. What does require explanation is the order of the tribal list. It is not at all like St. John to write it haphazard; but as it stands it makes no intelligible sense, and conforms to no known principle of reckoning the tribes. We will not weary our readers by an inventory and analysis of all the tribal lists which scripture contains, since the result would merely prove a negative. The solution of the difficulty is as follows.

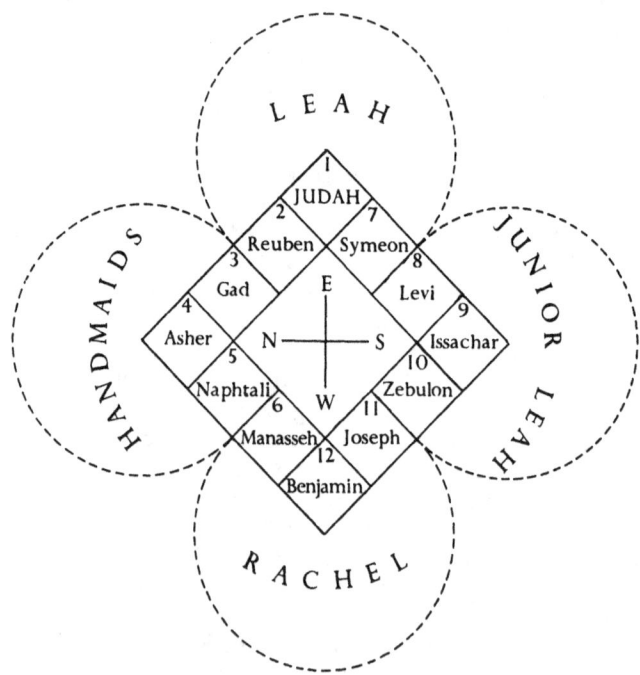

The tribes are a square (12 × 12). 'Square number', to us a metaphor, was a physical fact to the ancients. Having no cyphers to reckon by, they saw numbers as rows of dots equally spaced. We have just had the world set before us as a four-cornered square; the angel of the seal approaches from the east, and starts at Judah, the

THE LION OF JUDAH

tribe of the Dayspring (see above, p. 76). Does he not then go round the square Israel, taking the tribes in order? Since Judah is the head, it will be suitable to draw the square lozengewise with Judah as 'head of the corner': and to avoid going backwards or upwards, we may write the tribes in two lists, round the two bent sides of the lozenge. Such an arrangement counts from the east and north corners, then (making a fresh start) works to the south and the west corners. Now in chapter xxi. 12–13 and 17, St. John mentions the tribal names again, in connexion with the number 144, as attaching to the gates on the four sides of the four-square Jerusalem; and he uses the same broken order: those to the east, and those to the north; those to the south, and those to the west. But we need not look to the remote sequel for our present authority. The order St. John follows here in his vision of the four winds is the same order as he followed in the four horsemen. Judah is the Lion. If we put the cherubim at the four corners in their true astrological order, the Bull will have Asher, the Scorpion or Eagle Issachar, and the Man Benjamin. So we may say that in counting the tribes St. John starts from the Lion, goes on from the Bull, then, making a fresh start, goes to the Scorpion or Eagle, and on to the Man.

The list so arranged not only makes sense (as we shall presently show in detail) but comes very close to a list in Ezekiel which is also arranged round the gates of an ideal square Jerusalem, and which must surely have served St. John as a model. Ezekiel goes by sides, not by corners—St. John himself falls back into the Ezekiel pattern in xxi. Ezekiel arranges his four threes differently; but in themselves they are almost identical with St. John's threes. Ezekiel writes

NORTH: Reuben, Judah, Levi. (Senior Leah)
EAST: Joseph, Benjamin, Dan. (Rachel)
SOUTH: Simeon, Issachar, Zebulon. (Junior Leah)
WEST: Gad, Asher, Naphtali. (Handmaids)

All the tribal patriarchs were the sons of Israel, but by different mothers: the drama of the mothers' rivalry is told in Genesis xxix-xxx, and xxxv. 16–26. Leah had six sons, Rachel only two; there were in addition two sons of Rachel's handmaid, adopted by Rachel, and two of Leah's, adopted by Leah. Ezekiel's method of fitting the several families to the pattern of a square is to divide Leah into two threes, and build up Rachel into a three by crediting her with the eldest of her two adopted sons, Dan. He makes the point clear by putting in the junior Leah tribes between Dan and the other sons of handmaids. There is one other artificiality in Ezekiel's list. Judah was in fact the fourth of Leah's children. By exchanging him with Simeon, he brings the royal tribe into the senior group.

St. John revises both of these artificialities. He makes a genuine three for Rachel, by substituting Manasseh's name for Dan's. In fact, the tribe of Joseph had become two tribes, Ephraim and Manasseh. Since Ephraim was Joseph's principal heir, Joseph covers Ephraim; Manasseh is added. A by-product of this improvement is the disappearance from the list of Dan, one of the Twelve. Perhaps it will not have displeased St. John; let Dan be the Judas of the patriarchs. Dan had, in fact, a dubious reputation (Gen. xlix. 17, Lev. xxiv. 10–11, 1 Kings xii. 28–30, Jer. iv. 15 and viii. 16). In the end (Rev. xxi. 12–14) St. John puts the names of the apostles round the city, pairing them with the tribes. We cannot suppose that Iscariot's name would stand there, any more than Dan's.

Then as to the artificial promotion of Judah: instead of exchanging Judah and Simeon, St. John simply puts Judah up two places. The result is that Levi, not Simeon, is pushed out of the first three. The alteration is presumably deliberate, for in the new dispensation Levi is degraded. The priesthood is united with the kingship in the tribe of Judah, as the writer to the Hebrews so copiously explains; Levi has no special standing (see especially Heb. vii. 11–14).

St. John, further, rearranges the order of Ezekiel's four groups of three. The beauty of the new arrangement is obvious: it balances Leah and Rachel at opposite corners, it makes the two actual surviving lay tribes the top and the bottom, it allows us to read the three families of Leah, Rachel, and handmaids straight round the ring in the order of their dignity.

9 After these things I saw, and lo, a great multitude which no man could number, of every nation, of all tribes, peoples and tongues, standing before the throne and before the Lamb, arrayed
10 in white robes, and palms in their hands. And they cry with a loud voice, saying, Salvation to our God that sitteth upon the throne,
11 and unto the Lamb. And all the angels stood round about the throne, and about the elders and the four living creatures, and fell
12 before the throne on their faces and worshipped God, saying, Amen; Blessing, and glory, and wisdom and thanksgiving, honour and power and might, be unto our God for ever and ever. Amen.
13 And one of the elders spoke to me, saying, What are these that are
14 arrayed in white robes, and whence came they? And I said unto him, Sir, thou knowest. And he said to me, These are they which are to come out of the great tribulation, and have washed their
15 robes and whitened them in the blood of the Lamb. Therefore are they before the throne of God, and serve him day and night in his

THE LION OF JUDAH 109

temple; and he that sitteth upon the throne shall tabernacle with them. They shall hunger no more, neither thirst any more, neither shall the sun smite upon them, nor any heat. For the Lamb which is on the throne shall shepherd them, and guide them unto watersprings of life; and God shall wipe away all tears from their eyes.

16
17

The last vision of the three under the sixth unsealing shows the final consequence both of the sealing on the forehead, and of the martyrs' prayer. Those who were sealed come through to salvation; the martyrs need no longer wait for the family of martyrs to be complete; they are merged with the innumerable host of their brethren victorious in the great persecution, and arrayed as they themselves have been arrayed.

There is an obvious contrast between vii. 4 and vii. 9: 'I heard the number of the sealed, 144 thousands from every tribe of the sons of Israel' and 'a great multitude none could number, from every nation, all tribes, peoples, and tongues . . .'. On the face of it, a limited number of Israelites are sealed against danger; an infinite number of men from every race triumph over the great persecution. But the distinction is difficult; we have known since v. 9–10 that God's Israel of priestly kings is made up from every nation. Why should Israelites by fleshly descent be singled out for protection in an ordeal which all must face? St. John cannot be telling us that Jewish Christians stand firm by divine grace, while Gentile Christians make do on human virtue.

We must take the difficulty here with the similar difficulty in xxi. 9–xxii. 2. The New Jerusalem will be a four-square city measured in twelves, with the names of the twelve tribes over its gates. But the nations shall walk by its light, their wealth and splendour shall pour in through the open gates—not any impurity, however, nor any men but those inscribed in the Lamb's book. The tree of life planted there shall bear twelve fruitings (as for the twelve tribes) while its leaves shall serve for medicine to heal the nations. Now this picture, taken literally, is sheer Judaism. Israel endures the tribulation, merits the kingdom, and is enthroned in the imperial city. The nations are illuminated by her rule and come to share in the blessings of the true worship, glorifying the city they honour with their offerings. St. John keeps the picture, because it is in the prophets; he does not take it literally. The pouring in of the nations does not await the world to come; the *cadres* of God's Israel were filled out with Gentile recruits, in time to fight the battle against Antichrist's tyranny.

The paradox in vii is the same, only that it is taken several steps back, from the establishment of New Jerusalem to the sealing of a host to meet Antichrist. It is a foursquare Israel that is sealed, to guarantee the victory; yet uncounted multitudes of Gentiles swell the host, and they must have been sealed too. Such is St. John's way of saying that the triumph of God's people and their blessed future are secured by his promises to Israel, and that the Gentiles are nevertheless brought in to share the promises. How purely symbolical such a way of speaking is can be judged from the equalization of numbers sealed from the twelve tribes. In St. John's day there were only the tribes of Judah, Benjamin, and Levi; some Simeonites, perhaps, were merged with the Judaeans. No one but the heretical Samaritans claimed to belong to any other tribe; and the Samaritans' claim to be Josephites was disallowed. If a twelve-tribe Christian Israel is to be made up, Gentiles must actually fill the squares.

By the contrast between the numbered tribes and the innumerable host, St. John gives expression to two antithetical themes, both equally traditional. God knows the number of his elect; those who inherit the blessing of Abraham are numberless as the stars (Gen. xv. 5). Yet St. John cannot mean either that the number of Gentile saints is unknown to God, or that the number of righteous Israelites can be counted by men. What he tells us is, that his ear receives a number resulting from an angelic census; and that his eye is presented with a multitude he cannot count, as was Abraham's when called upon to look at the stars. The vision of the white-robed host, purified by martyrdom, must in any case reflect Daniel xi. 35. The theme is continued in Daniel xii. 1-3, where the same persons are described as 'registered in the book' and as 'like the stars'; it is easy to conclude 'numbered, therefore, yet uncountable'.

The setting of the picture in vii. 9-17 is developed quite simply from vi. 9-11. There the martyr-souls were seen in some sort of withdrawal or confinement beneath the altar of the heavenly temple. Now that their number is complete, they stand free before the throne. Palms of victory are added to their white robes. They cry 'Hosanna!' (salvation) and the choir of heaven takes up the doxology. The detail of the picture is not to be insisted upon. St. John sees the saints in their ultimate perfection, as is shown by the virtual repetition of vii. 15-17 in xxi. 3-6, xxii. 1-4. He does not think that the final state is to be reached by souls stepping up out of the crypt of heaven into the choir. The bodily resurrection, not to name the millennium, will have intervened; they will inhabit the earth, not the sky, after heaven has descended into it.

The elder's comment explains both the provenance of the multitude, and the whiteness of their robes. Beside the text of Daniel just cited (xi. 35) the elder may rely on the Lion of Judah oracle

(Gen. xlix. 9–12) which he quoted when he last spoke to St. John (v. 5): the tribe washes his robe in the blood of the grape. What the elder means is that they have died, or at least offered their lives, and that their sacrifice cleanses them, because it is the enactment in them of Christ's sacrifice; cf. xii. 11. He goes on to describe their blessedness, first generalizing the picture in verse 10—their crying Hosanna in festal array is the beginning of an endless priestly service in God's temple. But we are surprised to hear him continue in a different vein—God will pitch his tabernacle beside them or over them, to defend them from hunger, thirst, and heat; the Lamb will shepherd them, and lead them to springs of living water. It is the picture of Israel's miraculous preservation in the wilderness.

The clue to the connexion lies in the word 'tabernacle' (verse 15). Those who stand in festal array with branches in their hands, and shout 'Hosanna!' in the Temple (cf. Ps. cxviii. 25, 27 in the LXX) will be seen as keeping a Tabernacles Feast: a feast which celebrated the miracles of providence in the wilderness, when God tabernacled with them, or over them, in cloud and fire. What St. John is saying of that miraculous providence is that it finds its fulfilment in man's final blessedness.

That the festival of vii. 9–17 should be seen as a keeping of Tabernacles is specially appropriate. That feast was the feast *par excellence*, the feast which crowned the year, the 'feast of ingathering at the year's end' when all the work of the fields was finished. And looking back from 'Tabernacles' here, we can easily see the next preceding great feast, Pentecost, in iv–v, for Pentecost had become a celebration of the Lawgiving, and iv–v shows the giving of God's written word to a better than Moses. And since Moses is replaced by the sacrificial Lamb, in virtue of the offering he had made of himself at Passover, we can see back through the Pentecost of iv–v to the Sunday vision of the dead-and-living Christ in i–iii, if we remember that the primitive Church kept Passover as a weekly feast in the Supper of the Lord.

But in spite of vii. 9–17, we have not reached Tabernacles yet in St. John's scheme of symbolical time. The vision of final bliss is anticipatory, as is shown by the elder's first words, 'These are those *to come* out of the Great Persecution.' 'Coming' says the Greek; but 'coming' with St. John has the force of a future participle (see above, p. 61).

VIII And when he opened the seventh seal, there was silence in heaven for the space of half an hour. 2 And I saw the seven angels which stand before God, and there were given to them seven trumpets. 3 And another angel came and stood by the altar, having a golden

censer, and there was given unto him much incense, that he might offer it at the prayers of all saints upon the golden altar which was
4 before the throne. And the smoke of the incense went up at the
5 prayers of the saints out of the angel's hand before God. And the angel took the censer, and filled it with fire from the altar, and cast it to the earth. And there came thunders and voices and lightnings
6 and earthquake. And the seven angels that had the seven trumpets prepared themselves to sound.

The breaking of the seventh seal carries us back to the point at which the hurricanes restrained in vii. 1 are to be released, the danger against which the saints have been sealed is actualized, and the penitential season preliminary to Tabernacles is introduced. The Feast of Tabernacles is at the full moon of the seventh month. The first ten days of the month are penitential, from the ceremony of trumpet-blowing on the first, to the Day of Atonement on the tenth. The trumpet of 1 Tishri announces a new year. (It is confusing to our minds that the Jewish New Year begins with the seventh month, at Michaelmas, and not the first at Lady Day. Similarly the Jewish day began not with the first hour at dawn, but with sundown on the eve before.) A yearly trumpet which both announces a new era and prepares for the Great Day (Atonement) is an obvious symbol for the trumpet of Michael (Isa. xxvii. 13, 1 Thess. iv. 16–17, Matt. xxiv. 31). Michael's trumpet is basically a trumpet of assembly and of release (Num. x. 2, Lev. xxv. 9). Since most of those it summons are in the grave, it becomes a trumpet of resurrection.

That St. John's trumpets are Michael's trumpet expanded into a sevenfold series, is obvious. They are blown by the seven archangels (angels of the presence, viii. 2). We are to understand that Michael blows the principal blast, that is, the final one, and his name appears in the following scene (xi. 15, xii. 7). We shall find that Michael's trumpet, when it blows, is given the ceremonial trappings of a New Year. And as though the strata of symbolism were not thick enough, St. John superimposes another. Trumpets were blown at New Year; trumpets were also blown at the daily sacrifice, as soon as the dismembered lamb was thrown into the altar-fire. But the lamb could not be thrown in, nor the trumpets blown, until the censing priest had offered his incense on the golden altar within the Temple. He went in with his attendants; the congregation in the court waited quietly (viii. 1) for his reappearance; then the sacrifice proceeded and the trumpets blew.

This piece of ceremony allows St. John to tie up the trumpet-blowing with the prayer of the martyr-souls in vi. 9–11. They cry from beneath the altar—the only altar of heaven, the golden altar for incense. But it has been shown already that the prayers of saints are incense in heaven (v. 8). It is possible then to conceive of a censing angel-priest as offering the saints' supplications in incense on the golden altar, and as thereby releasing the trumpets of advent. The pause of quiet while the incense is being offered will be equivalent to the little while of vi. 11, during which the martyrs must continue to wait and to pray.

In the temple at Jerusalem, while it still stood, an attendant priest first spread the small square top of the golden altar with burning charcoal, and the censing priest overlaid the charcoal with incense. St. John is supplied with another image. Let the angel-priest refill his censer from the altar fire, and toss the contents to the ground, or earth. So coals of fire had been tossed over the doomed city in Ezekiel x. 2 after the righteous had been sealed in their foreheads. Thus it will be seen that when the trumpets blow, the prayers of the saints fall back on the heads of their enemies in coals of fire.

One of the few material obscurities of St. John's alien Greek besets the relation between the angel's incense and the saints' prayers in verses 3–4. It is not clear whether the incense is offered, and ascends, at the prayers of the saints, or *as* (for) their prayers. The latter may be preferable, but it involves a Semitism unsupported by any New Testament parallel.

Trumpet-like voices preluded both the seven of messages (i. 10) and the seven of unsealings (iv. 1), and so we are prepared for a seven of sheer trumpet-blasts. A fresh dignity is given them by the silence in which they are awaited. The four cherubs' cries made the plagues of the horsemen; the seven archangels' blasts will make the judgements of the trumpets. The archangels, previously unmentioned, are slipped in beside the cherubim, just as the altar, previously unmentioned, was slipped in beside the throne (vi. 9), or as the reed will be slipped in beside the scroll (xi. 1).

And the first angel sounded, and there followed hail and fire 7 mingled with blood, and they were cast upon the earth. And the third part of the earth was burnt up, and the third part of trees was burnt up, and all green grass was burnt up.

And the second angel sounded, and as it were a great mountain 8 burning with fire dropped into the sea. And the third part of the sea became blood; and the third part of the creatures which were 9 in the sea and had life, died; and the third part of the ships was destroyed.

And the third angel sounded, and there fell a great star from 10

114 THE LION OF JUDAH

heaven, burning as a torch, and it fell upon the third part of the
11 rivers and on the watersprings. And the name of the star is called
Wormwood; and the third part of the waters became wormwood,
and many men died of the waters, because they had turned bitter.
12 And the fourth angel sounded, and the third part of the sun was
smitten, and the third part of the moon, and the third part of the
stars; that the third part of them might be darkened, and the day
shine not for a third part of it, and the night in like manner.

The saints have been sealed. Ezekiel's saints were sealed against
the 'coals of fire' which rained on their city; the saints of Exodus
were sealed by the Paschal mark against the worst of the Egyptian
plagues, after having been miraculously exempted from several
others. St. John's symbolism will be complete, if, when the trumpets
blow, fiery bodies fall from heaven, and if their fallings produce
Egyptian plagues. How is this to happen? The rod of Moses drew
forth plagues from water (Exod. vii. 19, viii. 5), from earth (viii.
16, x. 12), and from heaven (ix. 8, 22, x. 21). So let the falling fires
touch the elements in order, and draw from them Egyptian plagues.
St. John, who has lately brought plagues from the world's four
corners (explicitly in vii. 1, implicitly in vi. 1-8) now brings them
from its four elements, in the order earth, salt water, fresh water,
luminaries. Land is smitten by the Egyptian plague of lightning
mixed with hail, sea by that of water turned to blood, fresh waters
by the plague of undrinkableness (in Exodus identical with the
former), and luminaries by the plague of darkness. As for fiery
things falling, the plague of lightning-and-hail provides its own; sea
is turned by a volcano dropped from heaven. The sudden appearance
of volcanic cones off Mediterranean shores is an observed phenomenon, though they do not literally 'drop from the sky'. The sea is
reddened by volcanic glare—we are asked to imagine it chemically
changed. In view of the common belief in astral 'influences', St.
John's readers would see no special difficulty in the fresh waters
being turned by the descent of a comet. When he comes to the
smiting of the heavenly bodies, St. John abandons the convention of
fiery things falling to earth; how could any such thing smite the
lamps of heaven?

Two further conventions of the vision need to be mentioned. The
passage from each plague to its successor is bridged by a common
feature. By borrowing a hint from Joel ii. 30 and mingling blood
with heaven's fire in (1), St. John prepares for the change of water
to blood in (2). (2) and (3) are joined by the common fact of water
changed, now to blood, and now to wormwood; and the deaths here

of fishes, there of men. And finally the torchlike star of (3) prepares for the sun, moon, and stars of (4).

The other convention is the pressing of the number *three*. We might expect plagues on the *four* elements, like the plagues from the four quarters, to smite a *fourth*. No, a third is smitten, for each tends to be threefold within itself. Fire, hail, and blood burn earth, trees, and grass—a third of the first two; St. John does not bother to divide grass, which is all burnt every year. The pattern is perfected, however, in the second plague, where three things are destroyed to the extent of a third part. The third plague is the third, anyhow; it spoils a third of the streams, and a third of the water is made bitter (the word *third* being written thrice). The fourth strikes the triad sun, moon, and stars, darkening the third of luminaries, the third of the day, and the third of the night. We cannot but feel that the series which has this triadic tendency will realize its principle, and release its full force, when it gets a three, instead of a four, to display itself in. Since we have now completed four out of seven, there is a three still to come; and we are prepared to learn, as we do in the next verse, that the remaining trumpets carry the weight of the seven.

III. WOES OF THE EAGLE

(A) FIRST WOE

13 And I saw, and heard an eagle flying in mid-heaven, saying with a loud voice, Woe, woe, woe to the inhabiters of earth, by reason of the other trumpet-voices of the three angels who are yet to sound!

In the previous series, the unsealings, a new urgency and an alteration of tempo came in at the fifth, when the cries of cherubim gave place to the cry of martyr-blood, appealing for vindication upon *the inhabitants of earth*. The phrase belonged to its context; all the blood of all the Abels cries from the earth on which it has been spilt, against the earth's inhabitants. The vengeance for which they cried, held back a while, is now in process of being released. Coming now to the fifth trumpet, St. John alters the tempo of the series, and introduces a new urgency—the three remaining blasts spell triple woe on *the inhabitants of earth*. Christ said that all the blood of all the Abels would come on the head of the generation which filled up the number of the martyrs (Matt. xxiii. 29–36). He also said that where the carcass was, the eagles would gather—where the murder had been done, the judgement would fall (Matt. xxiv. 28). St. John puts the new and triple woe into the mouth of a flying eagle, and by so doing brings the trumpets under the dominion of the eagle, as the unsealings came under the dominion of the lion: the four faces of the cherubim are to be distributed over the four parts of St. John's book.

The trumpets, unlike the two previous sevens, lack any impressive introductory vision of their own; they are released by the opening of the seventh seal, just as the three weighty visions in vi. 12–vii. 17 were released by the opening of the sixth. So it comes about that the figure of the Eagle actually appears earlier in the trumpet-apocalypse (viii. 2 ff.) than the figure of the Lion (v. 5) does in the unsealings (iv. 1 ff.), even though the Lion opens the whole series from the start, whereas the Eagle breaks in after the fourth item, to impress a character of new urgency on the remaining three. The seal-breakings are the work of the Lion, the trumpet blasts have an origin independent of the Eagle; yet it is natural enough that he should make them his own. As the lion's roar has an affinity with thunder (vi. 1), so has the eagle's scream with a bugle; the triple cry of woe (*ŭai*) put into his mouth reminds us what the note of a bird of prey is like. So the fifth, sixth, and seventh trumpets become the first, second, and third *uais* (ix. 12, xi. 14).

The Eagle of this verse is no more identical with the fourth cherub, than the Lion of v. 5 is with the first. The four cherubim simply supply animal themes, to be taken in order. As we said above, the cherubim are originally listed in anticalendrical order by St. John. They represent in fact the constellations at the middles of the four seasons: the sun was with the Bull in April, with the Lion in July, with the Scorpion and Eagle in October, and with the Waterer in January. And in assigning the cherubim to the several sevens of his Revelation, St. John very naturally takes them in the order of the seasons, reversing the order of iv. 7. Since we made this observation (p. 92 above), a further complication has arisen: the emergence of a symbolism connected with the Jewish calendar of festivals. The taking and opening of the scroll is a sort of Pentecost, while the trumpet-blowing is a New Year. How then is Pentecost related to the month of the Lion, or New Year to that of the Eagle? Or, to go one farther back, how is Passover related to the Bull?

The Jewish calendar as a whole wanders with the moon, as our Easter does; we can at the best speak of average positions for feasts in relation to the Zodiac. But speaking in this sense, we shall place Passover in March under the Ram, ranging forward into the days of the Bull: Pentecost under the Twins in May, ranging forward towards the Lion; and New Year at Michaelmas, between the Scales and the Scorpion or Eagle. So the Festivals introduce their respective cherubic signs, rather than the cherubim the festivals. The emergence of the Lion and of the Eagle well after the beginning of the visions which they characterize, and especially of the Eagle after the trumpets have begun to blow, need not therefore surprise us. The festival similarly leading on to the Waterer would have to be Dedication, at Christmastide. But St. John makes nothing of Dedication in connexion with the bowls. Their outpouring expresses from the start the work of the Waterer himself (xv. 7), and if the bowls are connected with the themes of any feast, it is in their sequel; and the feast is not Dedication but Purim, which comes after the Waterer, in the month of February. Purim is simply the commemoration of the events recorded in the Book of Esther. One can see Vashti deposed and Esther crowned in the overthrow of the harlot and the marriage of the bride, one can see the triumphant ride of Mordecai in the rider on the horse and the vengeance on Haman and his confederates in the day of the sword. But St. John's figures and episodes are sufficiently explained on other grounds and it is not at all clear that the Esther story makes any actual contribution to them.

IX And the fifth angel sounded, and I saw a star fallen from heaven
2 to earth; and there was given to him the key of the pit of the abyss.

And he opened the pit of the abyss, and there went up a smoke out of the pit, as the smoke of a great furnace; and the sun and the air 3 were darkened by reason of the smoke of the pit. And out of the smoke came locusts upon earth, and power was given them as the 4 scorpions of earth have power. And it was commanded them that they should not hurt the grass of the earth, neither any green herb, nor any tree, but only the men that have not the seal of God on 5 their foreheads. And it was given them not to kill them, but that they should be tormented five months; and their torment was as the 6 torment of a scorpion when it strikes a man. And in those days men shall seek death and not find it; they shall desire to die, and death 7 fleeth from them. And the shapes of the locusts were like horses prepared unto battle; and on their heads as it were crowns like 8 gold, and their faces were as men's faces. And they had hair as the 9 hair of women, and their teeth were as of lions. And they had breastplates as it were breastplates of iron, and the sound of their wings was as the sound of chariots, of many horses running to battle. 10 And they have tails like unto scorpions, and stings; and in their 11 tails is their power to hurt men five months. They have for king over them the angel of the abyss; his name in Hebrew is Abaddon, and in the Greek tongue hath he the name Apollyon.

Of fiery coals falling from heaven, we have seen lightning, volcano, and comet; now we have a falling star. Since a second series of 'elements smitten' begins here, in parallel with the first, it is the earth that is struck, as in viii. 7. There the plague was hail and lightning, here it is locusts, the pair to hail in the Egyptian list, where it finishes the destruction of such crops as the hail had spared. St. John gives a sinister twist to the Exodus contrast: the locusts are not to hurt 'grass, or green, or tree', the growths which the hail had smitten —no, not these, nor any other crops either; they are to smite men, like those other Egyptian plagues, the lice and flies. Their scorpion-like sting is a demonic and penal substitute for the stamp of God's seal, which their victims lack (verse 4). Though the locusts are compared in their several features with horses, men, women and lions (7-9), we are three times told that their power and effect is that of scorpions (3, 5, 10). That the first woe of the Eagle should be a plague of winged creatures who are also scorpions, is appropriate; they are winged for the Eagle, they are scorpions in honour of the Zodiacal sign for which the Eagle is substituted (see above, p. 91). Their scorpion-tails give them power to plague men for five months; there are five months, or zodiacal signs, from the Scorpion to the end of the zodiacal year (October to February) and, of course, this is the fifth of trumpet-plagues.

Exodus says of the Egyptian locusts, that there were never such seen, nor ever will be again (Exod. x. 6 and 14), an invitation to the sort of fantasy St. John indulges. Even so, it is impossible to take him as describing insects of any kind; these locusts are locust-demons and, in what we would call the literal sense, they are an infectious plague of boils, another of the plagues on the Egyptian list. The patriarch Job, smitten with boils from the sole of his foot to the crown of his head, opened his mouth and prayed for death, as a boon the wretched long for, and it comes not; dig for, but cannot find (Job iii. 21). Compare verse 6 in the passage before us. That it is boils the locusts bring is further emphasized by the fact that their evocation echoes that of the boils in Exodus ix. 8. 'The Lord said to Moses and Aaron, take handfuls of soot of the furnace and let Moses scatter it towards heaven.... Let it become dust over the land of Egypt, and there shall be boils on man and beast.' Here, since the irritants are not to be dust, but demons, our falling star, fully personified as an angel, is given the key of the abyss, to let out the smoke of the abyss, *like the smoke of a great furnace*; and out of the smoke come locusts. Even the special point St. John takes from Job is touched upon in the Exodus boils. 'For now', says the Lord to Pharaoh, 'would I reach forth my hand and smite thee and thy people with death; but for this cause art thee preserved, that I may show forth in thee my might' (Exod. ix. 15 f.). Boils are not 'death' (i.e. mortal pestilence) though the victims may wish, with Job, that they were. 'Death' is still to come; it was the last plague in Exodus, it is the next here.

As Job is the natural comment on a plague of boils, so Joel is on one of locusts; in ii. 2 he quotes Exodus on the unrepeatableness of the scourge, word for word. The whole passage, especially i. 6, ii. 2, 4 5, 10 11, supplies the features of St. John's description in verses 7–9. The most difficult trait to account for is the womanish hair. Perhaps it is a middle between the human and the lionlike: womanish hair is simply long hair, and prepares us for a mane. Proverbs xxx. 27 tells us that the locusts have no king. In Joel the Lord commands the terrible army. St. John follows later Jewish usage in giving the Lord an angelic deputy for such a part—the angel of the abyss from which the locusts came. The name 'Abaddon' is simply a synonym for Hades (= Sheol) in Psalm lxxxviii. 11, Job xxvi. 6, and elsewhere. The LXX translate *Apoleia* (Destruction) not *Apollyon* (Destroyer), but St. John wants a concrete masculine, not a feminine abstract. He may be specially influenced by Job xxviii. 22 where Abaddon, or Apoleia, is the pair and forerunner of Death.

(B) SECOND WOE

12 The first woe is past; behold, there come two woes more hereafter.
13 And the sixth angel sounded; and I heard a voice from the four
14 horns of the golden altar which is before God, saying to the sixth angel which had the trumpet, Loose the four angels which are
15 bound at the great river Euphrates. And the four angels were loosed, which had been made ready for the hour and day and
16 month and year, to slay the third part of men. And the number of the armies of horsemen was twice ten thousand times ten thousand;
17 I heard the number of them. And thus I saw the horses in the vision, and them that sat on them, having breastplates as of fire and of jacinth and of brimstone; and the heads of the horses as the heads of lions, and out of their mouths issue fire and smoke and
18 brimstone. By these three plagues was the third part of men killed, by the fire, the smoke and the brimstone which issued out of their
19 mouths. For the power of the horses is in their mouth and in their tails; for their tails are like serpents, and have heads wherewith they do hurt.

Moses's rod had drawn plagues from earth, from river-water, and from the skies. To obtain a list of four elements St. John spread the plague on water over salt as well as fresh (viii. 8–11). He has merely to return to the Exodus list as it stands, and he has the set of three elements he requires to make up his total of seven. So after earth in the fifth comes Euphrates in the sixth. Euphrates was 'the river' *par excellence* to ancient Israel, and from the fords of Euphrates had descended the great invasions of Palestine. The river is, imaginatively speaking, the right line on which to draw up an invading host, even if it be a host of demons.

As to the releasing agent, the series began with falling fires; the fire became a star in the third, and in the fifth a star personified, a keybearer, an opener of the abyss. It is but one step farther to the angel of the sixth, commissioned to unbind. The series of falling fires kept up the connexion between the trumpet-plagues and the incense-liturgy of viii. 3–5. The connexion is still more emphatically asserted, when a voice breaks from among the horns of the incense-altar, calling on the angel to act. This is the climax of the series, for the seventh trumpet-judgement, though weightier still, is not a plague of the same sort as the rest. The importance of the event is marked by the intervention of the trumpet-angel himself; it must be remembered that he is an archangel.

Why is the voice from the horns, not simply from the altar? The horns are the four (raised) corners, and in the letting loose of the four angel-captains, we are to be reminded of the four winds held back by angels at the four corners of the earth. That was in the sixth unsealing (vii. 1); we are now in the sixth trumpet; what was held back in the unsealings is let loose in the trumpets. Four angels all at Euphrates cannot be literally equivalent to four winds at the several corners of the earth; they are symbolically equivalent. The intrusion of the number *four* into the very heart of the province of *three* may seem an awkwardness, but St. John ties it in deftly by a descending series of numbers: '*four* angels prepared for the (1) hour, (2) day, (3) month and (4) year, to kill the *third* of mankind; and the number of their armies was *two* myriad myriads.' He then takes up the number three, and gives it a very strong base. The horses had breast-plates of three colours, fiery, smoke-blue, and brimstone-yellow; and they breathed three corresponding poisons, fire, smoke, and brimstone; by which three plagues the third of mankind was killed. We are to see in these horsemen, every one of whom has the three colours and the three plagues, an intensified antitype of the horsemen in vi, with their distinct colours and their distinct plagues. (Four horsemen, three with plagues, red, black, and livid; four cavalry commanders, leading innumerable hosts, all with three plagues, red, blue and yellow.)

Another feature of the sixth unsealing is recalled when St. John says that he hears the number of the muster; he had similarly heard the number of the sealed. God knows the numbers he has marked for salvation, and the numbers he has armed with destruction; just as he knows the hour, the day, the month, and the year.

There can be no doubt that the description of the cavalry is inspired by the same texts of Joel as the preceding vision. Joel describes the locusts as invading cavalry; St. John makes two pictures of it—cavalry-like locusts, and locust-like cavalry. He does not even wish to contrast them strongly. The locusts have lions' teeth, yet do all their damage with their scorpion-tails; the cavalry-horses have lions' heads, and do their damage with them; but they can hurt with their snake-headed tails as well. We observed that earlier trumpet-plagues were similarly linked to their neighbours by common features.

It seems that, in the sense in which the former host were scorpion-locusts, this latter host are lion-cavalry; they have lion-heads and they destroy with their mouths, even though they do not use them as lions do. The lion's mouth is proverbial of destruction. As we shall see, the lion-figure continues to play its part in the remainder of the sixth-trumpet visions; and we are bound to conclude that St. John has started upon a regular series of cherubic emblems. The first woe shows the dominance of the eagle-scorpion, the second that of the lion—we are going round the ring in the order of iv. 7. The third woe will show us the bull, the evangel brings us to the Man (xiv. 14).

20 And the rest of mankind which were not killed by these plagues repented not of the works of their hands, to cease from the worship of devils, and idols of gold, of silver, of brass, of stone or of wood, 21 which neither can see nor hear nor walk. Neither repented they of their murders, nor of their sorceries, nor of their fornication, nor of their thefts.

The prophecy of Joel is a liturgy of repentance. The locust-scourge is to turn the people towards a penitent supplication, in view of which the prophet promises them deliverance and peace. But, says St. John, in conclusion to his version of Joel's plagues, the heathen world, though lashed with the scourges of God, repented neither its idolatry nor its crimes.

X And I saw another strong angel come down from heaven, clothed with a cloud, and the rainbow was over his head, and his face was 2 as the sun, and his feet as pillars of fire. And he had in his hand a little book open; and he set his right foot upon the sea and his 3 left on the earth, and cried with a loud voice, as a lion roareth; and 4 when he cried, the seven thunders uttered their voices. And when the seven thunders uttered, I was about to write; and I heard a voice from heaven, saying, Seal up those things which the seven 5 thunders uttered, and write them not. And the angel which I saw standing upon sea and earth lifted up his right hand to heaven, 6 and sware by him that liveth for ever and ever, who created heaven and the things that are therein, and earth and the things that are therein, and sea and the things that are therein, that there shall be 7 no more delay; but in the days of the blast of the seventh angel, when he shall sound, then is accomplished the mystery of God, according to the good tidings he declared to his servants the prophets.

In view of heathen impenitence a great angel descends from heaven to declare that the final stroke of God's hand will be no longer delayed. The parallel between the sixth unsealing and the sixth trumpet continues. The four forces of destruction held back in vii. 1 have been released in ix. 13–19. In vii. 2 another angel (other, that is, than the four) carrying the seal of the living God, imposed delay on those ready to ravage sea and land. Here in x. 1–7 another angel (other than the four unbound at ix. 15) carrying an open (that is, an unsealed) scroll sets foot on sea and land to swear by the ever-living God that there shall be no more delay. The parallel with vii suggests the reason, that the destined number of martyrs will have been made up by Antichrist's persecution; the present context (ix. 20–21) suggests the reason, that the enemies of God will have demonstrated their final impenitence by joining Antichrist's rebellion. Both reasons are valid.

A 'strong angel descending from heaven' cannot fail to recall the 'angel of strength come down from heaven' in Daniel iv. 13 (see above, p. 93). That angel pronounced immediate doom on Nebuchadnezzar for his failure to make the repentance Daniel urged upon him. St. John combines the 'angel of strength' with the angel of the oath in Daniel xii, and it is very natural that he should. The angel of the oath is apparently the Gabriel of Daniel viii. 16, ix. 21, and the description 'angel of strength' suggests the meaning of Gabriel's name. A Gabriel-figure is proper enough to the sixth trumpet, the next in order and importance to the seventh; for if the seventh is blown by Michael, by whom will the sixth be blown but by Gabriel, the only other angel personally named in canonical scripture? Not that the 'strong angel' of xi can be actually identical with the archangel who unbinds the four at ix. 15; he is an angel in Gabriel's province, or under his command. But why, if he is less than an archangel, is he given a majesty of glory which the archangels themselves do not manifest in St. John's picture? Because the archangels are seen as citizens of heaven, overshadowed by the throne; this angel becomes a portent, and a bearer of divinity, by descending to earth. In this vision, as in i. 9 ff., St. John is a man on earth again, visited by glory. In iv he was lifted to heaven, and was there in vii. 9–viii. 5. He saw the trumpets blown, and the coals of fire cast from above; but has since more and more identified the sphere of his vision with an earth visited by their effects. He has just seen a supernatural invasion set in motion from Euphrates; and now he is on the Patmos of his personal inspiration.

The description of the angel fits his message, which affirms God's fidelity to his covenants (x. 7). The bow in the cloud is the token of God's covenant with all mankind through Noah, under which the impenitent heathen are judged (ix. 20–21). The pillars of fire walking sea and land are the sign of the angel of God's presence in the Red Sea and the wilderness, when the covenant was given through Moses; while the scroll which the angel brings to the Christian prophet recalls the writing of God's finger given to Moses on tables of stone, and read from paper scrolls by Israel. When the prophets describe the God of Exodus coming up from the wilderness of Sinai, they see the theophany embodied in a marching storm. St. John's angel may be seen as a strongly conventionalized figure of the sort; the sun in the rain-cloud makes the bow, and projects rods or pillars of light from the skirts of vapour down on shore and sea; the voice of thunder breaks like the roar of a lion.

The angel's lion-voice brings him into the series of cherub-themes with which St. John supports the three woes. The first began with the scream of the eagle; now we have the roar of the lion in the second; and both are portents of judgement to come. The eagle attached woe to the three last trumpets; the lion-voice attaches finality to the last of them, and brings in 'evangel' to balance 'woe'. ('As he *evangelized*'—gave tiding of joy to—'his servants the prophets' is the Greek of the last clause in verse 7.) The fulfilment of God's hidden purpose is woe to the inhabitants of earth, but evangel to his servants. The evangel follows the woe in due course (xiv. 6).

The lion-voice not only brings the angel's cry into series with the eagle's, it wakens the thunderous echoes of ancient prophecy. 'The Lord has roared from Zion, and uttered his voice from Jerusalem.... Shall the lion roar from the thicket when he has no prey?... Shall the trumpet sound in the city, and the people not be in alarm? Shall there be evil in the city, and the Lord not have done it? Wherefore the Lord will do nothing, without revealing the secret to his servants the prophets. The lion shall roar, and who not be afraid? The Lord hath spoken, and who will not prophesy?' (Amos i. 2, iii. 4–8). The influence of Amos's text on St. John cannot be doubted; it associates the voice of the lion with the sound of the trumpet, and with God's revelation of his secret purpose to his servants the prophets (cf. verse 7 in the passage before us).

When St. John is about to write down the thunderous echoes of the lion's roar, he may seem to be undertaking the duty which, according to Amos, a prophet cannot escape, and it is the more notable that he is prohibited from doing it. (The form 'Shut up the words, and seal' is supplied by Daniel's vision of the swearing angel (xii. 4, 9), but the form only; the intention is quite different. St. John is not to write at all, but seal with silence. Daniel was to write, and seal up for future generations to open.) The explanation of the prohibition is to be sought in the alternative offered. St. John is not to write the utterances of the thunders; he is to take and to digest the scroll. If he had written out the thunders, he would have been doing the same sort of thing as hitherto—reading the significance of cherubic exclamations beginning from a voice of thunder (vi. 1–8), of martyrs' cries (vi. 9–vii. 17), of angel-trumpets (viii–ix); portents all of them incidental to the Lamb's opening of the heavenly book. When the last trumpet shall have sounded, one might hope that portents incidental to the scroll-opening would be complete; the very angel who wakes the thunder-echoes shows the sign of an open scroll in his hand. But when the scroll is open, what then? According to Ezekiel iii, it is given the prophet to eat; in St. John's own theology, the revelation of Jesus Christ, given to him by God, is communicated to his servant John through the mission of an angel (i. 1). St. John has been translated in spirit to witness in heaven the giving of revelation to Christ in the form of a scroll, and Christ's making the revelation by opening the paper. Yet 'none hath ascended to heaven, but he that from heaven descended, the Son of Man in heaven' (John iii. 13) and there is something insubstantial about such flights of the Spirit as St. John's. He ascends, and remains below; sees, yet in a figure only. It is not when earth ascends, but when heaven comes down, that revelation is complete. Then the divine word enters the prophet's heart; then he prophesies. 'The lion hath roared, the Lord hath spoken; who can but prophesy?' Yes, but prophesy; not read lessons in the roaring echoes of the voice, but digest the word, and speak from the heart.

The theology of the text is plain; its visionary expression is not so clear. There ought to be a change in St. John's writing from now onward; he should appear less of a seer or portent-reader, and more of a prophet. Yet he has to go on with his tale, the prediction of things invisible; and the farther he goes into the world to come, the more figurative, not less, must his prediction be. In the passage directly following (xi. 1–13) he proceeds as a prophet, by acted sign and oracle; he soon falls back into the idiom of vision. The vision, indeed, is henceforward of greater substance, presenting great powers and great mysteries; there is less mere apocalyptic thunder. We cannot say that there are no more formal sevens of plagues, since St. John's balanced scheme requires the bowls (xv–xvi); but in spite of the bowls his vision moves more freely and is not restricted to the framework which formal sevens supply.

Had St. John listened to the suggestions of the seven thunders, and received corresponding visions, he would have added another seven to his book. Now, in a sense, he has made us expect two sevens more after the trumpets. The unsealings destroyed a quarter of things, the trumpets a third; it would seem that another seven, say of thunders, should destroy a half, before the bowls bring destruction on the whole. As the thunder-apocalypse is smothered at birth, the destruction of the half is omitted. Thus in declaring that there shall be no more delay, the angel seems actually to make St. John skip a part of his prefigured scheme, and go to the climax. God has indeed shortened the days, for the sake of his elect.

In setting out a scheme requiring four terms (quarter, third, &c.) and fitting it to three, St. John simply varies a theme on which he is constantly playing. The three which end the seven are built to the plan of the four which open it; there are four plagues of the horsemen, though only three of the horsemen carry plagues; the whole book is a four-part apocalypse, but only the last three parts carry the apocalyptic drama.

Let us return now to the angel's oath in Daniel xii. Lifting his right hand and his left to heaven, he swears by the everliving God. St. John improves. The distinction of right and left is transferred to the angel's feet, that they may be planted on sea and land. Lifting his hand to heaven, he makes his body a triangle of attestation, while he calls God to witness, who made heaven, land and sea (the usual pattern of inversion: sea, land, sky; sky, land, sea). A very proper form of attestation for an angel who has his being in the triad of elements which gives shape to the last three trumpets. (The angel of xiv. 6–7, picking up this angel's promise of evangel, attests the *four* elements in similar words; by the time he speaks, the *three* trumpet-woes are over.)

Daniel's angel swears that the breaking in pieces of the holy people will be accomplished in 'a time, times and half a time'; then all will be fulfilled. St. John is going to make free use of the Danielic half-week in a symbolical sense (xi. 2, 3, xii. 6, 14, xiii. 5). But since he cannot give it its literal meaning, it would be a mere mockery to put it into the mouth of the angel. What consolation could it be to St. John or to his hearers, that Advent must come after a period of uncertain meaning, counted from some uncertain date, but not from now? By making the oath bear on the movement of the drama, not the chronology of prediction, St. John avoids absurdity. If the space to be reckoned is space in St. John's written book, his readers may expect that 'the days of the seventh trumpet' will be proportionately longer than those of the sixth, as the days of the seventh unsealing have been proportionately longer than those of the sixth (see the Introduction, p. 15). Within these 'days' the vision of deliverance will be shown; and as it turns out, in chapter xiv.

8 And the voice which I had heard from heaven spake unto me again, and said, Go, take the book that is open in the hand of the angel
9 standing on sea and earth. And I went unto the angel, asking him to give me the little book. And he saith unto me, Take it and eat it up; and it shall make thy belly bitter, but it shall be in thy mouth
10 sweet as honey. And I took the little book out of the angel's hand and ate it up; and it was in my mouth sweet as honey; and when

I had eaten it, my belly was bitter. And they say to me, Thou 11
must prophesy again over many peoples and nations and tongues
and kings.

'The voice which I heard from heaven' presumably picks up iv. 1,
as iv. 1 picked up i. 10. We have anticipated the exposition of the
scroll in our discussion of the previous paragraph. We will only add
that, being a *little* scroll, it cannot be actually identical with the
great scroll of the heavenly synagogue opened by Christ in chapter v.
How could St. John be represented as eating that? Only the openness,
the availability of the word which feeds the prophet's heart
derives from the opening of all truth by the Lion of Judah.

According to Ezekiel, the book as spread open was seen to be
written with lamentation, mourning and woe (*uai*); and yet it was
sweet in the mouth of the eater. St. John puts the same point by saying
that, though sweet in the mouth (it is an evangel) it turns the
stomach; for it means prophesying on against peoples, nations,
languages, and kings; and the seer's first duty, as we know already,
will be to invoke the third and supreme *uai*. The addition of the
word 'kings' to the familiar Danielic formula (cf. Rev. v. 9, vii. 9)
seems to refer us from the vision of Ezekiel's call to that of Jeremiah's
(Jer. i. 9 f.), and naturally enough. For Jeremiah's call appears to be
the very text which Ezekiel himself elaborated in the powerful
grotesque characteristic of his art.

And there was given me a reed like unto a rod, with this command- XI
ment: Rise and measure the temple of God and the altar, and them
that worship therein. And the court which is without the temple 2
leave out, and measure it not; for it hath been given unto the
Gentiles, and the holy city shall they tread under foot forty and two
months.

The version of Daniel's swearing angel which St. John has just
given connects 'the accomplishment of all things' with the blowing
of the seventh trumpet. It must follow that the preliminary period
of 'a time, times and half a time' of which Daniel's angel spoke,
should be fitted in before the trumpet blows. It is, as many texts of
Daniel make perfectly clear, the period of the desecration of Jerusalem;
and as this period had both featured prominently in Christ's
prophecy, and proved already to be an historical fact, St. John can
scarcely leave it without mention. He finds a starting-point in the
corresponding part of his own previous vision-series which, as we are
in the course of observing, he is now reconstructing line by line. The

four destructive powers held back at vii. 1 are released at ix. 15. The angel with the seal enjoining delay in vii. 2 is answered in xi ff. by the angel with the unsealed scroll swearing that delay is at an end. The next piece of the model (vii. 4 ff.) numbers the saints as a four-square camp of twelve tribes, with the result that a multitude of every nation, tribe, people, and tongue become worshippers for ever in the temple of God.

St. John proceeds by way of contrast. The way of the heavenly Zion has been described in vii. She begins with perfect purity, uncontaminated by Gentile influences, and extends to embrace mankind without suffering any adulteration. The opposite way of the earthly Zion is now to be described. She begins by admitting the Gentiles to a close proximity with her sanctuary and ends by being fouled under their feet.

When St. John gave the figure of the twelve tribes in vii he took Ezekiel xlviii. 30–35 as his text. That passage is part of the description of the measuring of the temple and the city, performed under the prophet's eyes by an angel equipped with a reed (xl. 3). The purpose of the measuring of Ezekiel's New Jerusalem, as is made quite clear in the course of it, is to lay down boundaries ruling out all those secular and heathenish intrusions which had been the downfall of the old temple, and with it, of the city. It will be the same in St. John's coming picture of New Jerusalem, measured by the angel (Rev. xxi. 9 ff.). But a prophet, called upon to draw the line in the historical Jerusalem, must leave out of the area of sanctity the court of the Gentiles. The unconverted heathen, given a footing in God's courts, are destined to tread the holy city down.

We have said something about the relation of xi. 1–2 with its model in vii. 4 ff. We have still to see how it connects with its own context. It is characteristic of St. John's construction, that he is content with parallelism as justification for the introduction of a new feature. Having established the throne and its voices in iv–vi. 8 he takes for granted the presence of the altar, and proceeds to develop its voices in vi. 9. Having established the twenty-four who are seated with God in iv he sees the seven who stand before him as receiving trumpets in viii. 2. Having established in chapter x the picture of angelic hands giving the prophet a scroll with directions, he proposes for our acceptance the idea of his receiving a reed, likewise with directions. He does not feel it necessary either to encumber the angel of chapter x with a reed as well as a scroll, or to describe the descent from heaven of a second angel carrying a reed.

St. John says 'a reed', adding as a qualification, 'like a staff'. The gift of a reed, in supplement to a scroll, is immediately acceptable to our minds, because 'reed and scroll' are 'pen and paper', the instruments of a writing prophet's trade. Being confined on Patmos, St. John is forced to do what the author of 3 John excuses himself from doing—writing at length with ink and reed; or, as he says in 2 John, with paper and ink. But neither the paper nor the reed which St. John receives in x–xi is put to the use we expect; the paper is to be eaten, the reed used for measuring—and it will do, for it is not, after all, the sort of little reed to make a pen, it is 'like a staff'. And according to Ezekiel, a scroll eaten and a reed measured with are the alpha and omega of written prophecy: he begins with the one (Ezek. i–iii) and ends with the other (xl–xlviii).

St. John says, 'The temple of God and the altar and those worshipping in it.' Since they do not worship in the altar, St. John must surely mean 'The temple of God, the altar (in it) and those worshipping in it'; and it seems this is what he does mean, for he places the court of the Gentiles immediately round the temple. 'The court outside the temple put outside' (your area) is what he writes: and he uses for 'temple' the word *naos*, which designates the holy house, not the holy place, or whole complex of hallowed courts and buildings. So he presents us with the picture of a Gentile court containing a hallowed House, in which are the altar and the worshippers. Evidently he does not trouble to describe the earthly temple as it was, with its complexity of small sacred courts outside the House, accommodating altar and worshippers, and surrounded by the great Gentile court. He is content to describe it symbolically as the simple ectype, or earthly version, of the heavenly temple, which contains both worshippers and altar in the presence-chamber of glory. The only alteration he needs for his present purpose to make in the heavenly picture is to add the unhallowed Gentile court.

The nations are to trample the holy city, Daniel said, for three years and a half, or perhaps a fraction, of a year. He gave the period variously in years, and in days; it is not easy either to reconcile or to explain his several reckonings. St. John makes his own arithmetic perspicuous by adopting the simplest and most manipulable of all calendars—twelve months of thirty days each. Taking this simple basis, $3\frac{1}{2}$ years = 42 months = 1,260 days. Of the three modes of reckoning, St. John begins from the second. We shall see why he does so when we see what he hangs upon it.

And I will give unto my two witnesses to prophesy a thousand two 3
hundred and threescore days, clothed in sackcloth. These are the 4
two olive trees, and the two lampstands, standing before the Lord
of the earth. And if any man wisheth to hurt them, fire proceedeth 5
out of their mouths and devoureth their enemies; if any man

6 wisheth to hurt them, in this manner must he be killed. They have power to shut heaven that it rain not for the days of their prophecy, and have power over water to turn it to blood, and to smite the
7 earth with every plague, as often as they will it. And when they shall have finished their testimony, the beast that cometh up out of the abyss shall make war on them, and overcome them and kill
8 them. And their dead bodies are in the street of the great city, which spiritually is called Sodom and Egypt, where also their
9 Lord was crucified. And men of the peoples, tribes, tongues and nations look upon their dead bodies three days and a half, and
10 suffer not their dead bodies to be laid in the tomb. And the dwellers upon earth rejoice over them and make merry, and shall send gifts to one another; because these two prophets tormented the dwellers
11 upon earth. And after three days and a half the breath of life from God entered into them, and they stood upon their feet; and great
12 fear fell upon them which saw them. And they heard a great voice from heaven saying unto them, Come up hither. And they ascended
13 up to heaven in cloud, and their enemies beheld them. And the same hour there was a great earthquake, and the tenth part of the city fell. And there were killed in the earthquake seven thousand persons; and the rest were affrighted, and gave glory to the God of heaven.

St. John cannot be deeply interested in what happened to Jerusalem in A.D. 70. Evidently the end of the world was not implicated in the event, as it had looked like being, to St. Mark and St. Paul; nor is it to St. John, as it had been for St. Matthew, the triumphant vindication of Christ against his murderers. St. John is too far away from the event, and his Church is fighting on a different front. He hurries on into a description of the position of the Gospel in the intermediate age between the fall of the Holy City and the coming of Antichrist; that is to say, in the time of St. John. It may seem that heathenism has triumphed and the candle of the Lord has gone out. But no, the living witness, the dual ministry, the two lamps remain, and cannot be extinguished.

There is no break in the prophecy between verses 2 and 3. St. John does not tell us, either here or later, that he obeyed the command to measure the temple; the information would have added nothing to the purpose. The voice which commanded him to measure continues to speak, explaining the consequences of what he is commanded to do. 'Measure the temple (not the court outside: it is given to the Gentiles, and they will consequently trample the Holy City for forty-two months) and I will give [power] to my two witnesses, and they shall prophesy for that period, dressed in sackcloth.' A translator in contemporary style, embarrassed by the conventions of modern printing, has to decide where to close the quotation; St. John was under no such necessity. If we close the quotation after 'sackcloth', the history of the two witnesses is made to consist of a long comment written by St. John out of his own knowledge or wisdom, a feature unique in a book made up of voices heard and visions seen. The Greek original makes no such impression, but rather that of a divinely dictated oracle kindling into vision. As we said when we discussed St. John's inspiration, word with him easily passes into visual image, and back again.

The effect of the measuring is a Christian paradox. The line St. John draws round it is not to save the sanctuary in its physical form, but only the spiritual or personal substance of the worship offered there. The seven branched lamp was carried in triumph by Titus; the twofold lamp of witness continues to shine. Our minds have been prepared for the paradoxical conclusion by the paradoxical insertion of 'worshippers' among the things to be measured. The New English Bible is in a sense correct when it renders '*number of* worshippers'; but it weakens the suggestiveness of St. John's phrase. To take the number of the faithful, we remember from vii, is to set up the square figure of a spiritual camp, or city: the visible Jerusalem falls, but this does not.

The way in which St. John makes his transition from the words about the temple to the words about the witnesses can be appreciated a little better if we write down a literal translation of the Greek.

> For it is given to the Gentiles, and they shall trample the holy city for months forty and two;
> And I will give to my two witnesses, and they shall prophesy for days a thousand two hundred and sixty . . .

The parallel between the two sentences is the more evidently contrived, for being artificial; the construction 'give(n) . . . and' is verbally identical in the two cases, but quite different in meaning; in the first it means 'given over to . . .; and they shall . . .' in the second 'grant to . . . that they may . . .'. Besides forcing the parallel between the sentences, St. John has linked them by carrying the numeral 'two' from the end of the one to the beginning of the other. Since we have had abundant opportunity to observe the play St. John makes with numbers, we shall naturally ask what this means.

Why, to begin with, does he choose to state the Danielic period first in months, a form of statement Daniel never used? Presumably he likes the resultant number, forty-two. But why? Because forty is a suitable period for the punishment of Israel; were the tribes not made to wander in the wilderness forty years, when they had incurred the divine displeasure? But why forty *and two*? Forty for punishment, and two for witness; that *two* is the required number for witness, is a commonplace; and witnesses in the period of Israel's penance will be witnesses in sackcloth. The number shows us, moreover, who the witnesses are. Forty is a period inseparably connected with Moses's prophesying; it was at his word that Israel wandered for those fateful years. It was, indeed, forty-two years altogether; they had been two years in the wilderness already, before they incurred the forty years' penalty. Forty-two months is the period during which the word of Elijah brought a drought upon Israel—Scripture made it 'three years' simply, but St. Luke (iv. 25) and St. James (v. 17) show that common tradition had squared it with Daniel's sinister period. 'Moses and Elias' are a familiar pair in Christian tradition, the two witnesses at Christ's Transfiguration and, as St. Luke hints, at his Resurrection and Ascension also—the patriarchs of Law and Prophecy, pointing to Jesus.

The two witnesses are Moses and Elias, that is, they are a new Moses and Elias; but who are they in historical fact? The two martyr sons of Zebedee—on the improbable hypothesis, refuted by St. Luke, that they were both martyrs and died together—or the two good apostles, Peter and Paul, killed at Rome? Both these suggestions labour under a common defect; neither of the proposed pairs prophesied after the fall of Jerusalem or survived until the day of Antichrist. And unless we think that there were two outstanding Christian leaders in St. John's time, who had begun to prophesy in A.D. 70, and whose coming martyrdom at the hands of Antichrist had been specially revealed to St. John, we shall have to abandon the search after particular and personal identities for his Two Witnesses.

After all, the topic is a commonplace. Deuteronomy requires two or three witnesses to convict (xvii. 6 and xix. 15). New Testament writers allegorize the regulation, so that what appears to be one person or one reality speaks with the required number of voices. St. Paul counts as a stage-army of witnesses at Corinth, by walking across the Corinthian scenes two and three times (2 Cor. xiii. 1). The witness of Christ is twofold, says John viii. 17–18. 'It is written in your law that the witness of two holds good. I am a bearer of witness to myself, and the Father who sent me bears witness to me.' God's witness in the Chruch is threefold, says 1 John v. 7–9. 'There are three that bear witness, the Spirit, the Water, and the Blood, and the three are in one. If we accept the witness of men' (as we do in a lawcourt) 'the witness of God is greater; and this is the witness of God.' Three witnesses may be even better than two; yet where the Church's witness is being presented in the concrete form of apostolic or prophetical persons, two are appropriate. The Jewish custom was to send emissaries in pairs, jointly to witness the words of their principal. Christ sent the apostles two by two, and when they later separated, they took each a companion (e.g. Acts xv. 39–40). St. John presents us with a typical scene. The state of God's Israel in the world after A.D. 70 is typified by a Jerusalem in which a heathen multitude tramples the old sanctities, while two prophetic voices, in mutual confirmation, maintain the cause of God. So it might be anywhere; in Pergamum, for example, where Antipas had witnessed to the faith.

St. John has a special motive for snatching the number *two* from the forty-two months of Daniel's period, and for building it up in the way that he does. He has shown us the judgement of *four* in the unsealings, he is showing us the judgement of *three* in the trumpets, and he has just been directed to suppress the seven thunders, which should have shown us the judgement of *two*. But here now is an opportunity to give it alternative expression. God's two witnesses plague the dwellers upon earth (verse 10) and they are the manifest types of that *One*, the witness faithful and true, who returns in the day of the seven bowls to fulfil all judgement (xix. 11).

We have said that the two witnesses are a new Moses and Elias; but that is to over-simplify. They are the twofold witness; and they correspond to other appropriate types that scripture supplies. First of all, they are 'the two oil-trees' (i.e. anointed stocks) 'that stand before the Lord of the whole earth' (Zech. iv. 14). That is, they are principality and priesthood, Judah and Levi, David and Zadok, Zorobabel and Jesus—the two families of which Jeremiah had prophesied when the first temple fell, that they would never lack a representative (Jer. xxxiii. 14–26). Now we know that the Church is a body of priest-kings, or royal priests (Rev. i. 6, v. 10). St. John slips 'and two lampstands' into his Zechariah quotation. In Zechariah the two anointed stocks feed the seven-branched lampstand with the oil of their anointing—that is, they maintain the temple-worship. Now that the temple lampstand is removed, they stand in its place; they are the living lampstands, the twofold prophetic voice of the lampstand churches (i. 20).

But now considered as prophets, they show the character most central to St. John's present theme; they represent the two patriarchs of revelation, Moses and Elias, the man of the forty(-two) years and the man of the forty-two months. It is interesting that Elias is a lamp or torch according to Ecclesiasticus xlviii. 1 and that the description is applied to John Baptist in John v. 31–39, a passage which comes very close to the symbolism of this vision. Christ, citing the Father's twofold witness, scripture and miracle, identifies scripture with

Moses, adding as it were in the margin the witness of that 'lamp, kindled and shining' the Baptist. It is true that in this Gospel John denies that he is the Elias to come, still more, that he is the second Moses (John i. 21). Yet it seems that he is the as-it-were-Elias of the first Advent; the Elias and Moses of the second Advent are to be found in the Church. The apostolic minister, according to 2 Corinthians iii, is even a more-than-Moses.

The attributes of Moses and Elias which St. John draws out in verses 5–6 are those which exhibit them as a dual plague on the inhabitants of the earth, and so bring them into line with St. John's scheme of judgements inflicted by the four, the three, the two, and the one. Like Elias, they call down fire to devour their assailants, and lock up heaven from raining during the days of their prophecy, i.e. for forty-two months; like Moses, they turn water to blood and smite the land with every stroke of the rod. In thus summarizing the powers of the two prophets, St. John keeps up the triad of elements, sky, water, and earth, and brings the action of the witnesses into line with the trumpet-plagues, in so far as those are strokes of Moses's rod.

As on other pages, we may find it easier to understand St. John's scriptural pattern, than to determine its contemporary application. What does he mean, by attributing what looks like a baleful magic to the ministers of the Gospel? He would not doubt the duty of Christian prophets to denounce impenitence, and declare a coming judgement; or doubt that in so doing they were at one with the will of God. As the plagues of the trumpets might be said to be called down by the prayers of the martyrs, so they might be said to be wielded by the utterance of the prophets. Supported by the visible judgements of heaven upon their adversaries, they hold their own through the 'times of the heathen'. It may surprise us that St. John should in a sense justify the accusation of the pagans: Christians are the cause of plague, pestilence, and famine. The heathens say they are so by practising a cult hateful to heaven. St. John says they are so, because heathen attacks upon them call out the forces of nature in their defence.

St. John cannot mean that the support they receive in this way makes it impossible for any Christian witnesses to undergo a personal martyrdom during 'the times of the Gentiles'. What he does mean is, that the Church's dual witness cannot be silenced. Antichrist's killing of the witnesses means, on the other hand, that his persecution will be outwardly effective and drive the church, as we would say, underground, but as Christ had said, up the hills (Matt. xxiv. 16–18). The witness which the prophets complete according to verse 7 is their 1,260 days = 42 months. We have seen that, in relating this period both to Moses and to Elias, St. John takes the months both literally, and also as years. Now it is evident that unless St. John was writing before A.D. 74, he could not suppose that the period from the fall of the city to the coming of Antichrist would be a literal 42 months. But he might very well think of it as something like 42 years. Suppose he wrote in the year 100, he would see himself as a dozen years before the coming of Antichrist, a view perfectly compatible with the probable meaning of the indications in xvii. 9–11.

The beast 'that comes up from the abyss, makes war on the saints, and conquers them' must be interpreted from Daniel vii. 2–21, not from Revelation xiii and xvii which have yet to be written. The beast of Daniel, in the phase in which he makes war on the saints and conquers them, is the beast in his 'little horn' phase, i.e. in the person of the last in the dynasty, the 'Antichrist'. And when St. John does come to write the visions of xiii and xvii he makes it clear that the beast who comes up out of the abyss is the smitten head returning to life, the last and worst of emperors. Everything combines to show, therefore, that the days of Antichrist terminate and follow the forty-two months of trampling and of witness.

The 'great city' of verse 8 is still Jerusalem, of which this was a standing title; it recurs in xvi. 19. Hitherto Jerusalem has been described as a holy place which forfeits its sanctity, and is trampled by the heathen; they are the enemy, against them the witnesses wield the judgements of God. But now in his concern to show the martyrdom of the Church as an ectype of Christ's passion, St. John accuses Jerusalem; she is the murderess, the Egypt and the Sodom on which vengeance falls. Isaiah i. 8–10 calls Zion Sodom; Amos tells us that God brings on Israel the pestilence of Egypt and the fires of Sodom (iv. 10–11). The Sodomites rejected, and would have outraged, God's two witnesses (his angels in human form); Egypt spurned the witness of Moses and Aaron.

In the next verse St. John returns to the persecutors of the Church, the mixed multitude of the heathen, and applies to them and the witnesses the prophecy he had applied to Christ and mankind in i. 7, 'They shall look upon whom they have pierced, and all the tribes of the earth shall mourn.' St. John develops the suggestions of the oracle with great thoroughness. They make themselves the opportunity to look on those they have pierced, by acting as Psalm lxxix. 1–3 says that the heathen destroyers of Jersusalem do act; they leave the dead bodies of God's servants unburied. They are to mourn indeed, when their crime brings the city down about their ears (verse 13), but all the more dramatically, because they first rejoice, as the Jews rejoiced to be rid of their enemy Haman (Esther ix. 22). They look on whom they pierced in two senses—first they gloat over the wounds of the corpses, then they are confronted by the living gaze of their victims. The text has the same dual application to Christ (John xix. 37, Rev. i. 7). The Gospel also says that the world rejoices over his death (John xvi. 20).

The ascension of the witnesses shows them once more in the parts of Moses and Elias. Elias's assumption was scriptural; Jewish piety could believe no less of Moses. The last verses of Malachi, joining the promise of Elias's return with the exhortation to remember Moses's law, was built up into an expectation that they would both return in the last days from the heaven of their translation. According to St. John, when they do return (in the martyr Church) they repeat their ascension; for are not the dead in Christ to rise first, and be caught up in the clouds, to meet the Lord in the air? (1 Thess. iv. 16-17).

St. John is writing an allegory on the destinies of the Church and the ministry of the Gospel, under the form of a story of Moses and Elias returning to prophesy in Jerusalem. The whole eschatological truth, as St. John believes it, cannot be so much as symbolized in such a story; the cast is too small, the stage is too narrow. The 'ascension of Moses and Elias' is presented as a thing by itself, a vindication enforced by its own portents. In St. John's serious belief it is a thing inseparable from 'the Lord's own descent from heaven, with a signal note, the blast of the archangel, the trump of God'. To disclose the Advent here would not only break the frame of his picture, it would overthrow the order of his book, and anticipate his carefully reserved climax. He rounds off the episode with the conventional earthquake, and immediately proceeds to 'the blast of the archangel, the trump of God'.

The 'three and a half days' during which the witnesses lie unburied will stand for the 'half-week' of Antichrist's brief triumph. By strict arithmetic, where 42 months = 42 years, half a week would be only 42 days. But St. John is not to be pressed so closely; he sets a half-week of days beside a half-week of years, to show that the 'half-week' of Antichrist is brief indeed compared with the half-week of witness during the 'trampling' of Jerusalem. Since Antichrist has not yet come, St. John has no reason to suppose that his reign will be more or less than the $3\frac{1}{2}$ years Daniel assigned him.

By placing a short half-week of Antichrist after a long half-week of trampling, St. John compromises between St. Matthew (xxiv. 15-22) and St. Luke (xxi. 20-24). St. Luke simply substitutes the days of trampling for the days of Antichrist, as sequel to the predicted fall of Jerusalem. St. John cannot abandon the old tradition so lightly. The Lord had connected the great blasphemy of Antichrist with the desolation of the sanctuary. Very well; but the true, or spiritual sanctuary, the witnessing church, did not have its candle put out in A.D. 70. This is the sanctuary of which the desolation will coincide with Antichrist's coming; and it will happen in a second half-week, on a briefer scale altogether than the half-week of trampling.

(c) THIRD WOE

The second woe is past; behold, the third woe cometh quickly. 14
And the seventh angel sounded; and there followed great voices in 15
heaven, saying, The kingdom of the world is become the kingdom of our Lord and of his Christ; and he shall reign for ever and ever.
And the four and twenty elders which sit before God on their 16
thrones fell upon their faces and worshipped God, saying, We give 17
thee thanks, O Lord God Almighty which art and which wast, because thou hast taken to thee thy great power and reigned. And 18
the nations were wroth, and thy wrath is come, and the time of the dead to be judged, and to give their reward to thy servants the prophets, and to the saints and them that fear thy name, small and great; and to destroy the destroyers of the earth.

Among the scriptural types of St. John's trumpets we should probably reckon the trumpets blown against Jericho, and the more so, because they actually have the pattern of a seven-day week. For six days Israel compassed Jericho in silence, blowing trumpets; on the seventh they went round seven times and, at the last circuit, backed the trumpet-blast with shouting; and down came the walls. The trumpets were followed round by the Ark of the Covenant, which duly follows them here (in verse 19).

So, when the last trumpet blast is sounded, there are shouts in heaven, declaring the victory. But though the Jericho type may suggest shouting, the substance of the cries belongs most to the proclamation of the New Year of the world (see above, p. 112). First comes the theme of the initiation of God's kingdom (15–17) and second the dawn of judgement day (18). We have good evidence to show that in the beginning of our era the Day of Trumpets was observed as the renewal of God's enthronement over Israel, but also as a day of judgement when the moral accounts of all the living were brought up to date in the heavenly books, and a provisional balance struck. St. John brings the two themes together by developing Psalm ii; we will pick the appropriate phrases from the LXX:

> Why have the heathen raged . . .
>   against the Lord and his Anointed?
> The Lord shall speak to them in his wrath . .
>   Yet have I been set by him as king
>   upon his holy hill of Zion.

Serve the Lord in fear . . . take hold of instruction
Lest the Lord be angry, and ye perish . . .
Blessed are all they that trust in him.

The kingdom of the Lord and his Anointed, or Christ, is established in spite of heathen rage; the wrath of God comes upon their rebellion, and such as trust in him have their reward. We shall find the influence of Psalm ii dominant in the sequel, and as far as the Beatitude of xiv. 13. The hymns in 16 and 17–18 are constructed of phrases from a large number of psalms and prophecies, in a way that calls for no special explanation. By placing 'God's servants the prophets' first among those who merit reward, St. John continues the theme of his 'two witnesses' vision, which itself develops the theme of St. John's own prophetic calling (x. 7–xi. 1).

The mention of the angelic elders here by themselves and without the cherubim is appropriate to the occasion. When God is enthroned in his Messiah those who sit on thrones before him vacate them, and throw themselves on their faces. Equally pointed is the description of God as the Almighty who is, and who was—no longer 'and who is to come', for he *has* come—he has taken his great dominion, and begun his reign. In xvi. 5 God is still 'who is, and was'; and that is the last occurrence of the title in any form. It is found in the initial greeting (i. 4) and once in each of the four parts of the book, at i. 8, iv. 8, xi. 17, xvi. 5.

19 **And the temple of God in heaven was opened, and there appeared in his temple the ark of his covenant; and there followed lightnings and voices and thunders, an earthquake and a great hail.**

The Ark followed the trumpets in the compassing of Jericho; the day of the Ark followed the day of the trumpet in the sacred calendar; New Year's Day, the first of the seventh month, was but a prelude to *the* Day, the tenth of the same month, the Day of Atonement when (so long as a complete temple still stood) the High Priest entered the Holy of Holies and mortal eyes beheld the Ark of Covenant. The Day of Atonement was a solemn day, but it showed God's covenanted presence to be merciful; the covenant sufficed to cover the sins of the repentant.

Neither David nor Solomon had made an Ark, but built their shrines for the Ark Moses had made, and which had been restored to them by miracle. It was lost in the fall of the kingdom and the architects of the second temple did not dare to replace it. Their shrine was empty. All the more significance attached to the protoypic Ark, preserved in heaven. The earthly temple itself has now fallen (xi. 2), even the mystical lampstands are thrown down (xi. 4 and 7) but the Ark is in God's temple above.

St. John ought not to be taken to mean that the temple of God, hitherto closed to his eyes, now opens its doors, and that what the opening supremely reveals is the Ark. The temple of heaven, which is the presence-chamber of God's glory, opened its door to St. John at iv. 1. The Ark cannot be the central manifestation of divine presence there; to enter the temple is to see God on his throne. The Ark is a subsidiary symbol, a token above of God's covenant-presence with his people below. At the moment of vision St. John has reached, the Ark, usually 'hidden', appears, or is manifested; and the doors are opened, to show it to the universe. 'The Ark *was seen*' is a translation etymologically correct but idiomatically false. The passive of the verb *to see* was used idiomatically for the self-manifestation of a normally invisible reality; so Christ 'was seen', i.e. appeared, before his disciples after his resurrection (1 Cor. xv. 3-9, Mark ix. 4, Luke i. 11, xxii. 43, xxiv. 34).

This appearance of the Ark is the first of a series of heavenly manifestations, or appearances: the woman of xii. 1 is 'a great sign appearing in the sky' and the dragon of xii. 3 is another. Michael's battle in the clouds (xii. 7) does not have the formula, but fits the *genre*. With xiii. 1 St. John resumes his customary rubric 'And I saw . . .'. There are no more *optasiai* or 'appearances' in the book.

And there appeared a great sign in heaven: a woman clothed with XII the sun, and the moon under her feet, and upon her head a crown of twelve stars, and she with child; and she crieth out, travailing 2 in birth, and in pain to be delivered.

Before we plunge into the mysteries of chapter xii it will be well to recall the various expectations which the sequel to the seventh trumpet must satisfy. We may list

(1) the establishment of God's reign through the enthronement of his Messiah (cf. xi. 15);
(2) Antichrist's usurpation (cf. xi. 7);
(3) the seventh trumpet-plague, touching the luminaries of heaven (cf. viii. 12);
(4) the third woe, the woe of the third cherub, the bull (cf. viii. 13+ix. 3 and ix. 17+x. 3).

How are these several matters to grow into a unity of vision? St. John's selective quotations of Psalm ii have already shown the way to a combination of (1) and (2). The enthronement of God's Messiah itself provokes a last rebellion on the part of hostile powers; a rebellion which will certainly be crushed by omnipotence but which, for the short time it lasts, will be the reign of Antichrist. That reign, since it leads man into war against God and ultimate perdition, is the greatest woe (4) and, being the usurpation of power by Daniel's horned beast, is the woe of the bull. It begins by touching the luminaries of heaven (3) because it springs from a fall of angels, and falling angels are falling stars.

The two previous woes each built up into a separate incident that 'touching of the element' from which the plague springs. A star-angel falls from heaven to earth, and opens the pit of the abyss (ix. 1–2); on the occasion of a voice from the altar, the sixth trumpet-angel (presumably Gabriel) goes to Euphrates and releases the captains of the Death (ix. 13–15). In xii these two models are combined, and greatly enlarged upon. On occasion of voices in heaven, and a showing of the Ark, a drama breaks loose which results in the casting down of a captain of angels also called stars, by Michael (presumably the seventh trumpet-angel). The falling spirit draws forth demonic plagues upon mankind, first from the sea (xiii. 1), then from the land (xiii. 11). The monsters thus evoked are described in all their features and powers, as were those in ix. 3–11 and ix. 16–19.

The general force of the parallel between the three woes is that the third, like the two first, is under the direction of God and serves the purposes of his providence. The kingdom of Antichrist looks like evil getting out of hand, and afflicting the righteous. In truth it is not the righteous who are afflicted; they are sealed with the seal of God against spiritual harm, and offered the opportunity of a glorious conquest. The wicked are given the god they ask for and, in accepting the mark of the Beast, receive a print more deadly than the scorpion's sting.

The figure of the Scorpion, we recall, was astrological. It was evoked by the scream of the Eagle, because the Eagle holds his place among the four faces of the sky in substitution for the zodiacal Scorpion. Now the blast of the great trumpet, being treated by St. John as an eschatological trumpet of New Year, has a date in the calendar, and consequently a place under the Zodiac. The Jewish calendar follows the moon, and its fit with the sun's zodiacal positions is therefore irregular. But ideally speaking New Year, being the first of the seventh month, should come between the sixth sign (Virgo) and the seventh (Libra). Libra was a somewhat artificial sign, put in to make the months even; the impressive figure of the Scorpion appears to cover the space with his claws, and Claws was an alternative name for Libra itself. Virgil, looking out a place in heaven for Augustus, sees the Scorpion pulling back his claws to make ample room for the new Augustan month:

Or to the slow months addest thou a Sign
Where shrinks from following Claws the Maid divine?
Does not the very Scorpion check his pace,
Draw back his burning arms, and yield the place?
(*Georg.* i. 32.)

The Scorpion's drawing back is Virgil's poetical conceit; the ordinary thing to say about the beginning of the seventh month will be, that it is the point at which the Scorpion's claws seem about to catch the Virgin. So St. John begins with the Lady of the Zodiac, threatened by a monster. She is crowned with the twelve constellations. According to St. John's conventions, this means that she is the one among the twelve who reigns at the time. So the Lord's holding the seven planets in his right hand means that it is Lord's Day, the chief of the week; and the beast's being crowned with seven heads means that he is the crowning manifestation of a dynasty of seven kings. She is arrayed in the Sun, for the Sun's being *in virgine* is what is meant by her being the reigning sign; and she reigns over a month—she has the moon beneath her feet.

It cannot cost St. John more than a glance to see in the Virgin of Heaven the mother of Messiah; and the identification plunges him back into the second Psalm. 'I have been set as king by him on Zion his holy mountain, declaring the Lord's decree. The Lord hath said to me: *My Son art thou, this day have I begotten thee.* Desire of me, and I will give thee nations thine inheritance, and thy possession the boundaries of earth.' The Psalm makes Messiah's heavenly birth all one with his enthronement; if he is fathered by God, he reigns. So the rebellion against his enthronement, of which the Psalm speaks, will be an attempt to stifle his birth.

St. John's mind sets to work on the lines of a very old mythic pattern. It appears in different guises in so many traditions, that it is idle to ask from which St. John derived it. For he clothes it in the detail of scriptural themes, and twists it to dogmatic ends, beyond all recognition. The basic story is simply this:

(1) A true prince is to be born. He is fated to overthrow a usurper. The usurper tries to kill him at birth, but the child is providentially snatched away and hidden.

(2) The prince comes to maturity, kills the usurper and takes the throne.

The theme may be felt by the bible-reader in the story of Moses and Pharaoh or of Joash and Athaliah, and in a much softened form, in the tale of Joseph and his brethren. The Matthaean account of Christ's infancy makes it applicable to him. If St. John too were writing a Gospel he might show Satan vainly attempting to crush

Messiah in the manger, and triumphed over by Messiah on the cross. But for the purposes of an apocalyptic vision the triumph must be not the cross but the Advent. St. John contemplates the vulnerable infancy of the kingdom, rather than of the king. As Christ's temptations show, he was exposed to Satanic danger all the days of his flesh; his whole time on earth, until he was snatched from mortal sight, and from the jaws of Satan, was one with the exposed danger of his birth, a continuous miracle of divine protection. The last act of the drama, the victory of Christ and the saints, is deferred by St. John, while he shows us the attempt of Satan to attack in its earthly existence a power which, in its heavenly being, he has failed to touch. So the baffled enemy sets Antichrist in motion, and gathers that earthly power which Christ and the saints will overthrow in the triumph of the last fight.

Such are the main lines of the design. To return now to the beginning, here is the lady crowned with stars. Hers is the womb from which Messiah, or his kingdom, is to be born, and her position in the firmament may signify that her son's birth is into heaven, and takes effect in his enthronement there. But who is she? She is that Eve who in all history and in all the generations of her race has been travailing to bring forth the Christ and the age to come. The threat to her destined offspring has been from the beginning. Because of the Fall, God set enmity between the serpent and the woman, between his seed and her seed; he was to eye the serpent's head, and the serpent to eye his heel. We observe that, according to the words of Genesis, the threat of mutual attack leaves the woman out; it is between the serpent and her seed. And accordingly we see the serpent of St. John's vision wait for the child to be born; he does not attack the woman first. As for the woman, she suffers her personal penalty, according to the same text of Genesis: 'Multiplying I will multiply thy pains and thy groaning; in pain shall thou bring forth thy children.'

The Eve of St. John's picture is not a cartoon-figure like Britannia, a personified collective noun, the female sex. She is actualized in each of those mothers whose childbearing lay in a line towards Christ; in Rachel, who bore with such difficulty, whose first child was her miracle and the second her death; the mother of that Joseph whose destiny it was to be chief among the twelve stars, his brotherhood, and over sun and moon, his father and his mother (Gen. xxxvii. 9–10); who was said to have been devoured by a monster, but was found safely hidden in the throne of the Great King. Or again, we see her in the mother of Moses, threatened by the dragon of old Nile, and caught away to the safety of the throne; but above all in the Virgin Mother, already assimilated by St. Matthew to the other two we have mentioned.

Yet the person of the woman is not simply confined within the single body pregnant at any given time with messianic destiny. The whole community is Eve, and in Rachel or in Mary travails to bring forth. So the prophets had depicted the daughter of Zion, in labour to bring forth her salvation (Isaiah xxvi. 16 ff., Jeremiah iv. 31, Micah iv. 9 f.) Whereas the desired birth may be metaphorical for the prophets, it is actual for the Christian seer: Zion brings forth salvation in bringing forth a saviour, first from the womb, and after from the tomb.

And there appeared another sign in heaven; and behold, a great 3 red dragon, having seven heads and ten horns, and upon his heads seven diadems. And his tail draweth the third part of the stars, and did cast them to the earth. And the dragon stood before the woman 4 which was ready to be delivered, that when she was delivered he might devour her child. And she brought forth a man child who is 5 to rule all nations with a rod of iron; and her child was caught up to God and to his throne. And the woman fled into the wilderness, 6 where she hath a place prepared of God, that they may nourish her there a thousand two hundred and threescore days.

The dragon is a composite figure. Regarded as the sign of the Scorpion, he is 'fiery red' (*pyrrhos*) because of Scorpio's outstanding star, named Antares, i.e. 'the false Mars', from his red colour; and he has a third of the (zodiacal) stars at his tail, for four out of the twelve signs come after him. As to his casting them to earth, that is theology, not astronomy. Regarded as the enemy of Eve, the dragon is a serpent, the old snake of Genesis, and so deserves the name of 'dragon'; for 'dragon' in the Greek language means neither more nor less than 'serpent'; it was, however, specially used of monstrous serpents in the mythology. We are to see the dragon of St. John as a seven-headed snake, like the hydra of the Hercules legend. At the same time 'dragon' is the standing LXX translation for 'Leviathan' in the Old Testament. Two Leviathan texts are specially significant. Isaiah xxvii. 1 makes the Lord's smiting of Leviathan a sequel to his people's painful travail in bringing forth resurrection (xxvi. 16-19) and to their going into hiding for a moment until the indignation be past (xxvi. 20): the same text also equates the two names 'dragon' and 'serpent' just as St. John does. The other passage of special importance is Job xl. 15–xli. 34. It gives a high poetic description of Behemoth, prince of beasts, and Leviathan, king of reptiles. Now 'Behemoth' is a Hebraic 'plural of majesty'; literally, the meaning is 'cattle'. The LXX did not shrink from the literal rendering, except that, seeing Behemoth to be a wild creature, they used the plural of 'wild-beast' (one word in Greek). So 'Leviathan and Behemoth' becomes 'the dragon and the (wild) beasts'. Having shown us the dragon in xii, St. John will show us two beasts in xiii, of whom the former is *the* Beast *par excellence*.

Though the dragon is a reptile and the beast a quadruped, the beast is treated as 'the dragon's seed', and as made in his likeness. The dragon's many horns and heads have their proper meaning, and receive their detailed interpretation, in the beast. We shall find that they stand for his sovereignty, which he derives from the dragon (xiii. 2). And so they have to be shown in the dragon first. That the dragon or Leviathan is at least many-headed, can be proved from Psalm lxxiv. 14.

His casting down of the stars is a verbal reference to the sky-raking of the goat's horn in Daniel viii. 10. The meaning of Daniel's allegory is obscure and St. John has placed a different sense on it. He profits from the astrological fact that a third of the Zodiac is at the Scorpion's tail to make it a third of the stars that he trails after him and casts to earth; it belongs to the form of the trumpet-judgements that a third should be smitten; the assault on the stars darkened the third of them in the corresponding plague among the first four (viii. 12). But whereas that darkening was meant literally, this pulling down cannot be, since the context allegorizes constellations as spiritual forces. St. John is his own interpreter and tells us three verses below how the dragon involves an army of 'his angels' in his own fall from heaven.

The phrase about the woman 'She bore a son, a male birth' quotes Isaiah lxvi. 7-8. 'Before the woman in travail bears, before the labour of her travail comes, she has fled away and born a male birth. . . . Has a land laboured in a single day or a nation been born at a birth? —For Zion has laboured and born her children.' St. John would see no difficulty in applying the text to the Christian mystery. Satan was watching for the crisis of the birth, but it had happened before he looked for it; and in the person of Christ a whole new people was born to the daughter of Zion. He finds it necessary, however, for the purposes of his historical allegory, to reverse the order of the woman's childbearing and her flight. Cf. Matthew i. 25 and ii. 13. The description of the Manchild in verse 5 is the description of the destined world-ruler in Psalm ii.

No Christian writer who was not adapting the facts to a preconceived mythical pattern would wish to reduce the gospel to the two points of Christ's being born (whether from the womb or the tomb) and his escaping to the safety of the Father's throne. Yet the departure of Christ, his baffling of pursuit, and the Devil's inability to touch him are important themes of the Johannine Gospel (John vii. 30–36, viii. 14, 21–24, xii. 35–36, xiv. 1–6, 30–31).

It is as though the force of the divine oracle in Genesis obliging the serpent to enmity with the woman's seed, and to designs against his heel, makes him leave the woman untouched until the 'seed' is born. But when the seed has been born, and snatched from the serpent's jaws, the mother becomes the object of his rage. She escapes into the wilderness, as did Israel from Pharaoh. It is doubtless in her corporate capacity she is now to be viewed; the ecclesia of God, like the two witnesses, is divinely protected for a season. What the season is, and what the protection means, are questions we will defer until we reach St. John's enlargement on the theme in verses 13 to 16 below.

And there arose battle in heaven, Michael and his angels to battle 7 with the dragon; and the dragon battled, and his angels, and 8 prevailed not, neither was their place found any more in heaven. And the great dragon was cast down, called devil and Satan, the 9 deceiver of the whole world. He was cast to earth, and his angels were cast with him. And I heard a loud voice in heaven, saying: 10 Now is come salvation and might, the kingdom of our God and dominion of his Christ; for the accuser of our brethren is cast down which accused them before our God day and night. And 11 they overcame him through the blood of the Lamb and through the word of their testimony, and loved not their lives, even to the death. Therefore rejoice, ye heavens and the dwellers therein. 12 Woe to the earth and the sea, for the devil hath come down to you in great wrath, knowing that he hath but little time.

From verse 7 to the end of the chapter St. John writes what is virtually an extended comment on the previous six verses. He develops two points, the pulling down of the stars and the dragon's pursuit of the woman into the wilderness. It is to be noted that these two points, anyhow in the position St. John gives them, have nothing to do with the storybook theme of the usurper and the child of destiny. The enemy's pursuit of the mother *after* the birth and safe escape of her child, is an irrelevance; his pursuit of her *before* the birth, to prevent her safe delivery, is a proper enough part of the theme, but useless to St. John: the persecution of the Ecclesia followed Christ's ascension, it did not precede it. Even more irrelevant to the tale of the child of destiny is the dragon's pulling down of stars. But St. John wants to tell us that, as a consequence of Satan's failure against Christ, spiritual wickedness has ceased to work in the high places of heaven, and has mustered its forces on earth for the outbreak of Antichrist.

Naturally the extraneous features are the features in the story which require explanation; but equally, for St. John's purposes, they are the features that deserve exposition. St. John would never have added them, if they did not point in the direction in which he wanted to travel.

In the few verses xi. 19–xii. 6 there were three apparitions or portents in heaven, the Ark, the woman and the dragon. They were bunched together in the first half of the passage; the second half consisted of a narrative development. In xii. 7–17 there is only one celestial portent, battle in the skies; it supplies the fresh beginning St. John requires; the rest is narrative development. Armies contending in the sky have been seen by imaginative sign-seekers at all times, presumably in mutually confronted thunder-clouds. If that is what St. John has in mind, the fall of Satan may be seen in the fall of lightning, as at Luke x. 18. St. John writes a curious syntax, best explained as the transcript of vision: 'Battle in the sky—Michael and his angels to do battle with the dragon. The dragon and his angels battle back, but they cannot hold. . . .' The unequal introduction of the contending parties will be due to the fact that the dragon is already on the page, Michael is the new arrival.

It is commonly said that Judaism never entertained the barbarous idea, that the peace of heaven could be disturbed by fights between angels and devils. But St. John does not intend to assert anything so bizarre. He is describing a portent, battle in the clouds; and if we want to know what the portent means, the cry of heavenly jubilation, the thunder over Satan's lightning fall, will inform us. 'The accuser of our brethren is thrown, who accused them before our God day and night. They have won against him by the blood of the Lamb and the word of their witness; they loved their lives so little, that they died.' As we saw in connexion with v. 5, St. John is happy to profit by the ambiguity of the word 'win'. It is used of battles, it is used of lawsuits. There is an identical play on the word in Romans viii. 31–39. After his paradoxical description of the suit that justifies us in the court of heaven, where there is no longer any Satan to accuse us, the Apostle continues 'We are more than conquerors through him who loved us'. He then proceeds to describe the conquest in terms of victory over hostile circumstances and hostile spirits.

Who are the victors, then, the saints, or Michael and his angels? In a lawsuit successfully defended, who is the winner, the advocate, or his client? Both; if one wins, the other wins. Now Michael and his colleagues were held to be the defenders of Israel against the accusation of Satan and his minions. If the merits of the saints prevail, Michael drives the Accuser out of court. But Michael's forensic victory on the floor of heaven may be seen as all of a piece with his active resistance to satanic forces in the air of our world. The scriptural authority for such warfare is Daniel x. 13, 21 and xi. 1. Michael, with Gabriel's aid, first resists and ultimately (it would seem) defeats the invisible forces or 'captains' of heathen oppression. Satan is the supreme of such 'captains' in St. John's view and, like the 'captain' of Daniel's text, he puts heathen oppression into the field against God's people.

What sort of comment does the battle in the sky offer in exposition of xii. 1–4ᵃ? It explains the presence of evil angels in heaven and how they come to fall. Why are Eve and the snake among the stars? Her heavenly standing is threatened by satanic malice. Satan and his angels are 'stars', and so, we must suppose, they are true angels, though perverted. There were several Jewish myths about the first fall of angels; we have no evidence which of them St. John accepted. He tells us about that last fall, in which the rebels lose the last precarious footing they retained in heaven, their right to appear as accusers in the court. Eve, by the promise of her childbearing, is the reason why Satan will fall from the stars; but equally by the guilt of her first transmitted sin, she is the cause of his being there at all.

The last words of the jubilant cry raised over Satan's defeat show us that the third and greatest of all woes to 'earth and sea' is the convulsive struggle of a dying power. He knows that he has but a short time and, cast out of heaven, makes a last desperate fling on earth. We observe that St. John keeps in play the triad 'heaven, earth, and sea' as in x. 1–2, 5–6, and so prepares the way for the completion of a corresponding triad—the Leviathan from the sky, and the two Behemoth one from sea, and one from land. The theme of the baffled or defeated warrior, who turns to wreak his rage on the defenceless, is too natural to require a model, but also too inevitable to lack one; the most relevant is Daniel xi. 30.

And when the dragon saw that he was cast down to earth, he 13 pursued after the woman which brought forth the manchild. And 14 the woman was given the two wings of the great eagle, that she might fly into the wilderness to her place where she is nourished a time, times and half a time, away from the serpent. And the 15 serpent cast after the woman water like a river, that he might have her carried away in the stream. And the earth helped the woman; 16 the earth opened her mouth and swallowed up the river which the dragon cast out of his mouth. And the dragon waxed wroth with 17 the woman, and went to make war with the rest of her seed, which keep the commandments of God, and hold the testimony of Jesus; and he stood on the strand of the sea.

St. John continues his development of 1–6. The defeat of Satan by Michael was the equivalent of Satan's failure against the manchild; the exposition goes straight on with the flight of the woman and her providential sustenance in the wilderness. The Old Testament typology of the paragraph is easy to recognize; the contemporary application is more difficult to fix. We will take the typology first. The woman is treated as the congregation of Israel, saved from Egypt, lifted by the Lord on eagle's pinions and brought to Sinai (Exod. xix. 4). The dragon's pursuit of her by throwing a waterflood after her is a generalized image for the action of Pharaoh, who (1) commands Israelite children and especially Moses to be washed down the Nile, (2) comes out after escaping Israel with a host, and (3) counts on the Red Sea to shut Israel in. No doubt St. John is also influenced by the primitive association of waterfloods with the forces of evil, and especially, perhaps, by Psalm xviii. 4 (= 2 Sam. xxii. 5), 'The streams of Belial made me afraid.' Belial or Beliar had become a byname for Satan in New Testament times (2 Cor. vi. 15). The action of the earth in swallowing the river is a mythical version of the drying of the Red Sea and the swallowing of Pharaoh's chariots. It is based upon the fairly common phenomenon of streams disappearing down swallow-holes. And it has the additional merit of recalling yet another action of miraculous power in defence of the congregation in the wilderness, when the earth did open her mouth, and swallow a more domestic enemy (Num. xvi. 32).

St. John says that the woman was given *the* two wings of *the* great eagle. The point is astrological; there is the great Eagle of the starry heaven, with his two wings, and the Lady of the Zodiac may well receive their help in fleeing from the pursuing Scorpion; for we all hope to escape the baleful omen of his name by accepting the Eagle in his place, when we reckon the four faces of the sky. Apart from astrology, St. John's picture rests on a combination of Exodus xix. 4 with Psalm lv. 6–7 (O for the wings of a dove). It is after the woman has received the Eagles's wings that the dragon shoots a river at her. This is astrological, too; the great river of the sky, the Milky Way, goes up from the Scorpion and sweeps over the Eagle.

The continued presence of star-lore is perplexing, because Satan has now fallen from heaven, and hunts the woman into the wilderness. But then on the other hand, though Satan has fallen, the woman has not. She has a double existence throughout; the Church is in heaven and on earth; every one of the seven churches is a star in Christ's hand, as well as a lampstand at his feet. Her earthly

WOES OF THE EAGLE

destinies may be read in the stars of heaven and, indeed, it was about earthly destinies that the stars were commonly consulted.

After all that scripture or astrology can do to clarify the symbolism, we still do not know to what realities St. John is applying it. Three considerations may direct our conjectures. First, St. John underlines the parallel between the period of the woman's preservation and the period of the two witnesses' prophecy. Second, he makes a contrast between the dragon's pursuit of the woman in xii. 6–16 and his 'war on the rest of her offspring' through the instrumentality of the two beasts. And third, he must surely intend some correspondence between his description of the newly delivered mother's flight, and the words of Christ about women pregnant or lately delivered, according to Mark xiii. 14 ff. 'When you see the abomination that maketh *desert* stand where he ought not, let those in Judaea flee to the mountains . . . and *woe* to such as are with child or that give suck in those days! . . . Except the Lord had shortened the days' (to the Danielic 1,260, that is), 'no flesh had been saved.' Cf. Revelation xii. 12 ff. '*Woe* to the earth . . . for the devil has come down . . . and he chased the woman who bore the manchild . . . and she was given wings . . . to flee into the *desert* where she is nourished a time, times and a half away from the dragon.'

To take the last consideration first. If St. John is working from anything like the synoptic text, he has magnified the childbearing woman from typical sufferer to symbol of the whole community. But then he already had the symbol on hand. His woman is not literally the woman of Christ's warning; but will not her flight be literally the same flight? If it is, it is the flight from the Jewish War in A.D. 66–70 and the 'shortened days' through which the Ecclesia is to be preserved and nourished will be the time succeeding the fall of Jerusalem, the days of trampling and of the two witnesses' prophecy according to chapter xi. It should be so, since the last mention of the period in xi is picked up in identical form by the first mention of the woman's safe-keeping in xii. 6. But that is not all: the period of the witnesses squares Moses's forty or forty-two years in the wilderness with Elias's forty-two months of drought. And of these two periods, the Exodus-typology of the woman's escape is a direct reference to the first, while the second is hinted at in the language used to describe the divine preparation for the woman's nourishment or sustenance. For it is more like the language of 1 Kings xvii. 2–4, 8–9 than it is like that of any other scriptural text; and 1 Kings xvii tells us how, for the period of the forty-two months' drought, Elias himself was nourished in God's appointed place, first by the Brook Cherith, afterwards at Zarephath.

Now to take the second consideration listed above. Satan, baffled in his attempt to sweep the woman away with 'rivers of Belial', brings a new engine to bear. When Israel had endured the physical dangers of the wilderness, Satan brought Balak and Balaam against them with more seductive wiles (Rev. ii. 14) and so Satan brings against the woman's remaining seed the Antichrist and the False Prophet. Against the *woman's* remaining *seed*, for Genesis iii. 15 lays it down that the feud of the serpent with the woman will be continued against her seed by his seed; that is, by the two beasts. It is quite clear what the new threat signifies: it is the emperor-cult carried to all extremes and enforced with capital penalties. It is brought to bear upon 'the woman's remaining offspring', the Christians individually considered; for that was how imperial persecution operated. Christianity was made a crime on the part of any single subject or citizen and he was punished as such. Satan's previous attempt to 'sweep the woman away on a flood' ought to represent an earlier stratagem, aimed more at the total destruction of the people of God, corporately considered. What else can this Satanic stratagem be, than the destruction of the Jewish State in the war of A.D. 66–70? How could Satan—how could heathendom—be expected to guess that the Israel of God would survive the disaster, or be found to have escaped intact into the world of the Diaspora?

The language does not perfectly fit, because the Exodus typology does not fit. History does not absolutely repeat itself. Israel escaped from Egypt and the Church from Judaea. Pharaoh came out against old Israel with the sword when they were already in flight from his land. The Legate of Syria attacked a Jewry entrenched in positions of defence; the flight came afterwards. St. John uses the language of the Old Testament type. Satan has the woman already fleeing before him, when he casts the river after her.

This point being conceded, we can see that the parallel between xi and xii. 13–xiv. 20 is complete. In xi we have (*a*) the city trampled by the heathen, (*b*) the preservation of the witnesses, (*c*) the beast from the abyss, his slaughter of the witnesses, their assumption in the cloud and the punishment of the city. In xii. 13 ff. we have (*a*) the river of water aimed at the daughter of Zion, (*b*) her preservation, (*c*) the beast from the sea, the slaughter of the saints, and the reaper on the cloud who gathers them, while their enemies are cast into the vintage of wrath. We have to observe in this parallel, that in xi the weight falls upon the prophesying of the witnesses; their death at the hands of the beast and their vindication are merely sketched. In xii. 13 ff. the weight shifts forward; the woman's preservation is merely sketched and the tyranny of Antichrist occupies the middle of the picture.

And I saw a beast come up out of the sea, having ten horns and seven heads, and on his horns ten diadems, and on his heads names of blasphemy. And the beast which I saw was like unto a leopard, and his feet were as those of a bear, and his mouth as the mouth of a lion. And the dragon gave him his power and his throne, and great authority. And one of his heads was as it were smitten to death, and his death-stroke healed. And all the world gaped after the beast; and they worshipped the dragon for giving the beast his authority, and worshipped the beast, saying, Who is like the beast, and who is able to war with him?

We are told that the dragon took his stand on the seashore and that the beast came up. The relation between the two events is to be understood from what precedes. Having failed against the woman with a *river* the dragon turns his steps towards the *sea*, and receives the help of a monster from the deep. Nevertheless the emergence of the beast is a mystery and meant to be so. The descending star-angel of ix. 1 was given from heaven the key to the abyss, and let out the demons of disease. The dragon, a fallen constellation of stars, has no divine mandate to release the powers of the sea, and no ability in himself to evoke them. Yet, in the furtherance of his plans, they come. The forces of nature, and the passions of men, though they are under the hand of providence, serve the purposes of malice—for a time.

The beast in the previous brief mention of him rose from the *abyss* (xi. 7) and we shall find this to signify that he is a man returning from the dead—or as though from the dead. But the context here, with its emphatic triad of earth, sea, and sky, and the parallel of the river already mentioned, leads St. John to return to a more literal following of Daniel vii, where the beast comes up from the sea. As we have already seen, 'beast' or 'beasts' rather, *therion* or *theria*, when set beside 'dragon,' must mean Behemoth; and Behemoth meant simply 'cattle'. So the beast (with his companion beast) is the plague of the bull, in the sequence of woes—the first being the woe of the eagle (= scorpion), the second of the lion. The third woe is the woe of the bull, not of the dragon—the dragon, though his part is greatly developed, is in the position of the falling star or other angelic power who comes down and releases the plague. Now Daniel saw not one, but four beasts rise from the sea, of which the fourth was a monster whose animal kind is not described, apart from the fact that he is a horned creature. As such he is the most bull-like of the four, and he is for obvious symbolical reasons the figure of Antichrist; Daniel makes short work of the other three, while building him up as the last and greatest enemy of God and of his saints. This creature, then, St. John takes, but he views it as the epitome of its predecessors; they were all prefigurations of it. So he loads it with their salient characteristics, and produces a monster every bit as composite as the scorpion-locusts of the first woe, or the lion-cavalry of the second.

His method is perfectly systematic. He begins with Daniel's ten-horned monster; since the horns of Daniel's allegory stand for kings, St. John equips them with diadems. Then he proceeds backwards through the list in order. In general, the beast is like his immediate predecessor, the leopard, only that he has the terrible claws of the leopard's predecessor, the bear, and the jaws of the bear's predecessor, the lion. St. John prepares us for this summarizing of the characteristics of the four by giving his horned beast the number of heads they share between them. Since Daniel's leopard has four heads, and the rest a head a piece, he gets the number seven, which is very precious to him for his symbolical purposes. The horns may do with diadems —they will turn out to be a miscellaneous rabble of kings. The heads, being Roman emperors, are not crowned, but what is worse, they carry names of blasphemy, Worshipful (Augustus), Son of God, Lord God, and such like.

The dragon gives the beast his throne—for the dragon is the God of heathens, and the beast is his Anointed. When the heathen think they worship gods, they worship demons, according to Jewish belief; and they themselves set up their emperor as a quasi-incarnation of godhead. So Horace says:

> We knew that thunder ruled the sky
>   At Jove's behest; our faith shall find
> Caesar a present deity,
>   The Mede and Briton strong to bind.

Men worship the dragon because he has conferred authority on the beast. This is an epitome of political religion; gods are worshipped as the support of established power. It is also a parody of Christianity; the divine Father is worshipped, that is, given praise and glory, for sending us a saviour and a king.

A more striking feature of the parody is the beast's smitten yet living head; for the Lion of Judah is 'a lamb standing as though slaughtered'. To have one patched-up head among seven might seem a small matter; but that is not what St. John means. The heads being the successive members of a dynasty, the beast is actual in one at a time and fully bestial only in the smitten head returning. But that is a riddle reserved for exposition in xvii. We can see a hint of the truth, however, in xiii. 12, 14, when the monster is described as 'the beast with the healed death-stroke'. We shall naturally see his identity as carried by the first of the heads, and in the Greek St. John writes 'Seven heads . . . and *one* of them smitten . . .' tends to particularize the first, as in the counting of the cherubim and seals (vi. 1, 3, 5, 7). The smiting of the head is not simply an historical allusion, nor simply a parody of Christ's passion; it rests on Scripture. Because the serpent has attacked the woman, he is flung down grovelling on the earth, to carry on a feud with the woman, which is continued between his seed and the woman's seed: the serpent (in himself, or in his seed?) shall have his head ambushed, the woman's seed, his heel (Gen. iii. 13-15). We have witnessed the fulfilment of this oracle point by point; and now that the serpent takes up the feud with 'the rest of the woman's seed' through the instrumentality of his own 'seed' the beast, we are not to be surprised to see that the head of the serpent's 'seed' is smitten.

And there was given him a mouth speaking great things, and blasphemies; and authority was given him to act for forty and two months. And he opened his mouth in blasphemy against God, to blaspheme his name and his tabernacle in heaven. And it was given him to make war on the saints and to overcome them; and there was given him authority over every tribe, people, tongue and nation. And all that dwell on the earth shall worship him, as many as have not their names written from the foundation of the world in the book of life of the slaughtered Lamb. If any man hath an ear, let him hear. If any is for captivity, into captivity he goeth; if any slays with the sword, with the sword must he be slain. Here is the endurance and the faith of the saints.

'The mouth speaking proud things' belongs to the Beast of Daniel vii. 8 and is correctly interpreted by St. John as blasphemous pretension. The blasphemy is against 'the Name and Tabernacle' of God. God was said to have put his Name in, or upon, his temple in Jerusalem; but the dwelling of the Name in which Christians have part is in heaven. So reads our oldest MS., Papyrus 47 ('his name and his tabernacle in heaven'). It is possible, in view of other evidence, that the writer of the papyrus was correcting the false grammar of 'His name and his tabernacle *who* are (or, who tabernacle) in heaven'. If St. John wrote this, it is still uncertain what he meant. He may simply personify the Name and the Tabernacle as dwellers above, and so write a masculine plural when strict grammar would demand a neuter. Or he may allegorize the Tabernacle as consisting of those who tabernacle there in the Spirit—the beast blasphemes God's Name and his Church; both of them heavenly realities.

'To act for forty-two months', literally, 'to *do* forty-two months'. In spite of the parallel in James iv. 13, 'Do a year', the phrase is surprisingly flat, unless it carries an echo of the LXX Daniel, where 'to do' has the pregnant sense 'effect one's purpose', 'get away with it.' What forty-two months is intended? In xi we had two half-weeks, of years (fulfilled by the witnesses in the period of trampling) and of days (enjoyed by the beast and his associates between the murder of the witnesses and their resuscitation). Since the half-week here is reckoned in years, it should correspond to the former period; but since it is the time of the beast's success, it should correspond to the latter. The ambiguity is probably intentional and forms part of the riddle which chapter xvii will resolve. The beast is himself an ambiguous figure. Taken in the extension of his seven heads, he reigns for the period of trampling; taken in his acute phase, as the first head returning, he reigns for the period of the witnesses' lying unburied.

The beast's 'vanquishing' of the saints is the language of Daniel. It expresses one-half of the Christian paradox, of which St. John commonly prefers to state the other. Martyrdom is not defeat, but victory. Only in a description of Antichrist's numbered days, it must be shown that he enjoys to all outward appearance an unresisted triumph.

Perhaps our version of verse 8 above is a somewhat amiable rendering. 'It will receive worship from all the inhabitants of earth whose names are unwritten in the slaughtered Lamb's book of life from the foundation of the world' is what St. John means, and he goes straight on to describe the combined effect of idolatry and non-predestination to life, in a quotation from Jeremiah xv. 2. The prophet, like the seer, is speaking of those who are excluded from the divine mercy. They beg Jeremiah to intercede for them, but he cannot pray them back into favour with God—Samuel could not, nor Moses himself. Send them away, says the word of God. And if they ask 'Whither?' say 'Those for the death, to the death; those for the sword, to the sword; those for famine, to famine; those for captivity, to captivity'. St. John adds, 'Here is the enduring and trusting of the saints', i.e. 'this is the vindication of their blood upon *the inhabitants of earth* for which they have trustfully waited (vi. 10), for this is the third and final woe invoked on *the inhabitants of earth* by the eagle (viii. 13). That such is the meaning of the text is clear from the conscious echo in xiv. 11–12. The words of Jeremiah are quoted for their great rhetorical force; the distinction of punishments has no evident application to the followers of Antichrist. Whether they are captured or slain after Armageddon, it is all one, considering the judgement that is to follow. It is possible that for this very reason St. John has turned the point to that of exact retribution. He does not tell us, any more than Jeremiah does, what marks a man for captivity; but he has Christ's authority in Matthew xxvi. 52 for the statement that it is recourse to the sword that marks one for death by the sword. The disparity between the two limbs of St. John's sentence has naturally confused his copyists, and there is some variety of readings. A more interesting variant is that which attaches the name eternally unwritten in the book of life to the beast, not his worshippers. Not only the continuous sense of the passage, but the paraphrase below in xvii. 8, obliges us, however, to reject this alternative. The introductory appeal to those who have ears serves both to cover the oracular abruptness of the quotation from Jeremiah, and to contrast so sinister a message with the blessed promises similarly introduced in ii. 7, &c.

And I saw another beast come up out of the earth; and he had two 11 horns like a lamb, and he spoke as a dragon. And he exerciseth all 12 the authority of the first beast in his presence. And he causeth the earth and them which dwell therein to worship the first beast, whose death-stroke was healed.

The second beast is introduced on a level with the first, since Gospel tradition places the false prophet on a level with the false Christ (Mark xiii. 22, cf. Rev. ii. 14). He receives the name false prophet in xvi. 13, xix. 20, while the false Christ is called 'the beast' simply. The part he plays is in fact very secondary; nor is he comparable with the first beast in the manner of his advent. He comes from the land, like the rest of us; the first beast's origin out of the sea is allegorized as a returning from the dead. The trio is now complete, dragon from the sky, first beast from the sea, second beast from the land. We may call them a satanic triad; it is not, however, the Trinity of Father, Son, and Spirit they traduce, but the triad of revelation: God, his Messiah, and his servant the prophet—i. 1, not i. 4–5.

St. John scarcely troubles to describe the second beast. It would seem that he takes the next visionary creature of Daniel after the great beast of vii, the two-horned ram of viii. 3. He could not seriously suppose this figure to be meant for a false prophet, whereas he was entitled to think that the beast of Dan. vii was a figure of the Antichrist. But his ramlike look will serve: the false prophet comes in sheep's clothing, though inwardly he is a ravening wolf (Matt. vii. 15). Since the 'ravening' of a false prophet is expressed in his prophecies, St. John's way of putting it is that though he is horned like a young ram, his utterance is dragonish. It is surely childish to ask what St. John supposed dragon-speech to sound like. His dragon is the old serpent, who talked seduction in Paradise.

13 And he doeth great signs, so as even to make fire come down out
14 of heaven upon earth in the sight of men. And he deceiveth the dwellers upon earth by reason of the signs which it has been given him to do in the presence of the beast, telling the dwellers upon earth to make an image of the beast that beareth the stroke of the
15 sword and hath lived. And it is given him to give breath to the image of the beast, that the beast's image should speak, and cause that as many as would not worship the image of the beast should
16 be killed. And he causeth all, both small and great, rich and poor, bond and free, to be given a mark on their right hand or their
17 forehead; and that no man might buy or sell save he that had the
18 mark, the name of the beast on the number of his name. Here is wisdom. Let him that hath understanding reckon the number of the beast, for it is the number of a man; and his number is six hundred sixty and six.

According to verse 12 the second beast looks like a Grand Vižir, with the special functions of a Minister of Cults; now he begins to look like a juggling magician, such as were the Egyptians who counterfeited the signs of Moses at the court of Pharaoh. It is not very profitable to ask whether St. John expected to see one supreme personal embodiment of these various roles standing by the throne of Antichrist. It is more useful to consider in what present realities he saw the types of the false prophet. And it seems right to conclude that he found them in all powers or persons, priestly or political, who promoted the emperor-cult, whether out of fanaticism or out of servility.

The false prophet is a figure of the Gospel tradition and, further back, of Deuteronomy (xiii. 1–5). His characteristic there is misleading Israel to idolatry by signs and wonders. If he preaches idolatry, he is not to be believed, even though he obtains the signs he predicts; and so we are told that the second beast even achieves what Elijah did, and the prophets of Baal could not do—he brings down fire from heaven. Only, unlike Elijah's fire (xi. 5) it does not burn; it is a show before men's eyes. The speaking image is an obvious trick of idolatrous conjuring, but, like the fire from heaven, it gains a more vital interest by its apparent cancellation of a scriptural negative. 'The gods of the heathen are but idols; they speak not, neither is there any breath, or spirit, in their mouths' (Ps. cxxxv. 16–17, cf. cxv. 5, 7). More in general, the setting up of Behemoth in effigy may add another feature to the figure of Antichrist as the bull; see Exodus xxxii, 1 Kings xii. 26 ff.

It is not clear from St. John's Greek whether it is the false prophet or the speaking image which causes either the executions of verse 15 or the brandings of 16; nor does it make any difference, since the speaking image is but the mouthpiece of the false prophet.

The restriction of the right of commerce (*ius commercii*) to Roman citizens, or other privileged classes, was a well-known instrument of Roman policy; but St. John's model is more likely to be the synagogal practice of forbidding all dealings with the excommunicate. Christians of Jewish race may have felt the cruelty of this; John tells the churches that the Roman world will bar them out in the same way. It is evident that the stamping with the mark is to have a more systematic application than the challenge to offer idolatrous worship. If *all* recusants have been executed in verse 15, it will be superfluous to forbid them the market in 16. The stamping with the mark is a blasphemous parody of the divine sealing in vii. It may be that the addition of right hand to forehead as a place of branding would convey a suggestion of the branding of low-class slaves. All subjects of the Empire are to be the slaves of the god Caesar.

'Here is wisdom. Let the man who has wit reckon the number of the beast, for it is (the) number of (a) man, and his number is 666.' We may note first, that this oracular conclusion to the vision of the second beast echoes the similar conclusion to the vision of the first. There is once more the challenge to discernment—'He that has wit . . .', 'If any has an ear . . .'. And in view of 'Here is the patience and the faith of Saints', 'Here is wisdom' should mean 'This is where wisdom comes in'. The phrase following 'the beast' can mean, and probably does, 'for it is the number of a man', but grammatically speaking can equally well mean 'for it is human number' and so open to the analysis of human wit—not a baffling angelic or satanic mystery; cf. 'measure of man' in xxi. 17.

St. John does not tell us what kind of reckoning to employ. St. Irenaeus is certainly correct in relating the riddle to the practice of *gematria*, a game common to Jews and Gentiles. Since all the Greek and Hebrew letters were also used as numerical cyphers, any word in either language could be read as a sequence of numbers, and the numbers added up. The total was then 'the number of the name'. So far, we are on agreed ground. But when you had got your number, there were several uses to which you could put it. You might use it simply as a shorthand or cryptogram for the name, or you might use it as a basis for further ingenuities—you might see that the numerical value of your name stood in an interesting relation to the numerical value of some other name or names, and that the arithmetical relation appeared to symbolize some other relation. It was a sort of arithmetical 'punning'. (Puns relate words by mere sound, but they are not interesting as puns, unless there is a corresponding relation in the sense.) Let us speak, for short, of a 'punning' use of *gematria* and contrast it with the plain 'cryptogram' use. The simplest interpretation would be that St. John puts his *gematria* to a cryptogram use; but his oracular language suggests something more like a punning use. And we will proceed to show that a satisfactory explanation in terms of mere cryptogram cannot be found, whereas a punning interpretation fits the case quite readily.

If St. John is offering a cryptogram it is in fact no use to anyone who does not know the answer. There is no way of breaking down 666 so as to get one rather than another among several alternative Greek names. Now the name we think we want is (to anticipate future discussion) the name NERO. But neither in Greek nor in Hebrew is 666 the value of Nero. It is, however, the value in Hebrew of '*Caesar* Nero'. But this is both a roundabout solution (St. John is writing in Greek to Greeks; why go through Hebrew?) and a redundant solution (since we are asking 'Which Caesar?' the natural answer is just 'Nero'). Now it may be that St. John has gone as far about as this, to make out the equation 'Nero = 666'; but if he has, it is surely because he values the answer for its own sake; he *wants* Nero to be 666 rather than some number more obviously obtainable from his name by the Greek reader. And why? Because he has what we have called an 'arithmetical pun' in mind. And we need not look far to see what that pun is. St. John runs straight on into a vision of the Lamb and his hundred and forty-four thousands, bearing *his* name on their foreheads. Now the numerical value of the name Jesus in Greek is 888, and any Christian who had ever played at *gematria* must have known that piece of 'wisdom'. But why should the Name be a *triple* reiteration of *eight*? Why, Jesus rose on the *third* day, being the *eighth* of that week: he is the Resurrection and the Life. For *eight* signifying resurrection, see 1 Peter iii. 20–21, and 2 Peter ii. 5. But the third day on which Jesus rose is third from that sixth day (Friday) on which Antichrist had his apparent triumph; so if Christ has a name valuing 888, Antichrist should have a name valuing 666.

It will be seen that the punning solution is independent of the cryptogram solution and can stand on its own feet. We may, as St. Irenaeus says, not know the name of Antichrist till he comes. He may be a *Nero Redivivus* but he may not be called by that name. Still we may be sure that he will turn out to be a 666 against Christ's 888. So St. John's Greek reader can play the more interesting part of his game without knowing any Hebrew at all.

But there are still deeper veins of 'wisdom'. The ancients talked of 'triangular' as well as 'square' numbers. The triangular of a given number is the sum of whole numbers up to, and including, that number: 10 is the triangular of 4, because $4+3+2+1 = 10$. The formula is $n^{tr} = \frac{n(n+1)}{2}$. Now 666 is an unusual number in being the triangular of a triangular. $8^{tr} = 36$, and $36^{tr} = 666$. So the number which is all sixes is a 'power' of eight. We shall learn in xvii. 11 how Antichrist parodies Christ in being 'himself also an eighth'; yet an eighth (we see) which has run all to sixes.

Another obvious property of 666 is to be two-thirds of that standard quantity, the thousand; Christ's followers in the next verse are reckoned in whole square thousands. May we not fairly remark, that the kingdom of Antichrist belongs to the day of the trumpets, which destroy everything to the third part, so that Antichrist reigns in a two-thirds world, a world touched by the finger of judgement? He himself has received the stroke of the sword; his subjects have been one-third part killed in the pestilence (ix. 15, 18).

Last of all, a doubly triangular number is a most emphatic expression of three-sidedness; and this number is in immediate contrast with the square number of Christ's flock. The contrast marks the transition from the period of the three woes, in which the number three has run riot, to the period of the evangel, in which the number four will regain its rights.

(D) THE EVANGEL

And I saw, and lo, a Lamb standing on Mount Zion, and with him XIV a hundred forty and four thousand, having his name and his Father's name written on their foreheads. And I heard a voice 2 from heaven as the voice of many waters and as the voice of a great thunder; and the voice I heard was as though of harpers harping with their harps. And they sing as it were a new song before the 3 throne, the four living creatures and the elders; and no man could learn the song save the hundred and forty and four thousand, the people purchased out of the earth. These are they which in com- 4 panying with women defiled not themselves; for these are the virgins which follow the Lamb whithersoever he goeth. These were purchased from among mankind for firstfruits unto God and the Lamb. And in their mouth was found no lie; they are without 5 blemish.

This vision is a direct antithesis to the last. The wolf in sheep's clothing has built up a vast congregation and signed it with a name of blasphemy. While we saw him doing so, we recognized the parody of God's Israel as described in vii. The original of the parody is now brought back before our eyes, with the addition of the true Lamb, set in opposition to his counterfeit. While the vision of the sealed Israel refers us to vii. 2 ff., the figure of the 'Lamb standing' refers us to v. 6 ff. The combination of the two models joins earth with heaven; for the 144,000 were sealed on earth, whereas it was in heaven that the Lamb's taking of a book none other could open or look over, caused the elders and the cherubim to lead the choir of angels in a new song. The bringing together of the two levels, the earthly and the heavenly, is what gives the vision now before us its special character. St. John transfers the figure of the Lamb to the earthly scene, and in doing so continues the exposition of Psalm ii which has given form to the whole complex of seventh-trumpet visions. The 'rage' of the heathen, and their vain attempt to cast off the divine sovereignty, has been shown at length; it is time to remember 'Yet have I set my king upon my holy hill of Zion'. So here on Zion's hill he stands, and his people round him. He is the link of earth and heaven; he who opened the secrets above, which no other could touch, is the cause why his congregation on Zion 'learn' the new song sung about the throne on high, which thunders down to them from the skies, a song no others on earth but they can 'learn'. It was a new song, because it was concerned with the new wonder, 'men bought for God from every tribe and people' (v. 9); and it is fitting that only those so *bought* (xiv. 3) should be able to 'learn' the song. The word 'bought' is the same in the two texts. As to the 'learning' of the song, we cannot be sure whether St. John means 'learn to sing', 'learn to understand', or even 'hear'. Whichever is the literal meaning, the spiritual sense will be much the same.

The hill of Zion is an earthly site, but not any one literal place; John iv. 20–24 is the best comment. It is where Christian worship is offered through Christ; his congregation is ideally one though physically divided. The interpretation of the seal as the name of Christ and the name of his Father should not be taken as evidence of baptism in two names rather than three or one. Those marked with the seal bear the stamp of loyalty to 'the kingdom of the Lord and his Anointed' (xi. 15).

Verse 4ª may be seen as a comment on vii. 14 and 17. They have whitened their robes in the blood which has bought them—this is now interpreted in special relation to chastity. The Lamb shepherds them and leads them to living waters—and they follow him wherever he goes. The phrase about chastity does not express any other attitude to sexual relations than what is common to Christianity. St. John neither implies that to touch woman is pollution, nor that the sealed are all celibates. He says first, that in their dealings with women they have not defiled themselves, a commendation which will cover Christian husbands; and second, that they are 'virgins'. That is not the Greek for 'men who have never had to do with the other sex'; it is a violent and paradoxical metaphor, for 'virgins' in Greek means simply 'girls' with the added suggestion, 'still sexually innocent'. What St. John must be taken to mean is 'these are the dedicated virgins who accompany the bridegroom (the Lamb) wherever he goes'. We must put together Matthew xxv. 10 and 2 Corinthians xi. 2 to see what he means. St. Paul tells us which sexual relations are incompatible with 'chaste betrothal to Christ' in 1 Corinthians vi. 15–20. There is no reason why St. John should be taken to disagree with St. Paul, for anything that he says here, or for that matter in ii. 14, 20.

'Firstfruit' is ambiguous. It need mean no more than that the redeemed are taken out of humanity and given to God, as in James i. 18. It could mean that the 144,000 are the promise of a greater harvest, and this St. John anyhow believes: see pp. 109 f. above.

'In their mouth was found no falsehood' does not mean that they abstained from the distressing habit of social mendacity but that they made no compromise with the great lie of Antichrist. They are 'unblemished'—the word has sacrificial associations, strengthened by the suggestions contained in 'Lamb' and 'firstfruit'. They are an offering ritually acceptable to God.

'On their lips no lie' is particularly apt, for the way it brackets Isaiah liii. 7–9 with Zephaniah iii. 13. Zephaniah tells of a faithful flock, 'feeding and lying down' on Mount Zion, who shall not do iniquity nor speak lies. Isaiah shows that in this respect they are indeed the flock of the self-offering Lamb, in whose mouth was found no deceit.

And I saw another angel flying in mid-heaven, having an everlasting gospel to proclaim unto them that sit on the earth, to every nation and tribe, tongue and people, saying with a loud voice, Fear God, and give him glory; for the hour of his judgment is come; and worship him that made heaven and earth, sea and watersprings.

And another angel followed second, saying, Fallen, fallen is Babylon the Great, which hath made all nations drink the raging wine of her fornication.

And another angel followed third upon them, saying with a loud voice, If any man worship the beast and his image, and receive his

10 mark on forehead or hand, the same shall drink of the wine of the wrath of God prepared unmixed in the cup of his indignation; and
11 he shall be tormented with fire and brimstone in the presence of the holy angels and of the Lamb; and the smoke of their torment goeth up for ever and ever, neither have they rest day or night that worship the beast and his image, and whoso receiveth the mark of
12 his name. Here is the patience of the saints, that keep the commandments of God and the faith of Jesus.
13 And I heard a voice from heaven, saying; Write, Blessed are the dead that die in the Lord henceforth. Yea, saith the Spirit, let them rest from their labours, for their works go with them.

Even while Antichrist's overthrow is still withheld, the divine counter to him is not limited to the preservation of Christ's spiritual kingdom. There is, as we have heard, a heavenly music for the ears of the elect alone; but there is also an open proclamation to men of every tongue and tribe, inviting repentance before it is too late.

In recalling the heavenly hymnody of chapter v St. John has recalled a liturgy out of which four cherubic cries came, and four corresponding figures of horsemen. We observe further that the number of the elect being mostly fours (xiv. 1, 3) St. John brings it into juxtaposition with the *four* cherubim (3). A new series of *four* applying the four cherubic types seems a natural development here. *Three* has had a long innings; ever since the flying eagle of viii. 13 uttered his woes, we have been working through the three judgements arising from the three elements of nature and smiting the third part. These judgements have expressed three cherubic types, the eagle, the lion, and the bull; but there are, after all, four cherubim and it seems only proper that a new series should complete the number and, in so doing, take off the curse of three.

So, then, St. John shows us in contrast to the three woes a fourfold evangel. His method is to go over the three woes providing each with an antitype, and then to make the decisive step in going on to a fourth object of vision.

'An angel flying in mid-heaven' with good news for the inhabitants of earth is an evident antitype to the eagle flying in mid-heaven with cries of woe for the inhabitants of earth. It is to be remarked that this is the sole text of the Revelation in which an angel flies like a bird. Apart from the cherubim with their six wings each, St. John has no feathered angels but this. We observe that the angel calls on men to worship the creator of the *four* elements (contrast x. 6).

In parallel with the cry of the eagle introducing the first woe, St. John takes up the roar of the lion from the second woe (x. 3). To be more exact, what he takes up is the proclamation of a herald, crying with the voice of a lion; and such a proclamation cannot but recall the striking vision in Isaiah xxi. 6–9, where the fall of Babylon is tidings hearkened for by a desert-watchman, eyeing the caravans, and proclaimed at length with a lion's roar. (It is to be noted that here as elsewhere, St. John follows the Hebrew; the LXX miss the reference to the lion.) In chapter x, as we saw, St. John developed other associations of the lion-voice; but now, in the antitype, he brings out Isaiah xxi, 'Fallen, fallen is Babylon'. 'The great' belongs to Nebuchadnezzar's unlucky boast about Babylon in Daniel iv. 30, when pride went before a fall. So far as we have yet learnt, we are bound to suppose that 'Babylon', i.e. Rome, is associated with Antichrist in the same way as Babylon was with Nebuchadnezzar, and that the fall of one is the fall of the other. When we reach xvii. 16 we shall see a different picture.

Jeremiah li. 8 follows Isaiah xxi in declaring the sudden fall of Babylon; and this after calling her a cup in the Lord's hand, to poison or madden the Gentiles; they have swallowed her wine, and reel. If we compare li. 7 with verse 10 in the passage before us, we shall see that St. John doubles Jeremiah's image. If Babylon is a cup from the Lord's hand, to poison or madden the Gentiles, it is as a temptation permitted by God—a first judgement on their sins. But those who embrace the temptation merit the second judgement—they drink the bitter wine of God's wrath, that is, they undergo the torment of brimstone and fire.

For the woe of the bull St. John simply takes up the worship of the golden calf, or effigy of Behemoth, and the stamping with his name. As we have seen, he carries over the theme of poisonous wine from the denunciation of Babylon to this denunciation of beast-worship, as though the two topics were equivalent. The relation between the two 'wine' texts poses an insoluble problem to the English translator. The transition within verse 10 from wine of wrath to fire and brimstone, the punishment of Sodom and Gomorrah, shows that St. John has Deuteronomy xxxii. 33 in mind, where the LXX use 'fury' in the evident sense of 'poison'; 'Their vine is the vine of Sodom, their shoot is from Gomorrah; their cluster a cluster of gall, their grape bitter; fury of dragons their wine, and fatal fury of asps.' The translator would be in no difficulty if St. John adhered to one sense of the phrase 'wine of fury', but he chooses to play on an ambiguity. Babylon has made all nations drink the wine-of-fury (raging wine) of her fornication; the sinner shall drink the wine of God's fury, prepared undiluted in the cup of his wrath. (The translation we have offered verges on blasphemy: we ought not to speak of the fury of God. The divine heart is not subject to negative passions).

The overthrow of the sinners is as that of Sodom and Gomorrah—the smoke goes up (Gen. xix. 28) forever, unquenched night or day

(Isa. xxxiv. 9–10). 'Here is the patient endurance of the saints', i.e. here is the vindication they waited for; this is what makes all their fortitude worth while. This remark is closely parallel to xiii. 10^b and helps to explain how the proclamations of the three angels are 'gospel' or 'good news'. It is, indeed, said of the first alone that he carries 'everlasting gospel', that is, the tidings of a good that shall last for ever. But the others are in parallel with him and the analogy of viii. 13 on which he is so strongly modelled suggests a threefold counter to the three woes. Yet the design (if St. John intended it) was difficult to execute. The three woes already run counter to one another (or so it seems). The first two plague the enemies of God, the third gives them all the outward forms of a delirious success. This success is, like Hitler's victory in 1939–40, the worst thing that could possibly have happened to them; it carries a print more poisonous than the scorpion's sting, a fate worse than the death. All the same, how is one to write a counter-evangel to a programme of woe composed partly of plagues, partly of sinister successes? If the infliction of judgement is woe, the offer of repentance is gospel; if the enthronement of Antichrist is woe, the fall of Babylon is evangel; if the diffusion of Antichrist's service is woe, the destruction of his devotees is tidings of great joy—not, however, to the broad masses of mankind, who have conformed, but to the saints who stood out. So, having begun with a gospel for every tongue and people, we end with a gospel for the saints.

The voice from heaven (verse 13) turns the blessing to the special address of those who die under the persecution. The text is uncertain, the sense is not. If we read with the majority of our witnesses, 'Blessed are the dead that die in the Lord *ap'arti*; Yea, says the Spirit, let them rest from their labours . . .', the sense must be, 'Blessed from the moment of their death . . .' not 'From this moment forwards, blessed are the dead' as though there had been a former time when they were not blessed. So the sense is not altered, if we accept the minority of very early evidence and read '. . . that die in the Lord. From that moment, says the Spirit, let them rest. . . .' They are blessed to rest *because* the work they laboured to achieve goes with them in the form of a merit which will bring its reward at the resurrection. 'Work' in the New Testament very commonly means 'payable service'. If our work goes with us, it counts for pay. The voice of the Spirit audible in a blessing recalls the similar terminations of the messages to the churches; an echo recently evoked in the parallel passage xiii. 10.

14 And I saw, and behold, a white cloud, and on the cloud one sitting like unto a son of man, having on his head a golden crown and in his hand a sharp sickle.

And another angel came out of the temple, crying with a loud 15
voice to him that sat on the cloud, Put in thy sickle, and reap, for
the hour to reap has come, for the harvest of the earth is ripe. And 16
he that sat on the cloud put his sickle to the earth, and the earth
was reaped.

And another angel came of the temple in heaven, he also having 17
a sharp sickle. And another angel came out from the altar, who 18
hath power over fire; and he called with a loud voice to him that
had the sharp sickle, saying, Put in thy sharp sickle, and gather
the clusters of the vine of earth, for her grapes are ready. And the 19
angel put his sickle to the earth, and gathered the vintage of the
earth, and cast it into the great winepress of the wrath of God.
And the winepress was trodden without the city, and blood came 20
out of the winepress, even unto the horses' bridles, as far as
a thousand and six hundred furlongs.

The association between payable service and harvest work is
a commonplace of Judaism, see Pirqe Aboth ii. 19–20, John iv. 34–
38, vi. 27–29, ix. 4. So the transition from the saying about rest from
labour, with payable service credited, to the harvesting of the elect
is natural, though not logical.[1] Instead of the harvest-workers being
paid, they are themselves harvested. As in so many other cases, the
straining of the symbolism is due to multiplicity of reference. St.
John ended the last vision with the saints resting as labourers sure
of their reward, but he had ended the vision before that with the
saints as a firstfruit-sheaf taken out of the field of mankind. And the
picture he now presents is not only a picture of harvesting, it is
a picture of the cutting of firstfruits. The ritual is prescribed in
Leviticus xxiii. 9 ff. and Mishna Menahoth x. The harvest could not
be cut until the firstfruit-sheaf had been cut, nor the sheaf cut until
the sun had set on a given day. It was cut for offering in the temple,
from the nearest barley field which happened to be ripe. The local
peasants gathered round and joined in a ritual dialogue with the
appointed reaper (or reapers). It was only when they had assured
him that his sickle and basket were correct instruments, and that he
was now free to reap, that he could act. Hence the intervention of
the angel from the temple (where the firstfruit is wanted) who gives
the heavenly harvester his signal to begin.

A figure enthroned upon a cloud does not seem conveniently
placed for reaping but, once again, the symbolism is strained by the
multiplicity of reference. St. John has been over the woes of the

---

[1] The harvest-image is also suggested by the transition from 'Fallen is Babylon' to 'Corn of my threshing' in Isa. xxi. 9–10.

eagle, the lion and the bull in corresponding evangels, and now he takes the inevitable and decisive step of completing the cherubic circle in the evangel of the man. The man-figure who follows upon the bull-figure, that is, upon Behemoth, the great beast of Daniel vii, can be no other than the figure like a Son of Man who comes with the clouds of heaven in that same prophecy, to redeem the suffering saints and put an end to heathen usurpation. The evangel of the man is the evangel *par excellence*, and St. John breaks out of angelic proclamation into direct visionary experience for the presentation of it.

Though the Son of Man on clouds may seem a strange harvester, the connexion of ideas was ready to hand in the synoptic tradition. When the Son of Man comes with clouds, he will send out his angels to gather, or harvest, his elect (Matt. xxiv. 30–31). The connexion of such a prophecy with the seed-parables seems unmistakable, and in Matthew xiii. 37–42 it is explicit. But the formula most serviceable to St. John is in Mark iv. 29: when the crop is ready he sends forth the sickle, because harvest is come. The synoptic harvest-parables alternate between the interpretation of the crop as men's good deserts (Matt. xiii. 18–23) and as well-deserving men (ibid. 37–42). The ambiguity serves St. John perfectly; he is writing of men whose good deserts accompany them—human cornstalks with grain-packed ears.

The Son of Man is seen as *mounted* on the cloud with which he traditionally comes, and the cloud to be *white*; he wears a garland or crown of victory besides. All these strokes of the pen place him in parallel with the rider on the white horse (vi. 2), and no wonder; the series of four cherubic themes which St. John is working out is in antitype, as we said above (p. 162), to the four horsemen. It has surprised Christian commentators to see the Son of Man placed on a footing with the three angels of harvest and vintage; but the case is no different in the horsemen. The white rider is Christ, the three others are angels inflicting plagues. St. John sacrificed hierarchy to serial pattern in vi, and so he does again. For he runs on with another round of cherub-types: after the man, the eagle, lion, and bull, represented by the harvest-angels; and so we are ready for the great exposition of the man or Aquarius theme in the next vision (i.e. in chs. xv–xvi). The three harvest-angels are little more than numerically equal to the three gospel-angels who precede them; the match between the threes is commended to our notice, however, by the fact that the first angel in each triad says 'The hour is come'.

The cry of the first harvest-angel borrows the language of Joel iii. 13. Joel's oracle probably speaks of vintage only; if a 'harvest' is mentioned it is the harvest of grapes. But it is possible to read him otherwise, as speaking, that is, first of a harvest, then of a vintage. Even if he is so read, there is no place for any distinction between the things symbolized by harvest and vintage respectively. Both images are equally sinister: Harvest the corn of judgement, tread the vintage of wrath! Influenced by Christ's teaching, and by the needs of his developing story, St. John makes the distinction which is foreign to Joel's meaning: the harvest is blessed and the vintage accursed. The distinction does something to mitigate the seeming impropriety of an angel acting in absolute parallel with the Son of Man. The first and immediate act of Christ's advent is his gathering of his elect to himself. Meanwhile angelic forces drive the hosts of Antichrist into the 'winepress', that is, the field of battle. There the grapes will be trodden—by whom, we are not yet told, but we soon will be (xix. 13–15).

The Son of Man rides the air; his signal-giver comes out from the doors of the temple. The vintager comes likewise from the temple, his signal-giver from a temple within the temple, therefore—from the altar. And so the last act in the long drama stemming from the trumpets goes back to the source from which the whole began—the offering of the martyr's prayer in incense on the altar of their sacrifice (vi. 9, viii. 3). They prayed for vengeance on their murderers; and when the sixth trumpet brought death on a third of mankind, it was at the behest of a voice from the altar. Now the voice from the altar takes bodily form, to give the signal for a total destruction; and St. John takes occasion to say that the embodied voice, being the angel of the altar, is the angel of fire.

The vintage is trodden outside the city. St. John accepts the symbolism of Joel. Joel describes under the metaphor of a ghastly vintage a battle in which the nations, attacking Jerusalem, are smashed outside the walls. St. John no more supposes the act of judgement to be confined within the Valley of Jehoshaphat, than he supposes the blessed harvest to be reaped in a field of barley on the Judaean hills. The value of the phrase 'outside the city' is that it links Joel's prophecy with the last chapters of Isaiah and Zechariah respectively, both of which describe a final slaughter of enemies outside Jerusalem.

'Come,' says Joel, 'tread, for the winepress is full; the vats overflow, for their wickedness is great.' St. John's measurement of the ghastly overflow places a river of death in comparison with the river of life, as described in Ezekiel xlvii (cf. Rev. xxii. 1). Ezekiel's angel measures the river—which also issues from Jerusalem—and gives its increasing depth at several distances from the source by relation to the body of a man attempting to ford it. The river of life deepens as it flows; the vintage of blood grows shallower as it spreads, but even at 1,600 furlongs it is still up to the bridles of horses. The horses suggest battle—all St. John's horses are horses of war and all his warriors are mounted. It seems likely that he derived the suggestion from the last battle-scene according to Enoch c. 3: 'The horse shall wade to the breast in the blood of sinners, and the chariot plunge to its height.'

1,600 stades are roughly 200 miles, but to substitute the more familiar measure will not illuminate St. John's meaning. He is handling symbolical number, not real distance. Why 1,600? Chapter xiv is, as we have seen, a *four* passage in emphatic contrast with the long *three* passage preceding it. Now the expression of *four* in penal terms is *forty* (Num. xiv. 33, Deut. xxv. 3). We remember that the *three* passage ended with a triangular, that is, a three-sided number, whereas the *four* passage began with a square, that is four-sided, number (xiii. 18, xiv. 1). St. John now ends it with another, by squaring *forty*. The result is a number with a *six* in it. This is fortunate in two ways. (1) It chimes with the end of the last vision in the *three* passage, just as the end of the vision before it (xiv. 12–13) chimes with the termination of the penultimate vision of the *three* passage: so that a total formal parallel results between xiii. 1–10+xiii. 11–18 and xiv. 1–13+xiv. 14–20; between the kingdom of Antichrist and the divine answer to it. (2) A *six* number at xiv. 20 prepares us for the *seven* angels of xv. 1 as a natural sequel; and looking back, we may observe that we have seen six angels arranged in two triads, in the evangel-series which has been shown us.

IV. THE HEAVENLY MAN

(A) SEVEN BOWLS

And I saw another sign in heaven, great and marvellous, seven XV
angels having seven plagues, the last—for in them is accomplished
the wrath of God. And I saw as it were a sea of glass filled with 2
a fiery mixture; and them that had gotten the victory over the
beast and his image, and the number of his name, standing by the
sea of glass, holding harps of God. And they sing the song of 3
Moses the servant of God and the song of the Lamb saying:
Great and marvellous are thy works, Lord God Almighty; just
and true are thy ways, thou King of the nations. Who shall not 4
fear, O Lord, and glorify thy name? for thou only art holy. For
all nations shall come and worship before thee, for thy judgements
have been made manifest.

The new vision has a fourfold connexion with what precedes it.
(1) It is a group of seven angels all together, succeeding a series of
six in open order; (2) the last three of the six forming a set by themselves and representing the eagle, lion, and bull cherubim, it adds
a fourth to them, the man-cherub Aquarius; (3) as 'another great and
astonishing portent in heaven' it is the successor of the woman and
dragon (xii. 1, 3), as though everything in xii–xiv had been the
working out of that mighty conflict, and the next act were now to
begin; and (4) as a new and final seven of plagues, it is the successor
of the trumpet-vision in viii.

It is to be remarked that the man or Aquarius figure is reached
along no less than three convergent lines. According to (2) he completes a small-scale series of the cherubic types, and according to
(3) a similar large-scale series, since the woman-and-dragon drama
of xii–xiv, taken as a whole, is the story of the third woe, and the
three woes are eagle, lion, and bull. Both these cherubic series are
in the anti-calendrical order prescribed by the list in iv. 7. But, in
addition to the many examples of that order, the Revelation contains one grand example of the calendrical order: the great sevens
which give shape to the whole apocalyptic drama follow the quarters
of the year. The unsealings are a heavenly Pentecost introducing the
Lion (summer), the trumpets a New Year, or, as we should say,
Michaelmas, introducing the Eagle or Scorpion (autumn); and now
here are the bowls, bringing us Aquarius for winter. (On reflection,

we see that the Sunday of the messages was, like any Sunday, an Easter, and as such fell to the quarter of the Bull.)

The relation between (2) and (3) is significant, because it corresponds to the tension between St. John's two opposite principles of construction—his desire to round off his visionary themes, and his desire to leave them open in expectation of a fulfilment still to come. The small-scale cycle of cherubic types (xiv. 6–14, xiv. 15–xv) in the course of two revolutions has rounded off the theme of Antichrist by a vision of the advent of the Son of Man: whereas the large-scale cycle shoulders this development aside, as a mere promise or anticipation of things to come, and goes straight from the woe of the Bull to the judgements of Aquarius, who pours the rain of fiery vengeance on the kingdom of the beast.

The seven angels of the seven last plagues are mere angels, whereas the seven trumpeters were the seven angels of the presence, that is, the archangels. The apocalyptic drama steadily descends through the levels of the hierarchy. The seven unsealings are the work of Christ himself, the trumpet-blasts that of archangels, the bowl-pourings of angels. We may compare the descent of revelation from God to Christ, from Christ to the angel, and from the angel to the Christian prophet. The descent is not to be seen as an anticlimax of power, but as a climax of immediacy. The higher agents themselves worked through inferior agents, whether spiritual or natural—neither unsealing nor trumpeting was the direct cause of any plague, but a signal on which some lower force should act. The angels of the last plagues act directly, in pouring them on the earth. The parallel we have drawn between the descent of revelation and the descent of judgement is more than a parallel; St. John actually draws the two themes together. When, in the descending scale of judgement, he reaches mere angels, he reaches a sort of beings who can step out of the frame of the visionary picture and act directly as the guides of his inspiration (xvii. 1, xxi. 9).

The vision which presents the angels of the bowls is modelled on that which presented the archangels and their trumpets (viii. 1–6). First the seven are seen, then there is a brief episode of a liturgical sort, then the seven act. In viii such an arrangement was natural; the angels, like the temple-priests, are given their trumpets and stand by while the incense-liturgy takes place. The copy is artificial. The angels are introduced before the liturgy, with the vague statement that they have, or hold, the seven last plagues; but the plagues are not put into their hands until the liturgy is over (verse 7), and the mention of them in verse 1 is more like a heading descriptive of the chapter to come, than a genuine object of vision.

The true vision begins with a presentation of the great 'Sea' of the heavenly temple (iv. 6). The former mention of it placed it beside the seven lights, the waters of regeneration beside the fires of the Spirit. The seven lights were immediately taken up in the sequel—they became the sevenfold spiritual endowment through which the Lamb was alone qualified to open the seven seals. In the course of the seal-opening the seven trumpets were introduced, and so was the liturgical centre from which their action sprang, the altar of incense. But now, with the bowls, St. John makes an absolute fresh beginning—they are not introduced under cover of the trumpets, as the trumpets were under cover of the seals—and so he goes back to the starting-point, and takes up the sea of glass. What the lamps of the Spirit were to the unsealings, and what the incense of prayer was to the trumpets, the baptismal waters will be to the bowls.

Just as the spiritual meaning of the altar was set forth in viii. 3-5 (on the background of vi. 9-11) by relation to the saints and their prayers, so the sea or laver is interpreted here by relation to the saints and their purification. The 'sea' was to sanctify the priests, and here the saints are a priestly choir, ministering in heaven, and standing at, or by, the 'sea' which cleanses them—'by', not 'on'. The phrase 'stand *epi* . . .' with the accusative is used by St. John three times, once meaning 'on' (xiv. 1) and twice 'at' or 'by' (iii. 20, vii. 1). But in fact St. John does not distinguish *epi* with the accusative from *epi* with the genitive, and the decisive text for us, though it has the genitive, is the very model of the sentence we are discussing. The saints stand by the laver here, as the angel stood by the altar in viii. 3, to offer the incense of their prayers.

The relation of their ministry of praise to their purification is set forth by an exploitation of the ritual name, 'the sea'. Baptism is a 'sea' indeed, it is the Red Sea water through which the people of God are saved, and separated from heathen Egypt (1 Cor. x. 1-2); standing on the brink of the font, they sing with Moses and Israel the praise of redeeming love (Exod. xv). But 'the song of Moses and of the Lamb' is a double shot. The Israelites who had crossed the sea celebrated a redemption effected through Moses and the blood of the Paschal Lamb; but 'the Song of Moses' is a liturgical piece in Deuteronomy xxxii, celebrating the divine judgements, and described in 44 of that chapter as a song taught to the people by Moses *and by Joshua* (Jesus). It is characteristic of St. John that he is content with having made the references; the beautiful psalm he puts into the mouths of the saints is a cento of phrases from all over the psalter and elsewhere.

The baptism of the saints has proved a *Red* Sea indeed, a baptism of fire; their victory over the beast is their martyrdom. So the great glass bowl of the sea is seen 'filled with a fiery mixture'. What the Israelites are brought through to salvation, their persecutors undergo to their destruction; Pharaoh and his hosts perish in the returning waters. And so we know that the baptism of fire must fall on the people of Antichrist; the vision of the bowls will show us how. Well may the hymn of the saints celebrate the upright judgements of God.

The harping and hymnody of the scene take up those of xiv. 2–3. There the faithful on earth marked with the divine name were alone able to 'learn' the song of heavenly harpers. Here the conquerors of the beast's name themselves hold 'harps of God' and sing in heaven the song they have learnt; the song which Moses and Jesus have taught Israel (Deut. xxxii. 44). If they are martyrs like the souls in vi. 9 we have no need to suppose that the Son of Man's harvest of his elect, prefigured in xiv. 16, has yet taken place, to raise them from earth to heaven. The martyrs are now singing praises instead of crying for vindication, because what they cried for is now so certain and so near.

5 And after these things I saw, and the temple of the tabernacle of
6 the testimony in heaven was opened, and there came out from the temple the seven angels that had the seven plagues, clothed in linen clean and shining, and having their breasts girt with golden
7 girdles. And one of the four living creatures gave unto the seven angels seven golden bowls full of the wrath of God who liveth for
8 ever and ever. And the temple was filled with smoke from the glory of God, and from his power; and none was able to enter the temple until the seven plagues of the seven angels were accomplished.

The scene has hitherto been within the temple, one must suppose, since St. John saw the seven angels who have not yet left it. The great sea was outside the House in the Temple of Solomon, but the heavenly House seems to cover the whole consecrated area, being virtually equivalent to heaven itself. The doors are now thrown open so that the plague-angels may go forth and pour their plagues on the earth. The description '*Temple* of the Tent of Testimony' is artificial; the Tent of Testimony (LXX translation for Tent of Meeting) was with Moses in the Wilderness; the Temple was another thing, and replaced it. No doubt the Heavenly House is the archetype equally of both. St. John has previously spoken of the temple; he now doubles the description so as both to keep hold of his chain of 'temple' symbolism, and to bring in an appropriate reference to Moses and the Exodus. The Tent of Testimony was the house in which, when they had built it, those who triumphed at the Red Sea offered their worship to God. It was specially memorable as the place of the Ark which was made along with it; and so the phrase may serve another purpose—to remind us of a previous opening of the temple, when the Ark was manifested, and the last great 'portents in heaven' were displayed (xi. 19–xii. 3).

It may be supposed that the angels received their bowls from the cherub before they were actually clear of the Temple. St. John begins, as in xi. 19, with the opening of the temple, goes on to say what it was for (the angels went out) and then tells us how they got the plagues they carried. He can then go straight on to tell us how this dealing out of the divine wrath caused the house in which it took place to smoke with glory and power, so that (when the angels had gone out) no angelic minister could enter again until the plagues had all been poured. The reference is to what happened when Moses had consecrated the *Tent of Testimony*, and Solomon the *Temple*. The house was on both occasions filled with a cloud, so that the priests dared not go in to minister until it departed. When Isaiah saw God in the Temple, the house was filled with smoke, and with the proclamation of his glory; and the prophet thought it death to be there until he was reassured.

When the incense-angel of viii had emptied coals of fire on the ground from his censer, and the trumpeters went on to blow, fiery things came down at their blasts from heaven to earth. The relation between the censing angel's action and the subsequent rain of judgements was purely symbolical, or, as it were, magical. It is the same here—the Red Sea of the Saints' baptism is red with fire and we know that the 'Egyptians', their enemies, are destined to be consumed in it. But there is no direct or physical relation between the contents of the great laver and the bowlsful of smoking wrath which the seven angels receive.

It seems almost too good to be true, in view of the requirements of St. John's symbolism, that he has chapter and verse for the personal action of a cherub in giving fire to the angels of judgement. Nor need he look far to find it. In Revelation viii, the model he is now following, the penal scattering of fiery coals was in itself an allusion to Ezekiel x. 1–7. He takes Ezekiel's vision up again now, following (it would seem) the sense of the Hebrew rather than the LXX. According to the Hebrew, the cherub reached his hand into the midst of the divine fire which burnt among the cherubim and gave burning coals into the hands of an angel clothed in linen and girt with an inkhorn, for scattering over the city. Since for St. John the cherub here is the man-faced Waterpourer, and since he has already used the coals of fire in viii, it is very natural that bowls of wrath to pour should be substituted for coals of fire to scatter. The substitution has a dozen advantages—it carries on the image of the cup of fury, first in the hand of Babylon a divinely permitted temptation to mankind, then in the Lord's hand the wine of his vengeance, or, by transition to an associated image, a ghastly vintage flowing from the grapes trodden outside the city (xiv. 8, 10, 20). At the same time it squares with the great cup of glass, the sea filled with fiery mixture; and above all, it introduces the theme of the ritual drink-offering. The 'bowls', *phialae*, are libation-bowls. Now the libation, or drink-offering, was poured at the daily sacrifice just after the trumpets had begun to sound, so that by placing bowls in sequence to trumpets St. John maintains the sequence of ritual action which began with the slaughtered Lamb, continued in the incense-offering and passed into the trumpet-blasts. Because the drink-offering had such a position, it was the last ritual act, completing the service of the altar, and was proverbial in that connexion (Phil. ii. 17). The drink-offering, as St. Paul implies, was poured upon the slaughtered victim, burning in the fire. Because there is no bloody sacrifice in heaven, the angels pour their libations upon the terrible holocaust of vengeance which divine justice makes on earth.

The angel who receives fire from Ezekiel's cherub is dressed in linen and girt with an inkhorn. The LXX could make nothing of the inkhorn, and wrote, 'girt with sapphire'; the phrase recurs as a standing description of the man. Very likely St. John could make nothing of 'inkhorn' either. His seven angels (in whom Ezekiel's one is multiplied) are girt with gold and dressed, according to the accepted reading, in pure shining linen, but according to an interesting variant which has a good deal of support, in pure shining stone. (As between 'linen' and 'stone' in Greek there is only one consonant's difference.) Here is a pretty puzzle, though not an urgent one. If St. John wrote 'linen', it was a clever scribe who altered his text.

XVI And I heard a great voice out of the temple, saying to the seven angels, Go and pour out the seven bowls of the wrath of God upon the earth.

2 And the first went, and poured out his bowl upon the earth. And there came a noisome and grievous sore upon the men which had the mark of the beast and which worshipped his image.

3 And the second poured out his bowl upon the sea, and it became blood as of a dead man, and every living soul died of things in the sea.

4 And the third poured out his bowl on the rivers and water-

springs, and they became blood. And I heard the angel of the 5
waters saying, Righteous art thou, the Holy which art and which
wast, in judging thus; for they have shed the blood of saints and 6
prophets, and thou hast given them blood to drink; they are
worthy. And I heard the altar saying, Yea, Lord God Almighty, 7
true and righteous are thy judgments.

And the fourth poured out his bowl upon the sun, and it was 8
given him to scorch men with fire. And men were scorched with 9
great heat, and blasphemed the name of the God which hath
power over these plagues, and repented not, to give him glory.

'From the temple': the judgements of the trumpets came as from
the altar, because they expressed the prayers of the saints which are
the incense of heaven. The judgements of the vials are the overflow
of the wrath of God blazing forth and filling his temple, a visitation
or presence vouchsafed in response to the prayers of the saints. The
voice is not the personal utterance of the enthroned Glory himself,
for it names him in the third person. Like the other voices of the
Revelation, it is a sort of thunder, expressing his mind.

The plagues follow those of the trumpets in smiting the four
elements with strokes of Moses's rod. They differ from the trumpets
in this, that the plagues arising from the several elements attack
mankind directly, with appropriate retribution; the signal for such
a target of attack was given in the first woe (ix. 4). So the infecting
of the land becomes the plague of boils, as in Exodus ix. 10–11,
a hideous stamp avenging the mark of the Beast on the bodies which
carry it. The plagues on waters salt and fresh are scarcely distinguished—all waters of every kind are turned to blood. In this plague,
most properly characteristic of the Waterpourer's judgements, the
lesson of retribution is voiced by the angel of the waters; and since
he is immediately answered by (the angel of) the altar in the name of
fire (xiv. 18) it is reasonable to suppose that his own habitation is in
the great sea or laver of glass (xv. 2). In so far as it is a 'sea' it finds
expression in the plague on the sea; in so far as it is a reservoir of
clear water, in the plague on fresh waters; in so far as it is 'filled with
a fiery mixture' at this moment of judgement, it calls for the answer-
ing comment of the fiery altar. The omen is immediately taken up;
the next bowl, poured upon the sun, heightens his power to blister
men with fire.

The effect of the first round of plagues on four elements is recorded
as blasphemy and impenitence towards the God whose power is
shown in these (four) plagues; a response which exactly reverses the
angels' gospel in xiv. 7.

10 And the fifth poured out his bowl on the throne of the beast, and his kingdom was darkened. And they gnawed their tongues for
11 pain, and blasphemed the God of heaven because of their pains and their sores; and they repented not of their works.

The second round of bowls has nothing like the same development as the second round of trumpets; but it has its own distinctive colour. We may describe it as a triad of political, or historical, events; the darkening of the beast's dominion, the Armageddon muster, and the overthrow of the cities, especially 'Babylon', that is, Rome. Since St. John here begins a new series of plagues on the elements, the first must strike the land; but the land is narrowed down to the seat of Antichrist. His kingdom is plunged in darkness, as it was by the last Egyptian plague. St. John gets a direct antithesis to the plague preceding: there the sun's power was enhanced, here it is annihilated. We may recall that the plague on luminaries in the trumpet-series was a darkening, not an enhancing. 'His kingdom was darkened.' St. John's language suggests more than a failure of daylight. Babylon is in eclipse. The trouble, whatever it is, calls forth more blasphemy, and an intensified resentment against all the plagues, particularly the previous plague on land, the boils. The title 'God of Heaven' is used in Daniel ii where the supremacy of God is being asserted over earthly kingdoms. It comes with special force in Revelation xi. 13 where the witnesses, martyred on earth by Antichrist, are caught alive into heaven. Then the heathen 'gave glory to the God of Heaven'. Here they do the opposite. The verbal echo is no doubt deliberate.

12 And the sixth poured out his bowl upon the great river Euphrates, and the water thereof was dried up, that the way might be pre-
13 pared of the kings from the sunrising. And I saw three unclean spirits like frogs from the mouth of the dragon and of the beast
14 and of the false prophet. For they are spirits of demons working signs, which go after the kings of the whole world, to gather them
15 unto the battle of the great day of God Almighty.—Behold, I come as a thief. Blessed is he that watcheth, and keepeth his garments,
16 lest he walk naked and they see his shame.—And they gathered them together into the place which is called in Hebrew Har-Magedon.

Babylon has been darkened, now Babylon's river is dried up, as Jeremiah had predicted (Jer. l. 38). But the purpose is not so much to humiliate Babylon, as to let the armies pass, as in Isaiah xi. 15.

The parallel with the sixth trumpet is, so far, very close. But the armies now are of men, not demons. It is difficult to interpret St. John in terms of realities. Babylon stands for Rome, and Zion for the Church; a story which makes good sense in application to a literal Babylon and a literal Jerusalem is difficult to allegorize in relation to a world-wide Church and an Italian city. Kings from the East making common cause with the King of Babylon (cf. xvii. 12–13) would take the fords of Euphrates, and muster at the foot of Carmel (verse 16) for an attack on the Holy Land. Such is the familiar Old Testament picture. But the Church provides no target for military attack; a widely spread form of police action is required for the beast's 'war' against the saints as described in xiii. As in xi, St. John is simply giving us a prediction of the tribulations and deliverance of the Church through a myth about the historical Jerusalem. What he is symbolizing is nothing more nor less than a coming of all governments into line with the Empire in 'making war upon the saints'. St. John gives a hint of his meaning by forgetting the Orient and the fords of Euphrates in verse 14 and mustering 'the kings of all the inhabited world'.

Neither the drying of a river nor military invasion is an Egyptian plague. St. John brings the sixth bowl into the Egyptian list by an allegory on the plague of frogs. Invasion from the river is a plague of frogs, in the sense that the kings are brought by evil influences mysteriously insinuating thenselves (Their land swarmed with frogs in the chambers of their kings, says Psalm cv. 30 of the Egyptian plague). The frogs do not, indeed, come out of the river, but from the mouths of Satan, Antichrist, and the false prophet. They are embodied false prophecy, or lying propaganda, supported, as false prophecy is, by apparent miracle (xiii. 13, 15). Did not Pharaoh's magicians make frogs by their spells, that is, by the breath of their lips? (Exod. viii. 7). The threefold plague of the mouth recalls the plague of the sixth trumpet (ix. 17–18).

A muster against 'Jerusalem' becomes 'the battle of the great day of God Almighty' not by the kings' intention, but by Christ's intervention: he 'comes as a thief'. The abrupt insertion of the word of Christ fitly expresses the suddenness of his coming. There is the less need to name the speaker, because iii. 3 has made Christ say, 'I will come as a thief and thou shalt not know at what hour I will come upon thee.' The text before us speaks only of 'the day', but it stands upon the background of the corresponding trumpet-vision, when the hosts of God are prepared 'for the hour and the day and the month and the year, to slay the third of mankind' (ix. 15). The text in iii. 3 continues, 'But thou hast a few who have not defiled their garments.' The figure of the garments is differently developed here, and more in relation to the coming of the thief. The caretaker who undresses and sleeps may have his garments stolen, to his great disgrace when he runs out crying for help. Christ had said that when the great tribulation came, there would be no going back to get one's garment (Matt. xxiv. 18). The divine warning here is addressed rather to the disciples than to the heathen, and the garment, as elsewhere, is holiness.

The spirits bring the kings to Har-Magedon, that is, Mount Megiddo. No such mountain-name was ever current. Megiddo is a town on the southern side of the Esdraelon Plain, the nearest of known cities to the foothills of Carmel. 'Mount Megiddo' would have to designate Carmel, but why not say 'Carmel'? As well call Ben Nevis 'Mt. Fortwilliam'. One can only suppose that St. John wants to refer to Megiddo and to Carmel in one breath. Ahab, a renegade Anointed, or Antichrist, and husband of Jezebel (see ii. 20) 'sent unto all the children of Israel and gathered the prophets' of Baal and Ashtaroth 'together unto Mount Carmel' (1 Kings xviii. 20) there to try their strength against the Lord God of Elijah, and to perish by the sword. And (to complete the story) Ahab was himself to perish likewise on the day when a lying spirit in the mouths of false prophets enticed him and his allies into battle at Ramoth-Gilead (1 Kings xxii). The author of Chronicles transfers the exact circumstances of Ahab's death to the death of Josiah. He defied a true warning, he fought against God; though he went into battle disguised, he was shot by archers *at Megiddo* and carried out of battle in his chariot, to die. There was a great lamentation for him (2 Chron. xxxv. 20–25). The lamentation of Megiddo appears to be taken up by Zechariah in a very obscure oracle (xii. 9–14, esp. 11) where 'all the families of the land mourn', because they have 'looked on him whom they pierced'. Now we know from Revelation i. 7 (cf. xi. 9) what St. John made of this text. So in sum, Mt. Megiddo stands in his mind for a place where lying prophecy and its dupes go to meet their doom; where kings and their armies are misled to their destruction; and where all the tribes of the earth mourn, to see him in power, whom in weakness they had pierced. For there the stars in their courses fight against princes, and the floods of destruction sweep them away (Judges v. 19–21).

17 And the seventh poured out his bowl upon the air; and there came a great voice out of the temple, from the throne, saying, It is done.
18 And there were lightnings and voices and thunders. And there was a great earthquake, such as was not since men were upon the
19 earth, so great an earthquake as it was. And the great city split

into three parts, and the cities of the gentiles fell; and Babylon the great was remembered in the sight of God, to give her the cup of the wine of the fierceness of his wrath. And every island fled, and 20 the mountains were not found. And great hail came down like 21 talent-weights from heaven upon men. And men blasphemed God for the plague of hail, because the plague thereof is exceeding great.

The seventh bowl must, like the fourth, pour upon the sky; but now it is on the lower air, the region of cloud, to produce the Egyptian plague of thunder and hail. Thunder is a quaking of the sky, and St. John sees it as working out into a quaking of the earth. In Exodus it was the hail and lightning that were such as never were in all history; here it is the earthquake. The thunder is here as elsewhere associated with the utterance of a divine voice. By contrast with the voices from the 'sea' and from the altar, this voice comes from the throne itself, where it stands in the temple of heaven. The utterance is a single word, *ghĕgŏnĕn*, which is as thunderlike as the word *uai* is like the scream of an eagle (viii. 13). 'It is come to pass' is the seal of an accomplishment, like that other one-word speech, 'It is achieved', *tetelestai*, uttered by the Johannine Christ, as he dies upon the cross.

The moment at which Christ utters that word is the moment at which, in the older tradition, the veil of the temple was rent from top to bottom (Matt. xxvii. 51), in symbol of the fact that God was no longer to be sought through the curtains of that shrine. So the cry of accomplishment which greets the pouring of the last bowl puts an end to the very temple of heaven out of which it speaks. The liturgy is done; the temple is seen no more.

The course of temple-sacrifice, after a hint in vi. 9, is set firmly on its way at viii. 1 and extends to xvi. It neither begins nor ends the heavenly worship of the apocalypse. In fact it is a sort of great parenthesis enclosed within a Christian liturgy. The liturgy begins with the opening and exposition of the scriptures through Christ, an event which already leads to great prayers of thanksgiving, with ritual 'Amen' and 'Maranatha'. The prayer of thanksgiving accompanies the temple ceremonies of viii–xvi, but reaches its climax in xix when they are over and when the temple has vanished from sight. The prayer now takes on a sacramental colour (xix. 7–9), and the 'Amen' to it comes alive in the advent of Jesus. This is the decisive moment. It does not spring out of the temple ceremonies.

Verses 19–20 show the effects of the earthquake. Jerusalem splits into three, very likely an interpretation of Zechariah xiv. 3–5 where it is prophesied that rifts will extend north and south, east and west from the Mount of Olives, while the people of Jerusalem flee as they did from the famous earthquake in the days of King Uzziah. It would be not unreasonable to equate the quaking of Jerusalem here with the quaking in xi. 13, which also seems to coincide with the end of Antichrist's days.

The cities of the Gentiles also collapse and in particular 'Babylon', i.e. Rome; her reckoning is not forgotten, she drinks the cup of wrath. The language is phrased to pick up xiv. 8, 10; but there can be no doubt that a fall by earthquake is meant, since the description of the universal tremor is continued in the next verse as though the subject had never been changed. That is not to say that St. John wishes seriously to prophesy that Rome will fall by earthquake rather than by any other means. According to xvii. 16 she will be sacked and burnt by treacherous armies. The language of earthquake need express no more than the belief, that the Creator's vengeance lies behind the wrath of man.

Having done justice to the thunder, and drawn it out into earthquake, St. John adds on in verse 21 the second part of the Egyptian plague, the hail. This, too, smites the people, not their crops, and offers occasion for a repetition of the refrain about impenitence in face of heaven's scourges (cf. 9, 11). It serves at the same time to strengthen the parallel between the seventh bowl and the seventh trumpet (xi. 15–19). Both visions contain (*a*) a great voice or voices in heaven declaring accomplishment, (*b*) the announcement that the wrath has come, (*c*) utterance from the temple, accompanied by thunder and lightning, (*d*) grievous hail.

(B) BABYLON

XVII And there came one of the seven angels that had the seven bowls, and spake with me, saying, Come, I will show thee the judgment
2 of the great whore that is seated over many waters, with whom the kings of the earth have committed fornication, and the inhabitants of the earth have been made drunk with the wine of her whoredom.
3 And he carried me away in the Spirit into a wilderness; and I saw a woman seated upon a scarlet-coloured beast, full of names of
4 blasphemy, having seven heads and ten horns. And the woman was arrayed in purple and scarlet, and decked with gold and precious stone and pearls, having a golden cup in her hand full of
5 abominations and filthiness of her fornication; and upon her forehead a name written, a mystery; Babylon the Great, Mother
6 of the Harlots and Abominations of the Earth. And I saw the woman drunken with the blood of the martyrs of Jesus.

The pouring of the libations has had its proverbial effect—the ritual is complete, the action rounded off: we have heard the last of the temple, its furniture and its ministrations. And yet the supreme blessing which the sacrifice is offered to secure, the advent of Christ's kingdom, is still to come. Babylon has fallen, but the hosts mustered at Armageddon still await their divine antagonist. Having finished the ritual pattern, how is St. John to continue? Well, how did he continue when he had finished the trumpets? In a sense, he never did finish the trumpets—he did not finish them off with a double ruled line, like the bowls. The pattern of the three woes kept things moving after the sound of the last trumpeting had died away. Yet even the woes ended at last; and then what? The recurrent series of cherub-themes, already built into the woes, came round in a fresh cycle (xiv. 6–20) in comment upon the woes themselves; where we had had woes before, now we had good tidings. Three angels heralded the Advent, then the figure of the Advent Christ himself was disclosed; three more angels followed, as ministers of his 'harvest' and 'vintage'.

Here, in the short compass of fifteen verses, St. John has a model which not only lends itself to development, but cries out for it. The Advent has been sketched, it has still to be painted; and the old outline will serve for the full picture. The heart of xiv. 6–20 is the figure of the Son of Man on clouds; three angels lead up to him, and three lead down from him, so that we have the pattern

$$a\ \ a\ \ a\ \ C\ \ a\ \ a\ \ a.$$

In the development, St. John elaborates the symmetry, by matching the two extremes:

$$ba\ \ a\ \ a\ \ C\ \ a\ \ a\ \ ba.$$

The first and last angels are not only angels, but bowl-angels, and they have a very special function in common; they act as guides or interpreters, they show mysteries to St. John. Moreover the mysteries they show are an emphatic pair: Babylon the harlot, Jerusalem the bride. The intermediate pairs of angels are angels like others in the book, each with a single action, or a single cry. St. John helps them out with supplementary voices, or supplementary visions; voices for the herald-pair preceding advent, visions for the executive pair succeeding it. Such are the bare bones of the scheme to which he works in xvii–xxii.

The scheme is perfectly adapted for what St. John wants to do. As we have said, he is following the scheme of Christian prophecy, in which Christ's Advent is the final event; yet at the same time he wishes to round off his apocalypse with those traditional Last

Things which Advent will bring. What can serve him better than a scheme which puts the crowning event in the midst? The supporting part which follows will give scope for the treatment of the Last Things as consequential upon Advent. A proportional development of the herald-voices leading up to Advent will be required, if symmetry is to be maintained; and one might think that so many pages devoted to mere proclamation would overbalance the poem. In fact St. John moves on so dramatically from proclamation to exultation, and from exultation to thanksgiving, that a pause is scarcely felt; and the primitive Christian sense of eucharistic prayer, and of its invocatory power, allows St. John to see the very Advent of Christ as springing from the climax of the thanksgiving.

The subject of the thanksgiving is no mere anticipation of good things to come, but the manifest intervention of God in deliverance from Babylon; for Babylon has already fallen; Antichrist has yet to fall. The overthrow of Babylon is a foretaste of victory, occupying the same sort of position as the resurrection of Lazarus occupies in St. John's gospel, anticipating the resurrection of Christ; in both Gospel and Revelation the long tract of discourse intervenes, culminating in liturgical prayer (Rev. xvii. 1–xix. 9, John xiii–xvii).

The vision of the harlot, Babylon, then, fitly opens the series. But it also offers the necessary bridge of connexion with the preceding visions of bowls. The passage which we have called the model (xiv. 6–20) finds its connexion with the precedent trumpet-visions through the emphatic antithesis to the woe of the eagle offered by the flying angel's evangel. In xvii the flying angel of the model disappears entirely, because he could not perform his connective function in the new context. The bowl-angel who takes his place is admirably connective, for first, he is himself one of the Seven who have just poured the bowls; and second, he shows a vision which enlarges upon the effect of the seventh bowl in abasing Babylon.

There is no occasion, perhaps, for St. John's troubling any longer to keep in line with the series of cherubic types, eagle, lion, bull, and man. He experiences their influence at second-hand, in following a model which they helped to shape. Will he go over the head of the model and apply to the four cherubim direct, for further inspiration? Anyhow the man and his waterpouring (xv–xvi) have set the stage for the eagle, and our angel in xvii. 1–2 shows himself to be in so far an eagle, that he carries the seer away into the wilderness (cf. xii. 14). There is no symbolical identity, indeed, between the wilderness into which the woman flew on eagles' pinions, to be nourished in a place prepared, and the wilderness where St. John, carried by his angel, sees that woman's opposite. That was the wilderness of Exodus; this is an utterly out-of-the-way place, off the beaten track of vision, where St. John is led aside to contemplate an allegorical comment in picture-form. In xii St. John saw a woman-in-the-wilderness; here, in the wilderness, he sees a woman—a woman enthroned on 'many waters', or on a scarlet beast, or on the seven hills of Rome, but anyhow not a woman in desert country.

Babylon's seat 'upon many waters' reflects Jeremiah li. 13; her whoredom with kings, Isaiah xxiii. 17—though that was spoken of Tyre. Her making the world drunk reflects Jeremiah li. 7, already cited in Revelation xiv. 8, 10.

Having told us in the angel's words that the woman sits on, or over, many waters, St. John does not trouble to repeat the fact in his description of the vision; we may suppose the side-streams and canals of Euphrates spreading around her. As for the beast on which she sits, he is evidently the same as in xiii. 1 ff. No feature is altered; the only feature added is his scarlet colour. Perhaps we were inclined to think that his leopard-likeness was in his hide, but it may have been in his shape. His archetype the dragon was red, red as fire—a word suggestive of his astrological connexions (see above, p. 143). The word here, scarlet, suggests the dye of luxury fabrics and prepares us to see the harlot clad in scarlet and purple. We are already familiar with her cup (xiv. 8). St. John quite characteristically finds a second sense for it, based on xvi. 5–6. She makes the world drunk with the wine of her whoredom, she drinks herself drunk on the blood of the saints.

Her forehead is inscribed with a 'riddle-name'. It can scarcely be a riddle to any of St. John's readers, either that Babylon means Rome, or that Rome may be symbolized in such a figure. The riddle that needs to be read is not the name 'Babylon', but the Babylon characteristics set out in the whole detail of the vision; and it is these, in fact, that the angel undertakes to expound from verse 7 onwards.

Since part of her name is that she is the mother of harlots, it is possible that the brand on her forehead alludes to the branding of public prostitutes; but in view of vii. 3, xiii. 16, and xix. 12 the point can scarcely be pressed.

And when I saw her I wondered with great amazement. And the 7 angel said unto me, Wherefore didst thou wonder? I will tell thee the mystery of the woman, and of the beast that carrieth her, which hath the seven heads and ten horns. The beast that thou 8 sawest was, and is not, and is about to come up out of the abyss, and to perdition he goeth. And the dwellers upon earth whose names have not been written in the book of life from the foundation of the world shall wonder, when they see how the beast was, and

9 is not, and will come. Here is the wit that hath wisdom: the seven
10 heads are seven hills, on which the woman sitteth; and they are
seven kings; five are fallen, one is, another has not yet come, and
11 when he comes, must not continue long. And the beast which was
and is not is both an eighth and one of the seven, and goeth to
perdition.

St. John might be thought to be entitled to his astonishment, since figures such as he has described are not commonly to be met with, even in desert places. The angel must be taken to suspect that his astonishment is the superstitious awe, or heartfelt admiration, accorded to the object of idolatry in verse 8 below, or in xiii. 3 above. There is only one whose works merit unqualified amazement (xv. 1, xv. 3). The wonders of Satan are a sort of conjuring-tricks.

The angel's promise to expound the woman and her mount is executed in inverse order. So he reaches the woman herself at the end of the chapter and the denunciations, laments and exultings of which she is the subject can conveniently follow. Meanwhile he seizes the opportunity to explain the hitherto unsolved riddle of xiii. The angel takes up the beast as a creature at present non-existent, anyhow as 'beast', i.e. as self-deifying emperor. He does *not* personally live in his other six heads, of whom one now reigns (verse 10), any more than he does in his ten horns, who stand for future associates of his reign (verse 12). The angel does not, however, expound his present non-existence by contrast with the present existence of one or other of his additional heads; he expounds it as a defective parody of God's eternal being, reckoned in the three tenses of time. 'He *was, is not, and will come* up out of the abyss'—only that he may go to perdition. But the exact comparison is not between the beast and the eternal being of God, but between the beast as a falsification of the divine image, and the Lamb as a true offprint of it. Christ is the first and the last, the living who died and is alive for ever (i. 18, ii. 8). It is in parody of Christ that the beast has his first and second advents; but they are separated by a period of non-existence, and the second leads to perdition, not immortal life. The final perdition is not, in St. John's belief, absolute non-existence, but perpetual fire; the intermediate non-existence need not be absolute, either. It is absolute only in its ineffectiveness. Christ, now invisible, is an almighty king, victorious in the world by his Spirit. Nero in hiding (even if not literally banished to Hades) is no emperor until he reappears.

When St. John says that the inhabitants of earth *will* be astonished to observe the beast's former existence, present non-existence, and future existence, he means that they will do so when that future existence is manifested; they will marvel at Nero's power to return (cf. xiii. 12). For the eternal absence of their names from the Book of Life, cf. xiii. 8.

Only after these points have been made does St. John turn to the 'special subtlety' of the seven heads. Regarded as the seat of the harlot 'Babylon', they are the seven hills of Rome. Regarded as heads of the beast, they are a succession: the beast himself, and six successors of his first, or predecessors of his second, appearance on the throne. The statement that the beast is both an eighth and one (i.e. the first) of the seven would be baffling, if we had not the vision of the smitten head in xiii. 3. That text and this text mutually require one another and are scarcely intelligible in isolation.

We have discussed the historical identification of the beast's several heads in the Introduction, pp. 32–35, and the significance of his return as an eighth in our comment on the number of his name (p. 159). We will add the observation, that the 'week' of seven reigns corresponds to the period of trampling, or of witness, according to chapter xi, which we have identified with the period of the woman's preservation in chapter xii; whereas the eighth reign corresponds to the three-and-a-half days of the beast's triumph in chapter xi.

And the ten horns thou sawest are ten kings which have received 12 no kingdom as yet, but receive authority as kings for one hour with the beast. These have one mind, and give the beast their 13 power and authority. These shall do battle with the Lamb, and the 14 Lamb shall overcome them, for he is Lord of lords, and King of kings, and they that are with him called and chosen and faithful.

The ten horns, representing kings, are an embarrassing legacy from Daniel, in whose system they play the part which the seven heads play in St. John's. What is he to do with them? If they are not the beast's predecessors, what can they be but his associates? The statement that they 'have not received their kingship yet' merely places them in parallel with the seventh head 'who has not yet come'. We have no need to attribute to St. John the certain conviction that no king who will become associate to the beast is yet on his throne when St. John writes. He is merely telling us that kings associate with the beast belong to the times of the eighth emperor, not of his predecessors. His language might suggest to the student of Roman history that this emperor would institute puppet-kings in the provinces or dependencies of Rome. But the vision of xvi. 12–16 suggests such foreign kings as the Parthian; they are brought to Armageddon by the persuasion of propaganda, not by the command of a suzerain. The conspiracy of many kings against the Lord and his Anointed belongs to an old Jewish ritual pattern. For the form in which the pattern came to St. John we need look no further than Psalm ii of which the influence on his visions is so manifest. The conspiracy must take the form of a submission to the beast's leadership, so that the great Apostasy may take worldwide effect and the single issue 'Christ or Antichrist' may be presented to all mankind. It is the overruling will of God, which so shapes history as to oblige all men to declare for God or for Caesar (verse 17). St. John proceeds to relate the multitude of conspiring kings to the titles of Christ as Lord of lords and King of kings (Lord of lords, Deut. x. 17: *Lord* of Kings, Dan. ii. 47). He shows himself such by conquering them when they band against him. We will discuss the nature of the victory in connexion with the great battle of xix.

St. John does not tell us how the ten horns are related to the seven heads. We must suppose that they are all carried by the first—that is, the smitten and returning head. For (*a*) they are horns adding strength to the head that carries them, and the ten kings are not confederate with any other emperor than one; (*b*) there is no hopeful system for distributing ten horns among seven heads—let the reader try; and (*c*) though St. John credits Daniel's last beast with the heads of his predecessors in addition to his own, there is no reason why he should distribute the creature's horns over his predecessors' brows.

15 And he saith unto me, The waters thou sawest, where the whore
16 sitteth, are peoples and multitudes, nations and tongues. And the ten horns which thou sawest, they and the beast shall hate the whore, and shall make her desolate and naked, and eat her flesh,
17 and consume her with fire. For God hath put it in their hearts to fulfil his mind, and to come to one mind, and give their kingdom
18 unto the beast until the words of God are accomplished. And the woman thou sawest is the great city which hath kingship over the kings of the earth.

Having dealt with the beast, the angel makes a fresh start with the 'many waters' on which the woman is enthroned (see above, p. 183). Being allegorized as multitudinous nations, they are for political purposes equivalent to their princes. Since what St. John goes on to say about the rulers of the earth is that they turn against the city, and destroy her, it is possible that he takes an omen from the waters as being dangerous to her foundations: cf. 'The rain descended and the rivers came . . . and struck that house, and it fell' (Matt. vii. 27); or, for that matter, the river flung after the lady in Revelation xii. 15.

Babylon suffers the proverbial fate of a harlot: fallen from favour she is abandoned, stripped of her finery and left to naked shame. But having exposed her skin, St. John remembers that the beast is a lion-jawed monster, and his allies horns, the instruments of his violence; so he says that they devour her flesh. Then, considering that she is, after all, a city, he says they burn her down. So by God's overruling, his decree is accomplished.

Isaiah called Tyre a neglected harlot (xxiii. 15), but the true model of St. John's language is the prophetic denunciation of the cities of Israel. Unfaithful to their God, they flirt with foreign powers, yet their 'lovers' turn against them and destroy them (Ezek. xvi and xxiii). St. John has made a new and wholly realistic application of the figure to the Greco-Roman world. Since the days of Alexander there had been an uneasy balance between city civilization and military power. The cities are supposed to be sovereign and free, the centres of political as of cultural life. They are in fact propped up by an irresponsible armed despotism. They flatter the despots as gods and benefactors; from time to time the despots and their hungry armies get out of hand and sack the cities. The relation between city and monarch is not a stable marriage, but a shabby love-affair, disgraced by quarrels and darkened by murderous violence. Rome had not yet been sacked by imperial troops, but her time was to come.

Babylon's fate at the hands of the beast and his allies brings her into direct comparison with Zion. On the visible plane the suffering the two cities undergo is the same and, if Babylon is to be held guilty of Jerusalem's overthrow, the retribution is exact. In spirit and in reality, their fortunes are wholly different. Babylon, being no more than a hive of material culture, perishes in the waters of her flood. Zion, though driven into the wilderness, is preserved inviolate; the river cannot reach her.

XVIII *After these things I saw another angel come down from heaven, having great authority; and the earth was lightened with his glory.* 2 *And he cried with a strong voice, saying, Fallen, fallen is Babylon the great, and is become the habitation of demons, and the hold of every foul spirit, and of every unclean and hateful bird.* 3 *For all nations have drunk of the raging wine of her fornication, and the kings of the earth have committed fornication with her, and the merchants of the earth have waxed rich by the force of her extravagance.*

This angel is nothing but a more emphatic version of his model, the lion-voice of xiv. 8. Two points are, however, added: the 'doleful creatures' inhabiting the ruins, a prophetic commonplace; and the mention of kings and merchants as seduced by the 'wine of her fornication'. The mention of the kings reflects xvii. 2; the merchants are an innovation and prepare the ground for what is to come (xviii. 11–19).

4 And I heard another voice from heaven, saying, Come out of her, my people, that ye be not partakers of her sins, and that ye receive 5 not of her plagues; for her sins have reached unto heaven and God 6 hath remembered her iniquities. Render unto her even as she rendered and double unto her double according to her works; fill to her double in the cup that she filled. For all her extravagance 7 and her glorifying of herself, give her torment and grief in equal measure. For she saith in her heart, I am seated a queen and am no 8 widow and shall see no grief. Therefore shall her plagues come in one day, death, grief, and famine, and she shall be consumed with fire; for strong is the Lord God who hath judged her.

9 And the kings of the earth who committed whoredom and lived in luxury with her shall weep and lament for her when they see the 10 smoke of her burning, standing afar off for the fear of her torment, and saying, Alas, alas, the great city Babylon, the strong city! For in one hour is thy judgement come.

11 And the merchants of the earth weep and lament over her, for no 12 man buyeth their merchandise any more, merchandise of gold and silver and precious stones and pearls, of fine linen and purple and silk and scarlet; no fragrant wood, no ivory vessel, no vessel of 13 precious wood, of bronze, iron or marble; no cinnamon and spice, perfume and ointment and incense, wine and oil and cornflour and wheat, cattle and sheep, horses and carriages and slaves and lives of 14 men. The fruit of thy soul's desire is departed from thee, and all things dainty and fine are lost to thee, and shall no more at all be 15 found. The merchants of these things who were made rich by her shall stand afar off for the fear of her torment, weeping and 16 lamenting, and saying Alas, alas, the great city that was clothed in fine linen and purple and scarlet, and decked with gold, precious 17 stone and pearl! For in one hour so great riches is laid waste.

18 And every shipmaster, and every voyager, mariners and all that work by sea, stood afar off and cried out, as they gazed upon the smoke 19 of her burning, saying, What city is like the great city? And they cast dust on their heads, and cried, weeping and lamenting, saying, Alas, alas, the great city, whereby all were made rich that had ships in the sea, by reason of her costliness! For in one hour is she laid waste.

THE HEAVENLY MAN

Rejoice over her, thou heaven, ye saints, apostles and prophets, 20
for God hath executed your judgement upon her.

St. John has much to say in exultation over the fall of 'Babylon', but he will not so spoil the form of the short dramatic 'roar' of Isaiah's watchman, as to load it with all this matter. He starts again with a voice from heaven, summoning the people of God to get out before it is too late, as Lot was summoned out of Sodom. The warning is enforced by predictions of the sorrow awaiting those whose existence is bound up with the city; a sorrow which acts as foil to the rejoicing of the saints (verse 20). If we were following the conventions of modern printing, we should be faced by the dilemma whether to close the quotation of the heavenly voice after the first paragraph, or after verse 20. If we must choose, it is better to take the latter alternative. St. John, perhaps, forgets the heavenly voice somewhat as he becomes engaged with the object of description in 9–19, but we are not to suppose, any more than in xi. 4–13, that he has so far departed from the convention of his poem, as to write half a chapter which is neither 'heard' nor 'seen'.

The speech is surely one of the most brilliant patchworks ever composed. It is nothing but a cento of ancient prophecies, carefully selected and arranged. The centre is held by the merchants' lament (11–17a) flanked before and after by short laments from kings (9–10) and shipmasters (17b–19), the whole being contained by the divine voice's hortatory introduction (4–8) and conclusion (20). And beyond, on either side, are the two angels of 1–3 and 21–24. The whole passage has the form

A (B (C (D) C) B) A.

The introduction and conclusion (4–8, 20) are based on the denunciation of Babylon in Jeremiah li, especially 6–9, 13, 45, 48, but Isaiah, Ezekiel, and Deuteronomy contribute several phrases. The laments (9–19) are substantially based on Ezekiel xxvi–xxvii where Tyre, not Babylon, is the subject; while an important element in the refrain, 'the smoke of her burning' (9, 18, cf. xiv. 11 and xix. 3) belongs to Isaiah's oracle against Edom (xxxiv. 10). Because of this and similar prophecies, Edom came to be a cant term for Rome in rabbinic usage. St. John has, in fact, no reason for limiting himself to prophecies against Babylon, since the Rome he is denouncing is no more Babylon than she is Nineveh or Tyre. As an imperial city, Rome may find her type in Babylon; and in Tyre, as a mart of luxury. Old prophecies against tyranny and pride, though aimed at Babylon, will hit Rome just as well; if Tyrian merchandise was the mark of their arrows, Rome will be as good a target. Rome is now *the* city; and in the ancient world city life was the same thing as civilisation. It is agreeable to us to think of the ancient city as the centre of mental life and political vigour. When St. John wrote, the austere splendours of Hellas had departed, and so had the overpraised virtues of republican Rome. Rome, to St. John, is material comfort and social pride. He had not seen London or New York.

If we compare St. John's 'lament' section (9–19) with its archetype in Ezekiel, we observe that he has drawn together several lists of merchandise into one great catalogue. By way of compensation, he has distributed one lamentation among three parts, so as to produce a dirge-like refrain, and to prepare for the contrasting liturgy of exultation which follows (xix. 1–8).

The speech contains several linguistic barbarities but only one material obscurity. The 'voyagers' of verse 17 represent 'every one sailing to a place', i.e. booking a passage. Since the phrase comes in a list of mercantile people it should mean the merchant who lands with his goods.

21 And a strong angel took up a rock like a great millstone and threw it into the sea, saying, With such a cast shall Babylon the
22 great city be thrown, and found no more at all. And the voice of harpers and minstrels, of pipers and trumpeters, shall be heard no more at all in thee; and no craftsman of whatsoever craft shall be found any more at all in thee; and the sound of a millstone shall be
23 heard no more at all in thee; and the light of a lamp shall shine no more at all in thee; and the voice of the bridegroom and the bride shall be heard no more at all in thee. For thy merchants were the princes of the earth, and by thy sorcery were all nations deceived;
24 and in her was found the blood of prophets and of saints, and of all the slain upon earth.

St. John improves on the colourless third angel of xiv. 9 by looking out a figure of ancient prophecy both as appropriate and as dramatic as the watchman of Isaiah xxi with his lionlike cry. He finds what he wants in the same oracles of Jeremiah against Babylon which have provided the frame of the voice from heaven (4–8 and 20). Jeremiah sent his denunciations of Babylon to Babylon, directing his messenger, after reading the scroll aloud, to wrap it round a stone and sink it in the Euphrates, as a sign that the city should sink to rise no more, nor ever be again inhabited (Jer. li. 59–64). The same prophet had used a similar method in xliii. 8–13, for attaching a curse against Egypt to the accursed place. St. John retains simply the symbolism of the sinking stone. In allusion to such texts as Mark

ix. 42 it becomes like a millstone and sinks in the sea, not the river. The gospel allusion supplies a bridge to another text of Jeremiah. The irrevocable disappearance of the millstone is a sign of the disappearance from Babylon of the sound of the millstone and its accompaniments, the evidences of human life according to Jer. xxv. 10. St. John adds to Jeremiah's list the disappearance of every craftsman, in parallel with the silencing of female industry (the use of the handmill; cf. Matt. xxiv. 41). The effect of the addition is to maintain continuity with the industrial and mercantile picture presented by verses 11-19 above. The silencing of 'the voice of the bridegroom and the voice of the bride' as in Jeremiah xxv cannot but evoke the dramatic reversal in Jeremiah xxxiii. 11, where the return of these happy sounds to Zion is promised. St. John, having denied them for ever to Babylon, transfers them to Jerusalem in the spiritual form at xix. 7; cf. xxi. 2.

In verse 23 the change of person (from 'your' to 'her') may strike us as clumsy; but such changes of person are to be found in every page of Hebrew prophecy. St. John's object in doing so here, is to bring his conclusion back into line with his beginning (21). In fact 23b-24 is a typically disjointed semitic-style sentence, giving the reasons for the utter destruction of Babylon: 'Because thy merchants were the grandees of the earth, because by thy witchcraft all nations were misled; and in her was found the blood of the saints, and of all the slain upon earth.' The first 'because' would not be a reason for so drastic a punishment, if it were not coupled with the second—unless the splendid arrogance of Roman merchants were based upon the corruption of all mankind—and unless it were paid for by the martyrdom of non-conformists with the ungodly establishment.

In calling the angel who casts the stone a *strong* angel, St. John obtains a double point; his strength will serve him well for hurling the millstone out to sea; but as we have seen (p. 93 above) 'strong' angels are, for reasons of scriptural association, a class of heralds; and this angel's chief business, after all, is to make a proclamation. In spite of the angel's muscularity, there is no case for claiming any special expression in him of the bull-type; if he has any cherub-character, he derives it at second-hand through the angel of xiv. 9 to whom, in serial order, he corresponds.

After these things I heard as it were a mighty voice of a great XIX throng in heaven, saying, Alleluia; salvation and glory and power belong to our God, for true and righteous are his judgments; for 2 he hath judged the great whore which did corrupt the earth with her whoredom, and hath avenged his servants' blood at her hand.

192 THE HEAVENLY MAN

3 And a second time they said, Alleluia; and her smoke goeth up for
4 ever and ever. And the four and twenty elders and the four living creatures fell down and worshipped God who sitteth on the throne, saying Amen; Alleluia.
5 And a voice came out of the throne, saying, Praise our God,
6 all ye his servants, ye that fear him, both small and great. And I heard as it were the voice of a great throng, and as the voice of many waters, and as the voice of mighty thunders, saying, Alleluia;
7 for the Lord our God Almighty reigneth. Let us be glad and rejoice, and give him the glory; for the marriage of the Lamb is
8 come, and his wife hath made herself ready. And it hath been given her to array herself in fine linen, clean and shining; for the fine linen is the righteousness of saints.

The long laments over Babylon in xviii. 9–19 concluded with the contrasting invitation, 'Rejoice over her, thou heaven, ye saints, apostles and prophets, for God has wrought your vindication upon her.' The mention of the blood of prophets and saints in xviii. 24 revives the theme; and forthwith the heavenly rejoicing breaks out; the conclusion of the first paean being, 'for he has required the blood of his servants at her hand'.

The heavenly jubilation takes the form of four Alleluias, supported by sentences of praise. A liturgy of Alleluias cannot but suggest the Alleluia-psalms, or *Hallel*, sung in the worship of Israel at great festivals, e.g. at Passover and Tabernacles. Nevertheless St. John does not construct his liturgy from phrases of the *Hallel*-psalms especially: there is a half-sentence from Psalm cxv. 13 in verse 5, and an echo of cxviii. 24 in verse 7, that is all. (Similarly the Song of Moses in Revelation xv, though plainly antitypical to Exodus xv, scarcely quotes it.) The sequence of Alleluias is enough by itself to establish the reference; Alleluia is not found in any text of the Revelation but this.

The liturgy has a movement in two parts. The choir of heaven twice celebrates the sovereign glory of God (1; 6), assigning as the reason, first, the judgement of the harlot (2), and, second, the marriage of the Lamb's wife (7–8). Each hymn is followed by a short sentence (3, 9^a). The two movements are linked together by the Amen of the elders and cherubim to the doxological phrase 'for ever and ever' which closes the first part. In similar fashion they had crowned the universal praise of v. 12–13—cf. also xi. 15–16. But here they add to their Amen an Alleluia, that is, a further invitation to the praise of God; it is taken up by a voice from the throne, inviting the praise of all God's servants; and so the hymn of the second movement is given by the choir. The subject of it is more glorious than that of the former hymn, and the description of the thunderous voices more impressive.

There is no warrant for the taking of the last sentence in verse 8 out of the hymn, nor any difficulty in writing as one piece 'And it has been granted her to dress in clean and shining lawn, for the lawn is the virtues of the saints'. By bringing the allegory of the bride back to the flesh-and-blood of the saints, St. John brings the end of the second hymn into line with the end of the first. In judging the great harlot God has avenged his servants' blood; in adorning the bride for her wedding he has crowned their merits.

And he saith unto me, Write, Blessed are they which are bidden to the marriage supper of the Lamb. And he saith unto me, These are the true words of God. And I fell at his feet to worship him. And he saith unto me, See thou do it not; I am a fellow servant with thee and with thy brethren that hold the testimony of Jesus; worship God; for the testimony of Jesus is the spirit of prophecy. 9

10

The voices in heaven, which we have heard, comment upon and extend the message of the third angel (xviii. 21–24) as the voice from heaven (xviii. 4–20) extended the message of the second. So, in the vastly more ample scale he is using, St. John has reached the point marked in his model by the beatitude, 'Write, happy are . . .' (xiv. 13). It was the point of transition between the three angels, and the rider on the cloud. St. John is now about to make a corresponding transition to the rider on the horse. The beatitude in xiv was spoken by a voice *from* heaven. As we have been listening to voices *in* heaven, the change to a voice *from* heaven would lack emphasis. What is essentially required is a voice that speaks direct to the seer, 'Write'. St. John falls back upon the angel who is his guide. In the original Greek, the way this angel emerges as a person out of the divine message he relays is very subtly suggested. Literally translated, verses 9–10 would run as follows: 'And saith to me, Write, Happy are those. . . . And saith to me, These are the very words of God. And I fell at his feet to worship him. And he saith to me, see thou do it not. . . .' The voice which speaks is, initially, simply the voice of St. John's inspiration. It is only by the attempt to worship the messenger that he brings him to disclose himself as a 'fellow-servant'.

The influence of the model in xiv turns the short sentence following the hymn 6–8 into a beatitude spoken under heaven, whereas the short sentence following the hymn 1–2 was an alleluia spoken in heaven. In spite of the transformation, the parallel between the two liturgical movements 1–4 and 6–10 continues. After the short sentence in the first movement, elders and cherubim cry 'Amen' while they fall and worship. After the short sentence in the second movement (since the scene is transferred to earth) the angel who speaks with St. John himself adds a paraphrased Amen—'These are true words of God'—and it is St. John who falls and worships. The special occasion for the worship above is the declaration of God's fulfilled promise, and there is the same motive now for worship below; nor is it surprising that St. John should pay his homage to the angel who presents the authority of the divine Speaker on earth. Who is this angel? Scarcely the 'strong angel' of xviii. 21; he has entered into no intimate relation with St. John. It might be an unidentified angel of his inspiration, presumed present throughout; it might be that the part is at present sustained by the angel of xvii. 1, who was still speaking at xvii. 18 and may be thought to stand by through xviii. 1–xix. 8.

Whoever the angel may be, his rejection of St. John's proffered worship is appropriate to the model in xiv and to the development St. John is now making upon it. We are at the point where the figures of the three angels gave place to the figure of the Son of Man; and the function of the last angel in xiv was to denounce bull- or calf-worship, that is, Behemoth-worship. The suggestion lies ready to hand, that all worship is forbidden that is not paid to God in Christ; an angel must not only denounce idolatry, but refuse adoration. (For worship idolatrously paid to the minister of revelation, see Dan. ii. 46.)

The terms in which the angel makes his refusal are pregnant with meaning and offer the most serious exegetical problem in the book. The difficulty lies in the last sentence of verse 10. 'I am fellowservant of thee and of thy brethren who hold the testimony of Jesus. Worship God. *For the testimony of Jesus is the spirit of prophecy.*' The phrase 'testimony of Jesus' occurs also in i. 2, i. 9, and xii. 17. The ordinary meaning to a Greek ear would certainly be 'the testimony of Jesus', 'Jesu's testimony'. In fact the phrase can only acquire the alternative meaning 'testimony to Jesus' through the genitive case losing all distinctive force, so that 'the testimony of Jesus' means something like 'the Jesus-testimony'; and then you can take it which way you like. There is indeed plenty of analogy for such a weakening of the genitive. But the argument against the sense 'testimony to Jesus' is not primarily grammatical; it is the web of connexions surrounding the phrase. It is coupled with the 'word of God' (i. 2, i. 9, xx. 4), 'the commandments of God' (xii. 17). Since 'the word of God' is 'the word God speaks' and 'the commandments of God' are 'the orders God gives', 'the testimony of Jesus' ought to be 'the witness Jesus bears'. Moreover the first two occurrences of the phrase, which surely fix the sense, are in close conjunction with the ascription to Jesus of the title 'faithful witness'; the title occurs in iii. 14 and, as we shall see, is alluded to just below (xix. 11). When men are said to hold the witness of Jesus, or to suffer for it, it is meant that they stand by his testimony, and confirm his passion with their martyrdom (xii. 11); in supporting his testimony, they become also witnesses to him, his witnesses (ii. 13, xi. 3). Yet their being so does not alter the sheer sense of the phrase 'Jesu's testimony'.

But what is it that moves the angel, in turning St. John's worship away from himself and from his testimony, to talk about 'the Spirit of prophecy'? The model (xiv. 13) will instruct us. 'Write: Happy are the dead who die in the Lord. From that moment (says the Spirit) let them rest from their labours, for their merits go with them.' The beatitude, thus specially dictated, is the voice of the Spirit—the Spirit as inspirer of the Christian prophet. The text in xiv. 13 does not stand alone. Every one of the blessed promises with which the seven messages of ii-iii conclude is 'What the Spirit says to the churches'. And from the very form of the messages it is clear that *the testimony of Jesus* is the Spirit of the prophecy they contain. No angel can be more than a channel or an emissary. Now the angel of xix. 9 has uttered a beatitude and confirmed it with an Amen: 'These are true words of God.' Acknowledging the Spirit, St. John falls before the angel. No, says he; worship God. The testimony of *Jesus* is the spirit of (the) prophecy.

Even now we are left with a paradox. Worship God, not me who testify; the testimony of *Jesus* is the spirit of the prophecy. 'Worship God', would seem to exclude the worship of all who testify. Why then trouble to say, 'It is not *my* testimony, but Christ's, that is the spirit of prophecy'? The paradox is nothing else than the mystery of Christ's person; to worship him is not to direct worship away from God. As the Johannine Epistle says: 'We know that the Son of God is come, and has given us a mind to know the true God. And we are in the true God, (being) in his Son Jesus Christ. This is true God and life eternal. Children, keep yourselves from idols.' The angel seems worshipful because he brings 'the true words of God'. It is infidelity to worship the angel, but not so to worship 'the true and faithful word of God'. If we tell a beloved person 'I adore the things you say' we have not turned our love to another object. Jesus is the very Word of God; therefore his testimony is the Spirit of prophecy. The presence of the angel fades; St. John sees heaven open and One called Faithful and True . . . his name, the Word of God.

All the words of God are Christ, in some sense. What is it that makes the beatitude spoken by the angel so specially adorable, as to bring St. John down in worship at his feet, and open to him the vision of the Christ who stands behind the angel? It is the eucharistic reference which it contains. The primitive Church consecrated the eucharist by the great thanksgiving-prayer which names the rite. Lifting their hearts to heaven, they blessed God for his mighty acts of salvation, thereby both assuring their ultimate possession of Christ, and making real the foretaste they were about to receive in his sacramental body and blood. The exultation of victory has passed into eucharistic prayer in xix. 1–8, but it is the angel's beatitude which first makes explicit the allusion to that blessed feast eaten in the kingdom of God and anticipated in the Church. St. John falls to adore, and every intermediary vanishes between himself and Christ.

(c) THE LAST THINGS

11 And I saw heaven opened; and behold, a white horse, and he that sat thereon, called faithful and true, and in righteousness doth he
12 judge and make war; and his eyes a flame of fire, and on his head many diadems; having a name written which none knoweth but
13 himself, and clothed with a vesture dipped in blood; and his name is called the Word of God.
14 And the armies which are in heaven followed him on white
15 horses, clothed in fine linen, white and clean. And out of his mouth proceedeth a sharp sword, that with it he should smite the nations, and he shall rule them with a rod of iron; and he treadeth the winepress of the fierceness of the wrath of Almighty God.
16 And he hath on his vesture and on his thigh a name written, King of kings and Lord of lords.

The temple of heaven opened its doors to let out the bowl-pourers, the very sky has opened wide to let the rider pass. The coming of the white-horsed rider in vi. 2 accompanied the opening of the first seal; that was the beginning of a revelation now made complete. But the opening of the skies, removing every barrier between Christ and his servants on earth, awakes another set of echoes in its present context. The white raiment of the bride, or of the saints (xix. 8), and the eucharistic beatitude on those called to the Supper of the Lamb, bring back the conclusion of the last among the seven messages—the door is down—Christ comes to sup with the disciple, that the disciple may sup with him, and sit with him on the throne of his victory (iii. 18–21: for the special relevance of the text here, see above, p. 85). The Christ who gave such promises was the Christ who designated himself 'the Amen, the witness (the) faithful and true, the beginning of God's creation' (iii. 14). It is as such that Christ is manifested now.

The 'Amen' has been spoken by the cherubim and elders (xix. 4) and paraphrased by the angel as 'true words of God'—the repetition in xxii. 6 gives *faithful and* true words of God', the two adjectives expressing in combination the root-meaning of the Hebrew 'Amen'. And so Christ appears as the *Amen* in flesh and blood—the faithful and true, the witness whose testimony is the spirit of prophecy, the Word of God—and, as such, the beginning of God's Creation (Gen. i. 1-3, John i. 1-3).

It is as the faithful witness, the prince of martyrs, that Jesus rides to victory. In xii. 7-12 we have seen the testimony of Jesus and his martyrs, enforced by his blood and theirs, barb the spears of Michael and the angels, so that they drive Satan out of the heavenly court. Faithful witness is victory. From the first unsealing of apocalypse Christ rode forth conquering, and to conquer; he has been conquering every since; the power of his death and resurrection have taken effect in the passions of his martyrs. It has been a paradoxical victory. The Saints conquered the beast, yet it was given him to conquer them, anyhow in earthly appearance. In Christ's advent appearance comes into line with reality. The battle has been fought to a finish. The adversary has committed the folly of fighting against God and it is manifest who is the victor (xvii. 14).

It is the postulate of New Testament thought that the triumph of Christ and the Saints has to be merited. It seems the Advent needs no preparation, being the act of naked omnipotence. There is no question of a host gathered at Armageddon meeting the Son of God in the shock of spears. They can only beat their breasts, when they once look on whom they had pierced. So it was with Christ's resurrection; Hell could but groan, and cower away in fear. Nevertheless, neither act of omnipotence, neither Resurrection nor Advent would have place, but for the preceding paradox of visible defeat and invisible victory. Neither at his Easter nor at his Advent can we *see* Christ conquer his enemies. We can either see them conquering him, in his own flesh and in the body of his church; or we can see them calling on the hills to cover them. If Christ is shown in visionary portrayal overthrowing his enemies on a contested field, the reality symbolized is the agony of martyrdom, looked back upon from the triumph of Advent.

It must follow that the tokens of carnage have a double sense. Following Isaiah's terrible prophecy against Edom, the Lord treads the winepress of blood; the blood has soaked his raiment (Isa. lxiii, Rev. xix. 13, 15, cf. xiv. 20). In shedding his own blood he defeats his enemies and (in the ultimate effect) treads down their lives to the earth. The paradox is in St. Paul; when Christ suffered his flesh to be gibbeted on the cross, he was gibbeting principalities and powers (Col. ii. 15).

THE HEAVENLY MAN

A modern Christian might prefer to say that Christ's victory is over enmity, not enemies; that he conquers hate by converting it. But it is plain that St. John is not saying this. He knows, like any Christian, that Christ's death throws open the gates of forgiveness to mankind, but he does not see the world brought under the kingdom of God by a general conversion. The events of the last days, enlisting all mankind either under Christ's banner, or Antichrist's, will leave Antichrist a vast preponderance of numbers, and a full possession of political power, till the hour of Advent strikes. So the warfare of Christ in the present age is judgement; he drives men either into his own or his enemy's camp, so sealing their fate. And such also is the consistent doctrine of St. John's Gospel.

The description of the Advent Christ is, as it ought to be, the most poetically powerful paragraph in the book; but only when read in its place. For the effect is made by a concentration of echoes. The Advent is the fulfilment of hope; all the promise of earlier visions or oracles is here fused in a picture. The picture is lyrical, not visual; a unity of voices and ideas, not of imaginable forms.

Since the warrior on the white horse is the faithful and true witness, his warfare is righteous judgement (verse 11). His eyes are piercing as truth itself (12). The brow above them is laden with crowns. These 'many diadems' make him the king of kings and lord of lords, the master of the beast and of its crowned horns, the kings (xiii. 1, xvii. 12–14, xix. 16). The ineffable Name is mentioned after the diadems, because Aaron and his high-priestly successors wore the tetragrammaton JHVH in a gold plate on their foreheads. It is not possible to decide whether St. John sees the same letters on the forehead of Christ and reflects that the full meaning of the mysterious name is known to its divine bearer alone; or whether he sees letters of no known character, a divine archetype of the tetragrammaton itself. Perhaps iii. 12, 'My own new Name' might incline us to the latter view: cf. also ii. 17.

Just as the ineffable Name goes with the diadem, so does the name 'Word of God' with the warrior's blood-stained raiment. For not only does the title show Christ to be the testimony to the true words of God, as being himself embodied faithfulness, truth, and word (9, 11, 13); it shows him also in the part of the Warrior-Word of Wisdom xviii. 15–16, a text easily associated with Isaiah lxiii. 1–6. He leaps down 'from heaven out of the royal throne (Rev. xix. 11) a stern warrior . . . bearing as a sharp sword God's unfeigned commandment' (cf. 15 below), to give the *coup de grâce* to Egypt, and to deliver Israel.

Christ is the executive will of God, and the armies of heaven follow him, mounted as he is. In view of xix. 8 and xvii. 14 we are

THE HEAVENLY MAN

to see in this heavenly host saints rather than angels; the battle is of Christians against Antichrist, not of Michael against Satan. Christ's raiment is blood-stained, theirs is white; the antithesis reflects vii. 14, 'They have washed their robes, and bleached them through the blood of the Lamb.'

Verse 15 resumes the attributes of the Warrior-Word, reflecting previous visions; 16 gives him the final titles to all victory. We have already seen the mantle associated with his name; now names are written on it. This is as pictorially as it is symbolically intelligible; the royal titles are his glory, he is arrayed in them; the mantle is blood-stained, it is his glory and his victory to have died (v. 12); the letters are embroidered in the borders. 'And on his thigh' is difficult both as symbol and as picture. What is commonly said to be on the thigh is the sword. We may see Christ as the victor bridegroom of Psalm xlv. 3: 'Gird thy sword on thy thigh, mighty prince, in thy grace and thy majesty'; and we may suppose that St. John forces the paradox: as the word of Christ's lips is a sharp sword, so the armament of his thigh is a prevailing name. All the comment we require is offered by xvii. 14, 'They shall do battle with the Lamb and the Lamb shall conquer them *because he is Lord of lords and King of kings.*' So much for the symbolical sense. We cannot be sure of the pictorial. Does the border of the horseman's cloak hang across his thigh, so that the two localizations of the inscription are one? Or does St. John see a scabbard with the legend running down it?

And I saw an angel standing in the sun; and he cried with a loud 17 voice, saying to all the fowls that fly in mid-heaven, Come, gather together to the great supper of God, that ye may eat the flesh of 18 kings and the flesh of captains and the flesh of warriors, the flesh of horses and of them that sit thereon, the flesh of all whether bond or free, small or great.

The Advent was the climax of Christ's prophecy to his disciples, and Christ's prophecy lays down the main lines of St. John's vision. St. John will add the Last Things of Christian and of Jewish belief, but he will add them by way of appendix. The model he has provided himself in xiv and followed hitherto will serve the purpose well. A second triad of angels completed the harvest-work of the Son of Man (xiv. 15–20). So now let one angel preside over the great battle of Advent Day (xix. 17–18+19–21) and another, by imprisoning the defeated dragon for a set period, both make room for the millennium and plant the seed of its termination, a termination carrying with it Last Judgement and New Creation (xx. 1–3+xx. 4–xxi. 8).

A third angel can show the glory of the New Jerusalem, as a former angel showed the judgement of Babylon (xxi. 9–xxii. 5).

The three angels of xiv. 15–20 offer nothing but empty form to St. John's new purposes. The one usable detail is the river of death in which their action concludes, and which St. John matches with the river of life at the end of his new series (xxii. 1–2). In appreciating what he does with these three angels we have a guide in what he has just done with their predecessors, the three angels of xiv. 6–11. One of them he has put in charge of the great show of the harlot (xvii); the other two he has helped out with supplementary visions, or voices, rather (xviii. 4–20, xix. 1–8). He does the same thing again, only changing the order for reasons we have explained (p. 181); it is the last angel that is put in charge of the showing of the bride, the first two that are helped out with supplementary visions (xix. 4–8, xx. 4–xxi. 8).

The sequel to the rider on the white cloud offers St. John little in the way of material for elaboration; the sequel to the former rider on the white horse is more promising. (1) After the rider and his companions in vi we had the souls of the martyrs, crying for judgement and constrained to patience (vi. 9–11). The millennium may show us the same souls—judgement is now given to them, they live, they are enthroned. Nevertheless, even this reward, like the gift of white robes in vi. 11, is provisional, and for a time. There is still battle and final victory to come, and the rounding of the number of the elect. (2) The vision of martyr-souls in vi was followed by the great earthquake which foreshadowed the last judgement and the end of the old creation. The things so foreshadowed were held back then for the sealing of the saints. But now they can go forward. (3) In fact the sequel to the sealing of the saints did show what their final bliss would be (vii. 9–17). That scene will be largely reproduced in the descent of New Jerusalem after the great judgement.

We must deal with these matters when we reach them. Our present concern is with the first of the three angels. We have just seen the figure of the Son of Man, or, to speak in terms of the four cherub-faces, the man. St. John is so far conscious of the cherubic pattern as to give it some emphasis in the beginning of a new cycle. After the man, the eagle. This angel calls the vultures to that very scene of which Christ had said, 'Where the carcass is, the eagles will gather.' St. John's concern to get his eagle-theme where he wants it is all the more evident, because it leads him to take a piece of Ezekiel's last visions out of order; an order which he otherwise follows without deviation in xix–xxii. The summons to the birds of prey is part of Ezekiel's vision of Gog; and the Gog-episode, according to both Ezekiel's order and St. John's, comes after the millennium. In Ezekiel it is the prophet himself who preaches to the birds (Ezek. xxxix. 17-20). St. John improves on his original. The kites, who have such an astonishing power of vision from their high point of vantage, seem to assemble on a scene of slaughter even from behind the horizon; just as though summoned by a message from the sun, who surveys all things from his even higher station, and whose eye, in proverbial phrase, nothing escapes. The shocking comparison between the two invitations to the great supper (xix. 9 and 17) must be deliberate on St. John's part.

And I saw the beast and the kings of the earth and their armies, gathered together to make war against him that sat upon the horse and against his army. And the beast was taken, and with him the false prophet that wrought the signs in his sight, wherewith he deceived them that had received the mark of the beast, and that worshipped his image. They were both cast alive into the lake of fire that burneth with brimstone; and the rest were slain with the sword of him that sat upon the horse, the sword proceeding out of his mouth; and all the fowls were filled with their flesh. 19 20 21

The hosts which (in the symbolism of vision) gathered on the hills behind Megiddo must be supposed to have marched on Jerusalem, there to confront the army of the Lord, who has come down to defend his holy place. One may think of such a text as Zechariah xiv. 2-4 or Isaiah xxxi. 4. 'The lake of fire which burns with brimstone' is Gehenna and belongs to the same picture. For, typically speaking, Gehenna is the Vale of (the Son of) Hinnom, situated just outside the Holy City (Isa. xxx. 33, lxvi. 24). By calling it a 'lake' St. John can evoke the memory of the asphaltic lake, that is, the Sea of Sodom; and by saying that the two beasts are thrown alive into it, he can recall the Exodus: 'Sing unto the Lord, for he hath triumphed gloriously; the horse and his rider hath he cast into the sea.' St. John's battle is, indeed, seen very much as a cavalry engagement (verses 14, 18).

By falling alive into Gehenna, to suffer physical torments for ever, the beasts share with Korah, Dathan, and Abiram (Num. xvi. 28-33) the awful privilege of anticipating the penalty reserved for other sinners until the last day. The rest of the host being killed, that is, parted from their bodies, lead a shivering half-life until resurrection shall restore them to bodily being, divine judgement, and everlasting fire (xx. 12-15).

And I saw an angel come down from heaven, having the key of the abyss and a great chain in his hand. And he laid hold on the XX 2

dragon, the old serpent which is the devil and Satan, and bound
3 him for a thousand years, and cast him into the abyss, and shut
and sealed over him, that he might deceive the nations no more,
until the thousand years were finished. After that he must be
loosed for a little while.

Apart from the reminder of Daniel's den (Dan. vi. 17) in verse 3 there is nothing of the lion about this angel's action. The type is certainly faint when compared with the eagle-type of xix. 17, but, such as it is, it is in parallel. The Armageddon host is consigned to the kites, the dragon to the den of the abyss.

Satan did not appear as a warrior on the field of battle, for Satan is an incorporeal spirit. Why, then, is his binding by the angel a sequel to the victory over the beasts? The demon of Tobit, having sustained a check to his malice against mankind, takes flight and is bound by the angel (Tobit viii. 3). But the logic of St. John's thought can be more closely studied from his own work. We observe that the description of the dragon as seized here is identical with the description of him as cast down in xii. 9, and that both texts equally reflect the description of him as smitten by the Lord in Isaiah xxvii. 1. Now in xii. 9–11 we were told that Michael's casting down of Satan was equivalent to, or due to, the saints' victory over him 'through the blood of the Lamb and the word of their testimony—they loved their lives so little that they died'. That is to say, that Christ and the saints having triumphed in the contest of martyrdom, the devil is thrown down by his angelic antagonist. The paragraph now before us shows a later phase of the same battle. The devil has brought earthly forces into play through the tyranny of Antichrist; and these forces having been defeated by the Lamb and his saints, the angel can carry the abasement of Satan a stage farther: not from heaven to earth, but from earth to the abyss.

But why is Satan merely bound and why is he ever to be loosed again? No doubt St. John's scriptural warrant is Daniel vii. 12. When the great beast's body is given to the burning of fire (cf. Rev. xix. 20) the other beasts' dominion is taken away, yet their lives are prolonged for a season and a time—Yes, as it were shut and sealed in the den of beasts, says St. John, turning back the page to Daniel vi. 17. The lions were bound from hurting Daniel, and yet in God's time the spell was removed, and they sprang again (vi. 24). Who are 'the other beasts'? Behemoth is burnt with fire; Leviathan (with his angels, presumably) is bound. Such a method of allegorizing Daniel is quite in the style of its time, but the motive for it must be sought elsewhere than in the text of Daniel.

In fact the measure of defeat imposed on Satan corresponds to the nature of the kingdom which Christ's advent establishes. St. John sees the millennial reign as an earthly kingdom very much in the spirit of Old Testament prophecy. The empire had been held by the Babylonians, the Persians, the Romans; now it is held by the saints. The power of heathenism is crushed, and so Satan is bound; but only bound; there are unconverted hearts, 'Gog and his Magog, the people in the four corners of the earth', and a rebellion is always conceivable, should God permit it. And he will permit it; all enmity must come out into the open, and be annihilated, before God's reign is made absolute.

The millennium is a reign of Christ on earth, as God's Messiah or viceregent. But his viceroyal function is only required so long as there is opposition to God. The universal King employs a champion, so long as there is a war. He cannot descend into the arena of his creatures to take part against rebellion. God is the enemy of Satan, as of all mischief, but cannot be his antagonist. It is by the power of God that Satan exists, by his permission that he rebels, and by his will that the kingdom of Messiah subdues him. Once he is destroyed, and the kingdom of Christ is coextensive with the kingdom of God, the Messianic reign terminates: the throne of God and of the Lamb is one.

Though St. Paul did not (for anything we know) believe in the millennium, he supplies the form of thought which is required for understanding it. 'As in Adam all die, so in Christ are all to be brought to life, but each in his own order: Christ the firstfruit, then they that are Christ's at his coming; then the completion, when he delivers up the kingdom to God the Father, when he abolishes all rule, authority and power. For he must reign *until he puts all enmity under his feet*; the last enemy to be abolished is death. . . . But when all things have come under him, then the Son himself shall come under him who has brought all things under him, that God may be all in all' (1 Cor. xv. 22–28). There is no reason to suppose that St. Paul foresaw a thousand years' standstill in the completion of Christ's victory. Christ rose himself on Easter Day, his faithful will rise to join him at his coming, together they will achieve the conquest and the judgement of the world, and that will be the end. That Christ remains for St. Paul the head and focus of the redeemed creation in the Kingdom of God, goes without saying.

But why did St. John believe in a millennial standstill, if St. Paul did not? It seems that the doctrine established itself in rabbinic theology towards the end of the first century A.D.; St. Paul would not have learnt it at the feet of Gamaliel, the Seer of the Revelation might well learn it at whose ever feet it was he sat. The doctrine rested on a triple basis: first, on the cosmic importance attached to the seven-day week by Genesis i–ii; second, on the supposition that Ezekiel xxxv–xlviii offered a continuous prediction of the last things; and third, on the difficulty of referring all the messianic prophecies of scripture to a final state beyond time or change. Of these three arguments, the third does not appear to have weighed with St. John; he found no difficulty in a symbolical application to the final state of prophecies which in any literal sense would have to refer to a millenium (xxi. 24–27). We have considered the first argument in the Introduction (pp. 12–13 above). In view of St. John's evident belief that divine action in the world's affairs has a seven-act structure, we can well understand his acceptance of the view that all historical time forms a week in which every day is a thousand years (Ps. xc. 4 cited 2 Peter iii. 8), the last day being the world's sabbath, the restful dominion of the saints. His acceptance of the argument from Ezekiel is manifest in the arrangement of his own final chapters. In Ezekiel xxxv–xxxvi God overthrows Edom and restores Israel, and in xxxvii raises the dead of Israel from the valley of dry bones, that he may make them one kingdom under David, that is, King Messiah. In xxxviii–xxxix he defeats the rebellion of Gog, and in xl–xlviii reveals New Jerusalem and the Age to Come. Evidently, then, there is a first resurrection and a messianic reign before the overthrow of Gog makes room for the final state. As to the general resurrection and the Last Judgement, doubtless they will usher in the final state, though Ezekiel was not inspired to prophesy about them.

4 And I saw thrones, and they took their seat on them to whom judgment was given. And the souls of them that had been beheaded for the testimony of Jesus and for the word of God, such as had not worshipped the beast or his image, neither received the mark on their forehead and their hand—they lived again and
5 reigned with Christ a thousand years. The rest of the dead lived not until the thousand years were finished. This is the first
6 resurrection. Blessed and holy is he that hath part in the first resurrection; on such the second death hath no power; but they shall be priests of God and of Christ, and shall reign with him a thousand years.

The consequences of the action of the second angel and of Satan's imprisonment are set out in three further visions—the thrones of the saints (verses 4 ff.), the throne of God (11 ff.), and the New Jerusalem in which the two are united, for God comes to tabernacle with men (xxi. 1 ff.). There is no separate vision of the war of Gog; the millennial vision trails away into a prediction of it, much as the oracle of the reed trails away into a prophecy about the two witnesses (xi. 3–13) or as the vision of battle in the sky trails away into a prediction of the dragon's pursuit of the woman (xii. 13–18).

We are surprised to find that in the kingdom of Christ, Christ is mentioned only by way of allusion. The explanation can be found by attending to the introductory phrase and its place in the vision-series. 'I saw thrones, and they sat on them' leads on to 'I saw a throne great and white, and him that sat thereon' (verse 11) which in turn refers us back to 'I saw . . . and lo, a white horse, and he that sat thereon . . .' (xix. 11). The royal majesty of Christ has been shown already in the mounted warrior; what needs now to be said is that saints are enthroned with him.

St. John profits by the ambiguity of Daniel's vision of the Son of Man. In the primary vision the Son of Man is given dominion, but in the exposition, the equivalent is that 'judgment is given to the saints of the Most High and . . . the saints possessed the kingdom'. It is a common, though not certainly true, opinion among the learned, that Daniel's Son of Man is nothing more or less than an emblem standing for the saints themselves. But no primitive Christian read Daniel so. St. John has Daniel's authority for describing the Fifth Monarchy as the empire of the saints, and does so describe it. It is axiomatic with him that the saints can only be enthroned as assessors to Christ.

'Judgment was given to them', says St. John, as he puts them on thrones; evidently understanding Daniel to mean that they are given judicial authority; the same interpretation is implied in 1 Corinthians vi. 2. Daniel's words are at the least ambiguous—they may more naturally mean 'judgment was given in their favour'. What is curious is that the phrase apparently acts for St. John as a link with the vision of martyr souls in vi. 9 crying for judgement to be *done* them—not put into their hands. The evidence for the linkage is St. John's going on immediately to say that he sees *souls* of men done to death for the testimony of Jesus and the word of God; though he sees, in fact, nothing of the sort—these souls have come to life again and recovered their bodies; they were mere souls when he saw them under the altar in vi. We can only conclude that St. John was able to give Daniel's words both senses and that he saw no contradiction between them. The saints cry for justice to be done them; God sees they have justice by putting justice into their hands. That it would be so was indeed the common Jewish expectation.

St. John does not make clear the relation between the enthroned judges and the souls of the martyrs. Are all of them enthroned as judges? They will all 'reign' in some sense (verse 6) but this may not involve their enthronement. Those who 'reign' in xxii. 5 are not (apparently) enthroned; they have access to the enthroned Majesty ('see his face'). Perhaps the enthroned persons are those to whom Christ made the promise recorded in Matthew xix. 28. Some ambiguity also attaches to the second half of verse 4. Is St. John saying that those who live are men who not merely happened to be killed for their Christian profession but who had also been stalwart in refusing idolatrous homage; or is he saying that in addition to actual martyrs, steadfast confessors will live whether they happen to have been killed or not? Since they are all brought under the description 'This is the first resurrection' we must suppose they have all died, and we may as well say that they are all martyrs.

Does St. John mean to confine the 'First Resurrection' to the martyrs alone? It seems most likely that he does, though we do not know what he would have said if we had pleaded the case of famous names. Would he have found a corner for Abraham, Isaac, and Jacob, for Moses, Samuel, and Elijah? But as it stands, he must be taken to mean that where many fought against Christ, only the two beasts had their hell forthwith; and that where many stood for Christ, only the martyrs had their resurrection-life forthwith. The chief moral significance of the millennium in St. John's book, is the special promise it makes to the martyr; and is not his whole work an exhortation to martyrdom? St. John parallels 'first resurrection and second resurrection' with 'first death and second death'. The two deaths were a rabbinic commonplace, the two resurrections were not. A man might die (even under punishment) to this world, and not die for the world to come; the incurable sinner might die to both. The parallel St. John draws is not exact. The 'first death' is virtually universal (with the possible exception of saints who live to see the Advent); the second death is selective (it spares all true Israelites). The first resurrection, on the contrary, is highly selective (only the martyrs rise), the second absolutely universal (all rise for judgement, even sinners; or how could they undergo a 'second death'?) The first death leaves men's ultimate destiny unaffected; the first resurrection prejudges it.

A selective resurrection can be supported from Daniel xii. 2; it directly follows the overthrow of 'Antichrist', as St. John would have it to do. What is less convenient for him, is that it is a selective resurrection of the evil as well as the good: 'some to agelong life, some to shame and agelong abhorrence'. We cannot say what St. John made of this; unless the sinister resurrection has been exemplified in the single person of Antichrist himself, returning from the dead to reign, and cast into Gehenna.

It is unprofitable to ask how St. John pictures the millennium.

'Those who have part in the first resurrection' reign unaging for a thousand years, like Christ in his resurrection-being. But meanwhile, what of the rest? Do other faithful men continue in a natural life and die after seventy years? Have they any share in the kingdom? Do they enjoy the privilege of being a priesthood on behalf of mankind to Christ and to God? Is there a world-wide mission and if so, do the converts become 'kings and priests'? St. John did not picture the millennium. Even supposing a millennium, we must know infinitely less about it than about the world to come. Though the world to come may be further removed from our present state, we know it to be the fullness of all God has to give, that we are able to receive. Just how much it might please him to bestow upon a middle state between this life and eternal life, who can hopefully conjecture? St. John is too wise to make the attempt.

And when the thousand years are expired, Satan shall be loosed out of his prison and shall go forth to deceive the nations which are in the four corners of the earth, Gog and Magog, to gather them together to battle, the number of whom is as the sand of the sea. And they went up over the breadth of the earth, and compassed the camp of the saints about, and the beloved city. And fire came down out of heaven and devoured them; and the devil that deceived them was cast into the lake of fire and brimstone, where are the beast and the false prophet; and they shall be tormented day and night for ever and ever.

We have already discussed the significance of Gog's rebellion as the final confrontation of forces, and total elimination of opposition to the kingdom of God. St. John takes the story from Ezekiel and leaves the symbol undecoded. St. John says that the nations, or 'gentiles' beguiled by Satan are 'in the four *corners* of the earth' and perhaps he means this, i.e. that the unreconciled are tucked away in lands remote from the centre. The simple pairing of 'Gog and Magog' must not be taken as fixing on St. John the error of understanding both names either as tribes or as princes. In Ezekiel it is perfectly clear that Gog is the prince, Magog the people. St. John is innocent of the mistake; he says simply 'the nations in the four corners of the earth, Gog and Magog', i.e. the power so described by Ezekiel—as an English orator might have said 'the forces of frustrated nationalism, Hitler and Germany'. It is certainly curious that St. John equates without explanation the tribes in the four corners with a tribe in one corner; only he does exactly the same thing in the Armageddon vision. Euphrates is dried to let the kings of the East pass; the three demons beguile *all the kings of the earth* to come to Armageddon. The old biblical picture of invasion from the North East is in both cases given an ecumenical interpretation.

In Ezekiel heavenly fire is only one of the weapons brought against Gog; he is apparently overthrown in battle.

'The camp of the saints and city beloved' is a double description, like 'the temple of the tent of witness' (xv. 5), combining the camp of Moses with the Jerusalem of Solomon. Perhaps St. John means that the Jerusalem of the millennial Kingdom, Jerusalem though she may be, is a provisional habitation when compared to the everlasting Zion of the world to come, as was the camp of Moses compared to the city of David. In any case we are in a world of symbols too shadowy and distant even to be disputed. We know that the Zion of Christ's spiritual presence in our own age (xiv. 1-5) is not a literal Jerusalem. As for the throne of the millennium, has it a place or has it not a place? And if a place, why not Jerusalem as well as any other?

The conclusion brings the result of the war of Gog into line with that of the war of Antichrist. Leviathan is sent to join Behemoth in the lake of fire: the host of Gog is destroyed, but will rise for judgement at the Great Assize.

11 And I saw a great white throne, and him that sat upon it, from whose face the earth and the heaven fled away, and there was
12 found no place for them. And I saw the dead, the great and the small, stand before the throne. And books were opened; and another book was opened, which is the book of life; and the dead were judged out of the things written in the books, according to
13 their works. And the sea gave up the dead that were in it, and death and Hades gave up the dead which were in them; and they were
14 judged every man according to their works. And death and Hades were cast into the lake of fire—this is the second death, the lake of
15 fire; and whosoever was not found written in the book of life was cast into the lake of fire.

The idea of a 'white throne' may perhaps have been familiar to St. John's hearers as the distinguishing character of the local bishop's chair in the church. The practice of spreading a white cover over it was certainly early; whether so early as St. John's date, we cannot prove. Even if it was already in use, the custom would do no more than make natural the otherwise somewhat strange idea of a 'white throne'—unless we are to think of the ivory-and-golden throne of Solomon (1 Kings x. 18). It is certainly not St. John's purpose to present God as presiding in the 'congregation of God'; iv. 2 ff. would be the place for that. The symbolical value of the white seat is determined by its predecessors, the white cloud and the white horse (xiv. 14, xix. 11). The whiteness stands for victory. While the fight is on, the champion rides into the conflict. Now it is over, it is enough that the Godhead, timelessly enthroned, should be revealed in judgement. Nothing can stand before him. Earth and heaven flee away; the things previously shaken (vi. 14, xvi. 20) are now removed.

Nothing can stand before him; yet the dead must.

> Though death recoils and nature cries
> Yet the creature shall arise
> To answer at the last assize.

'Books were opened'. St. John now quotes Daniel vii. 10 in something closer to the literal sense, for Daniel was presenting a scene of judgement, not a scene of revelation as in Revelation v–vi. Yet Daniel's vision is not a judgement of the souls of men according to personal merit. It is a judgement passed in favour of the oppressed saints as a body; it condemns the persecuting power to dethronement and destruction, and restores the saints to the seat of empire. Nor can Daniel's 'books' or 'papers' be given the sense St. John requires; they need be no more than paraphernalia of the Court—most likely the minute-book, in which the acts and judgements of the day are recorded. The Old Testament does not contain the picture, so familiar to rabbinic Judaism, of the trial of souls. To that picture belonged 'the books of deeds', in which recording angels had written all actions of men, whether good or bad; and which served as written evidence on which sentence could be given.

A more ancient piece of biblical lore is 'the Book of the Living' or 'of Life', also known to Daniel (xii. 1). It had originally been conceived as a muster-roll of God's living subjects; to have one's name expunged was simply to die (Exod. xxxii. 32–33, Ps. lxix. 28). But by St. John's time it had come to be seen as a roll of those destined to receive the life of the world to come (Phil. iv. 3). The relation between the books of deeds, and of the living, is not perfectly clear in St. John's vision. He introduces the records of deeds first and we think we are to see a judgement assigning rewards and penalties in strict accordance with merit. Then the book of the living is introduced, and takes charge of the conclusion (verse 15). We wonder whether, after all, we are witnessing a trial of crimes and deserts, or a scrutiny of the citizen-list of the New Jerusalem. Such scrutinies and revisions were periodic events in ancient cities. No doubt the mysterious confrontation of the Last Day is both a scrutiny and a trial. If we wish to

210   THE HEAVENLY MAN

harmonize the features of St. John's vision so as to make a consistent human story, it seems inevitable that the scrutiny of the citizen-list should be taken as the starting-point. All conceivable claimants of citizenship, that is, all mankind, appear. Their names may not be on the roll at all, like those whom prescient wisdom omitted from the first (xiii. 8, xvii. 8). They may have forfeited their place, and have been expunged (iii. 5). If not, their claim to remain receives a last assessment on the evidence of the 'books of deeds'; and the same evidence is available for making plain to the claimants the justice of previous expungings, or of previous inclusions. The list, in its final or revised state, admits to New Jerusalem, which immediately descends (xxi. 1). Exclusion from the city, and eternal death, are equivalents; Gehenna is an everlasting bonfire just outside the gates. Compare xxii. 14–15.

The references to the book of the living in iii. 5 and xiii. 8 show the 'slaughtered Lamb' to be the keeper of it. The entry of a name is equivalent to Christ's testimony that the bearer is his (iii. 5). The absence of Christ's person here from the scene of judgement and from its immediate sequel is due to a point of style. St. John is presenting a simple contrast—the advent of Messiah and the advent of Godhead, the society of Christ in the millennium and of God in the world to come. He makes ample amends in the final expository vision, by uniting the throne of the Lamb with the throne of God (xxi. 22, 23, xxii. 1, 3).

The sea (verse 13) being regarded in old semitic fashion as an abyss of death, holds those who have drowned in it. Not so the kindly earth—those whose bodies earth has received are held in the subterraneous hollows of death and Hades. Death and Hades are so far personified, that they can be said to be flung into Gehenna, in accordance with St. Paul's sentence, 'the last enemy to be abolished is death' (1 Cor. xv. 26). The same cannot appropriately be said of Sea; but St. John hastens to add, that it is omitted from the new creation (xxi. 1).

XXI And I saw a new heaven and a new earth; for the first heaven and
2 the first earth are passed away, and the sea is no more. And I saw the holy city, new Jerusalem, coming down out of heaven from
3 God, made ready as a bride adorned for her husband. And I heard a great voice out of the throne, saying, Behold the tabernacle of God is with men, and he will tabernacle with them, and they shall
4 be his people, and God-with-Them himself shall be their God, and shall wipe away all tears from their eyes. And death shall be no more, mourning and crying and pain shall be no more; for the

THE HEAVENLY MAN

former things are passed away, and he that sitteth upon the throne 5
hath said, Behold, I make all things new.
And he saith, Write that these words are faithful and true. And 6
he said to me, They are come to pass. I am the Alpha and the
Omega, the beginning and the end. I will give unto him that is
athirst of the fountain of the water of life freely. He that over- 7
cometh shall inherit these things; and I will be his God, and he
shall be my son. But the fearful and unbelieving and abominable, 8
the murderers, whoremongers, sorcerers, idolaters and all liars,
their part is in the lake that burneth with fire and brimstone,
which is the second death.

This vision completes the triad of visions which follow the second angel and work out the implications of his binding of Satan in the abyss. The kingdom of God comes 'on earth as it is in heaven' and unites men to the Godhead. That is the last of the Last Things and the end of the visionary drama. Nothing happens after the end of happening. The rest of the book is expository; this is the text it expounds. The sad note on which the text concludes brings it back into line with a series originating in conquests and penalties (cf. the conclusions at xix. 20–21, xx. 2–3, 10, 14–15). But St. John does not allow this to be the last note in his book.

It is natural that such a paragraph should be full of echoes, since all anticipations are here realized and all promises fulfilled. The promise of the marriage, which ushered in the Advent, is at length taken up in the mention of the bride adorned, and the paraphrased Amen 'Write, that these words are faithful and true' supports the reminder of that most interesting passage (xix. 7–10). The happy promises which make up most of the utterance from heaven in 3–4 and 6–7 give detailed echoes of the bliss enjoyed by the countless multitude in vii. 15–17 and, as we said above (p. 200), these echoes form part of a systematic reproduction of the sequel to the first vision of a white horse, in the sequel to the second. Especially notable is the return of themes attaching to the Tabernacles Feast (see above, p. 111).

We have also to observe that the pouring of the bowls, extended through its sequels or appendices, has reached a second conclusion comparable with the seventh bowl-vision itself. There old Jerusalem was shattered and Babylon destroyed; here New Jerusalem is established. The comparison is made perfectly explicit by St. John when a bowl-angel steps forward to show Jerusalem, the bride (xxi. 9), just as a bowl-angel had stepped forward in the former occasion to show the harlot, Babylon (xvii. 1). But there is further matching of detail as between the seventh bowl-pouring and the paragraph now before us. Babylon was destroyed in a shaking of heaven and earth, a flight of mountains and islands; heaven and earth have fled away to make room for the new Jerusalem. In both visions there is a great voice out of the throne; in xvi it speaks from the midst of the temple, in xxi it declares the tabernacle of God to be with men. The thunderous confirmation '*Ghegonan*' ('They are fulfilled') matches the *Ghegonen* of xvi. For the confirmatory force of 'I am the *A* and the *Ω*', see p. 63 above.

Going back behind St. John's previous inspirations to his scriptural authority, we find the master-text for the whole paragraph in Isaiah lxv. 13–22: 'Behold, they that serve me shall drink, but ye shall thirst. . . . They shall be called by a new name which shall be blest on the earth; for they shall bless the true God (*ton theon ton alēthinon*). . . . They shall forget their former tribulation, it shall not come to their mind. For the heaven shall be new and the earth new. . . . For behold, I make Jerusalem a rejoicing and my people a delight . . . and there shall no more be found in her the voice of weeping or the voice of crying . . . for as the days of the tree of life shall be the days of my people.'

St. John improves the contrast between those who suffer thirst, and those who drink while enjoying days like the days of the tree of life. He makes it a contrast between drinking the water of life, and having part in the lake of fire. The 'true God', the source of the blessing, is found affirming that his words are faithful and true (*alethinoi*). Justice is done to the themes of new heaven and earth, the renewal of Jerusalem, and the abolition of sorrow; but as elsewhere, St. John makes these points by an anthology of the most speaking phrases from all over the Old Testament. He adds the bridal glory of Jerusalem from such texts as Isaiah lxi. 3, 10; God's tabernacling with men in the holy city from Ezekiel xxxvii. 27; 'They shall be his people, and God their God' from a refrain running though Jeremiah and Ezekiel after first appearing in Hosea ii. 23. The text of verse 3 is, indeed, uncertain. There is good authority for 'They shall be his people, and God himself shall be with them', but it does not seem likely that St. John wished to cheat our ears of the expected antithesis 'shall be their God'. We may therefore prefer the equally well-supported text, 'And God-with-Them himself shall be their God', an allusion to the name 'Emmanuel' as it stands in Isaiah viii. 8, &c.

A further uncertainty of interpretation attaches to verse 5. It is possible to cut short the voice from the throne and take 5 as an actual utterance of the enthroned Glory himself; the writer claiming to see the sovereign lips move, and to hear the tongue of omniscience speak. He nowhere else makes such a claim and there is no reason to suppose he makes it here. Moreover, the sense is absolutely continuous. We should be better advised to translate

> For the old order hath passed away and he that sitteth upon the throne hath said, Behold I make all things new.

(The authority for his having said it is in Isaiah's text.)

We shall then have a paragraph in the very common semitic form which brings the end back to the beginning; the Matthaean Beatitudes are a famous example. Here it is: 'I heard a great *voice out of the throne, saying, Behold,* the tabernacle of God is with men ... the former things are passed away, and *he that sits upon the throne has said, Behold I make all things new.*' Having rounded his paragraph, St. John resumes with his customary and indefinite 'And he says to me . . .', the divine voice speaking in inspiration though the instrumentality of the angel (cf. xix. 9, xxii. 6, 10). When he comes to go over this vision in the long commenting vision next after it, St. John takes 'And he says to me, ... these words are faithful and true' for the start of a new paragraph (xxii. 6).

It is vain to hope for an exact answer to the question, what literal meaning St. John would have us attach to his language about new creation. Are heaven and earth new, i.e. rejuvenated and transformed; or are they created afresh, i.e. abolished and replaced? The best short answer is, that a primitive Christian might think of the world what he thought of his own body; raised again and transformed, yet without loss of individual identity. 2 Peter iii. 5-7 compares the future destruction of the world by fire and its re-creation afterwards, with its destruction by water in Noah's time and its re-creation as we have it. The 'first heaven and earth' only perished in a very qualified sense; and though the perishing of the second by fire will doubtless be more radical, it need not be seen as removing all continuity. The most uncompromising picture of new creation is provided by a Jewish work roughly contemporary with St. John, the Esdras Apocalypse. Esdras applies the type of the first creation to the second. The old world goes back into chaos and nothingness; after a certain season a new world is created. There is no evidence that St. John subscribed to this view. He has no clear doctrine and no consistency of language. He mixes two figures: (*a*) Old things are made new, (*b*) Former things have fled away, and other things have come in to take their places. New Jerusalem is not newly made; she comes down from God out of heaven.

There is no reason to suppose that St. John felt these two ways of talking to mean different things. If he preferred to say that Jerusalem came down, rather than that she was new created, it will be because of traditional language about the heavenly pre-existence of the city or of her archetype. It was based on such texts as Exodus xxv. 40, Isaiah xlix. 16. Moreover it had become a Christian commonplace that the citizenship of Christians was in Jerusalem above; we may quote St. Paul in Galatians iv as well as the author to the Hebrews for that. It seemed, then, only right to say that such a spiritual reality would descend to embrace her children on earth and to take physical shape in the world to come. Going behind symbols, we may say that the Jerusalem we are speaking of is made what she is by the divine presence; she is 'the city of the Great King'. She cannot be established on earth, unless the divine presence is bestowed; she descends because God descends into the heart of his redeemed creation.

(D) JERUSALEM

9 And there came one of the seven angels who had the seven bowls full of the seven last plagues; and he spake with me, saying, Come
10 hither, I will shew thee the bride, the Lamb's wife. And he carried me away in the Spirit to a mountain great and high, and shewed me Jerusalem the holy city descending out of heaven from God,
11 having the glory of God; her luminary like a stone most precious,
12 like jasper crystal clear; having a wall great and high; having twelve gates, and at the gates twelve angels; and names written thereon which are the names of the twelve tribes of the children
13 of Israel; on the east three gates and on the north three gates, on
14 the south three gates and on the west three gates. And the wall of the city had twelve foundations, and on them twelve names of the twelve apostles of the Lamb.

The third angel is the antitype of the third and last in xiv only by being the third and the last, and by bringing us at length to the river of life (xxii. 1), a stream antitypical to the river of death (xiv. 20). He borrows all his character from the bowl-angel who acted in so similar a fashion to his own in xvii. 1 ff., showing the vision of the harlot, as he is to show the vision of the bride. The harlot is introduced as a woman, and only gradually revealed as a city. It would be absurd to go through the same mystery twice. The bride is seen as a city from the start. The mysterious figure of the harlot is suitably encountered in a 'solitary place'. The form of the city can be seen at one place only—at the mountain which Jerusalem descends from heaven to crown. Old Jerusalem was a hill-top town, and it was prophesied that in the last days the mountain of the Lord's house should be established in the top of the mountains, and exalted above

THE HEAVENLY MAN 215

the hills (Isa. ii. 2, Mic. iv. 1). So Ezekiel saw the New Jerusalem on an 'exceeding high' mountain and St. John follows him.

There is no detailed parallel between the harlot vision and the bride vision beyond the setting of the scene; and the text St. John takes up for exposition is the paragraph he has just written (xxi. 2–8). He deals with it in order and almost verse by verse. xxi. 2, the city descending in her bridal adornment, is set forth in the jewelled architecture of verses 10 ff. 3–5ᵃ, the divine presence which brings all healing, is taken up in xxii. 1–5. xxi. 5ᵇ–6ᵃ, 'These words are faithful and true: I am Alpha and Omega', is developed in xxii. 6–13. xxi. 6–9, warnings and promises (especially of living water freely given), are the theme of xxii. 14 ff. Even so, the direction given by the model is the merest outline; and of the four parts into which we have just divided it, only the first two bear upon the description of the city (xxi. 10–xxii. 5). St. John's chief sources of material are Ezekiel's visions of the city, and of the angel who measures her; and the visions of Zion's coming glory in the last few chapters of Isaiah.

If we wish to see how St. John finds his way into his theme we must take account of certain earlier passages in his book. The bride is never described as a lady adorned, but the omission may be made good by the figure of the mother in xii. 1. For though the mother of Messiah is not, as such, the bride of Christ, both figures are allegories of the same reality, the 'daughter of Zion', the congregation of God. She stands on the moon, is clothed with the sun, and wears a crown of twelve stars. It cannot be doubted that the description alludes to Joseph's second dream, according to which the twelve 'stars' (i.e. constellations) are the sons of Israel, the moon is their mother, the sun their father. So then, the lady of xii is the mother of the patriarchs, standing on the moon as her own station, crowned with her children and arrayed in the honour of her husband. In the new allegory of xxi her husband, or bridegroom, is divine. She comes, therefore, having the glory of God (verse 10), having no need of sun or moon to light her, for the glory of God has shone on her, her lamp is the Lamb (23). Her crown of twelve stars becomes a crown of twelve bastions, which are precious stones, with twelve gates between them, which are pearls; the pearls and bastions standing for the twelve sons of Israel and for the twelve apostles assigned to them. The transition from a crown on the lady's brows to a ring of city walls was mere routine for St. John's contemporaries; the standing emblem for a city was the figure of a lady with a battlemented crown.

The particular form which the crown will take, when it becomes a periphery of walls and gates still expressing the twelve tribes or patriarchs, is determined by the list of tribes in vii. In commenting on that list, we observed the following facts: the list is based on the list of tribal gates to the square city of Ezekiel xlviii; the list is consequently arranged in a hollow square; the sides of the square are taken not in Ezekiel's order, but in the order East, North; South, West, that being the order of the four faces of the sky as cited in St. John's directly preceding context. The names of the tribes are put round the gates of the city in the same order here (verse 13). St. John adds angels to the gates, and gives the names of the apostles to the twelve blocks of wall-bottom each reaching from gate to gate. (The *foundation* or bottom of the wall is broken into twelve by the gates; above the level of the gates the wall is continuous all round.) Christ had coupled the apostles with the tribes in the world to come (Matt. xix. 28) and made St. Peter a foundation-stone (Matt. xvi. 18) and made his colleagues assessors to his special powers (Matt. xviii. 18); the Epistle to the Ephesians says roundly that the divine building is founded on apostles and prophets (ii. 20).

So far everything is clear, but verse 11 requires special comment. The city, modern expositors like to say, has the *radiance* of some priceless jewel. St. John says that her *phōstēr* is like a stone of great price. Now *phoster* ought, both by its grammatical form and by its common usage, to mean 'luminary' not 'luminosity', the '*phosteres* of the sky' means 'the sun, moon, and stars'. Although our dictionaries allege that the sense 'luminosity' is found, the cases they quote do not bear them out; they are at the best ambiguous; the sense 'luminary' can be read everywhere and therefore should be. What is the present context? St. John has merely said that Jerusalem *has* the glory of God, without defining in anyway the sense of 'has'. If we read what St. John wrote, and in the order in which he wrote it, we do not yet know that the jewel-like quality of the city's *phoster* is to be extended to herself and reflected in her walls. That comes later. At present St. John is expounding the lady. She has the glory of God; her *luminary* (which clothes her as the sun clothes the lady in xii. 1) is like a jasper crystal-clear—and what do we know about the jasper? It is the colour of the divine Glory himself (iv. 3). We have had no other mention of the stone hitherto. Having dealt thus with the lady's 'luminary' (her sun or moon) he goes on to deal with her crown of stars. In so doing he continues to bear the divine Glory in mind. The jasper-like presence of iv. 3 was surrounded by a ring of twice twelve enthroned elders. St. John, by interposing apostle-foundations between the tribe- or patriarch-gates, surrounds the city also with a double twelve. The patriarchs and apostles have all the dignity of eldership; the apostles had been enthroned by the Lord (Matt. xix. 28) in, or beside, the thrones of the patriarchs.

15 And he that spake with me had a measure, a golden reed to measure
16 the city and the gates thereof and the wall thereof. And the city

THE HEAVENLY MAN

lieth foursquare; the length thereof as large as the breadth. And he measured the city with the reed, twelve thousand furlongs; the length and the breadth and the height of it are equal. And he 17 measured the wall thereof, a hundred and forty and four cubits, by the measure of a man, that is, an angel. And the building of the 18 wall of it was jasper; and the city was pure gold, like unto pure glass. The foundations of the wall of the city were garnished with 19 all manner of precious stones. The first foundation was jasper, the second sapphire, the third chalcedony; the fourth was emerald, the fifth sardonyx, the sixth sardius; the seventh was chrysolite, 20 the eighth beryl, the ninth topaz; the tenth was chrysoprase, the eleventh jacinth, the twelfth amethyst. And the twelve gates were 21 twelve pearls, every several gate of one pearl.

St. John's approach to the city has brought him to the walls and gates, that is, to the very last piece of Ezekiel's vision. After listing the gates, Ezekiel adds 'the periphery is eighteen thousand', a remark only intelligible in relation to the measuring angel and the 'reeds' in which he measures. One is, in fact, referred back to the beginning of the vision: 'A man, the look of him like the look of shining brass, with a line of flax and a measuring reed in his hand' (xl. 3). St. John begins again from there, but the measures he gives are those of the walls and gates, not those of the temple or its courts, which Ezekiel's angel was chiefly and first concerned to measure. But then St. John himself has measured them in xi. 1–2. His purpose there was to discriminate between the holy and the profane and to show that, because not all was holy, profanity would trample holiness. Now, by contrast, all is holy save the outer darkness of Gehenna, quite beyond the walls (xxii. 14–15). The whole city is measured for consecration; there is no reserved area of special holiness within it (verse 22).

St. John gives two measures, neither of which is Ezekiel's. Having said that the city is a square, equal in length and breadth, he says that the angel measured it 'to an extent of 12,000 stades'. He then goes on to say that its *height* is the same—it is a cube. Now a cube has twelve edges; so if it is measured along all of them, so as to be marked off and hallowed in its entirety, the measuring-rod will have covered 144,000 stades. 144,000 is the sacred number of God's Israel, that Israel which the city is, or contains; and St. John goes on to state the number for us in the measure of the wall—144 cubits. Are we to understand that the height or the thickness of the wall is meant? Ezekiel's angel measures thicknesses mostly; St. John has proposed to measure the city, its gates and its walls, and the second item in the programme will not have been covered unless to measure the walls *is* to measure the depth of the gate-openings. The city of God may well be walled 144 cubits thick. 'And when I say cubit,' St. John continues, 'I mean the cubit, or forearm of a person, that is, of the angel.' It is just possible to render 'In human measure, which is what the angel used'. But St. John cannot, surely, want to tell us that the dimensions he is giving us are literal human measure; he may well wish to suggest that everything in New Jerusalem is proportioned to angelic stature. 'Height of stature' was one of the glories which, according to rabbinic lore, man was to recover in the world to come. According to St. Luke, Christ said that those who can die no more will be *isangelic* (Luke xx. 36).

What can St. John mean by saying that the city's height is equal to her length and breadth? Perhaps it is most reasonable to see the height as that of a great acropolis, crowned with walls. St. John no doubt wants the cube for its own sake. It is a shape mathematically perfect, like the sphere; it symbolizes, as we have explained, the completeness of the number of the elect; it is the form of the Holy of Holies (1 Kings vi. 20) and as such appears as the central feature of Ezekiel's city (Ezek. xli. 4).

Isaiah lxi. 3, 10 can be quoted in support of St. John's describing the walls as the adornment of a bride; and it seems natural to take up the same prophet's further testimony, that they are set with jewels (liv. 11, 12). St. John begins by saying that the *endōmēsis* of the wall is jasper. The meaning of the word is not certain; to say 'the *building* of the wall' tells us nothing. Since for St. John jasper is the most precious and 'divine' of stones, he can scarcely be saying that the core, or mass of the wall is jasper, embellished with the jewels he goes on to mention. He must surely mean that the visible superstructure raised on the twelve diverse foundations is all the colour of the divine glory. And this would agree with Isaiah's text, 'Thy battlements (*epalxeis*) of jasper.'

A Jerusalem walled with precious stones is a dream of the prophets; but the historian (1 Kings v. 17) records that Solomon had 'great stones and costly' hewn for the foundations of his temple; and the word 'costly' can just as well mean 'precious' in the technical sense. If we like, then, we can imagine Solomon's temple as an enormous jewel, for as it was built of 'precious' stones, so it was all lined with gold; and this will presumably be the model St. John follows, when he makes the city within its jasper walls to be of pure gold, clear, or bright, as glass.

Having stated that the walls are jewelled, and the interior golden, St. John proceeds to take up the two parts of his statement in turn. He begins with the jewelled periphery. Each of the twelve 'feet' by which the wall, continuous over the gate-arches, takes hold of the ground between them, is laid with a distinct precious stone, and bears the name of a distinct apostle. Now twelve different stones, bearing the names of the Sons of Israel (i.e. tribes) were sewn in four rows of three on the breastplate of Aaron, so that he might bear the names of the Sons of Israel on his heart, when he ministered (Exod. xxviii. 17, 29). If the four rows are taken to be arranged round the breastplate in a hollow square, then Aaron carries the plan of New Jerusalem on his heart—except that the names of the tribes are now on the gates; their companion-apostles are inscribed on the jewel-foundations.

St. John does not adhere either to the order or to the names of the stones in the LXX Greek of Exodus, and any query we may raise about translations of the Hebrew names which he might have preferred to those offered by the LXX can only land us in an abyss of uncertainty. It is reasonable to suppose that he did not trouble to do more than give a euphonious list in some general correspondence with the Exodus catalogue. He has so arranged the Greek names, as to emphasize the division by threes. All but three of them end with *s* sounds, and the three exceptions with *n* sounds. He has placed the *n* endings at the points of division, thus: Jaspis, sapphiros, chalcedon; smaragdos, sardonyx, sardion; chrysolithos, beryllos, topazion; chrysoprasos, hyacinthos, amethystos. Why should he trouble to do more? If he had made a list perfectly worked out, what could it have done but answer exactly to the list of tribes which he has already arranged for us in vii? And how would our wisdom be increased by that? St. John wishes to give body to his vision by listing the tribes; but he has already listed the tribes. So he lists stones which (as we know from Exodus) are to be deemed equivalent to the tribes. He makes two points: first, that the names of the apostles can be substituted for those of the tribes—and, after all, the new mystical twelvefold Israel is more truly to be described as companies gathered round the Apostles, than as the actual descendants of Reuben, Simeon, Levi, and the rest. Second, he puts the jasper up to be head of the list and so, no doubt, to stand for Judah and its apostle (cf. vii. 5). And jasper is both the general stuff of the walls above, and the colour of the divine glory. The meaning of the allegory is plain. Messiah is the chief corner-stone; it is by being founded on him that the whole city, or Church, acquires the substance and colour of the divine glory.

Each gate is a single pearl. It is, presumably, the sole entrance for the man assigned to any given tribe. Did not the Lord say that entrance to the Kingdom of Heaven was that single pearl of great price, which the prudent merchant would sell all he had, to buy? (Matt. xiii. 46). These are the true riches, not that list of precious things which went to the mart of Babylon, and which occupied the same central place in the taunting of the harlot (xviii. 12–13) as the list of jewels occupies in the praise of the bride. This contrast between the true and false riches is another of the themes which pass over from the Last Message (iii. 17–18) to the last vision-series of the apocalypse.

22 And the street of the city was pure gold, as it were transparent glass. And I saw no temple therein, for the Lord God Almighty
23 and the Lamb are the temple of it. And the city hath no need of the sun, neither of the moon, to shine upon it; for the glory of God
24 hath lightened it, and the lamp thereof is the Lamb. And the nations shall walk by the light of it, and the kings of the earth
25 bring their glory into it. And the gates of it shall not be shut at all
26 by day—for there shall be no night there—and they shall bring the
27 glory and honour of the nation into it; and there shall in no wise enter into it anything unclean, or any man that worketh abomination or falsehood; but only they that are written in the Lamb's book of life.

Having finished with the jewels in the walls, St. John takes up the second part of the sentence in verse 18 above, and proceeds to the gold-lined interior of the city. He says of the main street, or square, what he there said of her inward aspect altogether; it is transparent gold. He turns next to the only feature of the city-centre that we could expect him to single out. In the street or square, he says, where you might look to find it, there is no temple. There is, however, the divine presence, enthroned, according to xxii. 1, in the midst of this same street or square.

The absence of a temple cannot surprise us, where all ground is holy and there are no veils between God and his saints. What may surprise us is that there ever was a temple in heaven; are walls interposed between God and his angels? But a little reflection will remind us that the heavenly temple has always been mentioned in connexion with a cult designed to implore the intervention of God upon earth, or to give that intervention effect. Heaven is a temple to which men's prayers gain access through angelic priests; which sometimes seems closed from us, but at other times thrown open to send forth the ministers of judgement, or the hasteners of advent. Once the history of salvation is achieved, there are no temple-doors for prayer to storm, or for mercy to throw wide; the blessed live always in the presence of God. In previous texts their perfect access has been described by saying that they are wholly within the temple and never go out (iii. 12, vii. 15). That is only to say in other words that their city of residence is their temple; it contains within it no temple whose walls or doors intervene between them and the God they adore. God is temple to the city, and the city is temple to God.

They have no need of any other temple, having the Godhead, nor any need of sun or moon, possessing Light himself. The prophecy is already contained in Isa. lx. 19. From the same chapter of the same prophet (3, 5, 11) we have nations and kings walking by Zion's light, bringing wealth and glory through gates which shut not night or day. St. John draws in verse 20 of the same chapter, to show that, the Lord being their everlasting light, there will be no night there, during which the gates might be conceivably barred.

St. John is content to accept from Isaiah the picture of an Israelite Zion, enriched by the tribute or the pious offerings of gentiles and kings, as they make their pilgrimages thither. The reality to which this corresponds is, doubtless, an Israel enlarged by the entry of converted nations, merged in her heavenly citizenship. It delights St. John to see them pouring in, though when he entertains the picture, he is seeing the future and everlasting reality as the goal of a pilgrimage trodden in the present time; and such appears to be the attitude of the author to the Hebrews in a passage like xii. 18-22. In discussing chapter vii above, we found there the same tendency to define the company of the elect in purely Israelite terms, and then to see the nations admitted.

The other side to the fact that the Gentiles bring in their honour and glory, is that they do not bring in their abominations. It is significant that where Isaiah lii. 1 excludes the uncircumcised, St. John excludes the unenrolled. The access of the Gentiles here is in strong contrast with their access in xi. 2. The mere presence of unregenerate heathen in the outer court spelled the ruin of Old Jerusalem; the New admits them sanctified, to her undivided precinct. St. John was to leave the court out in surveying the Holy Place; the angel-surveyor has taken in the whole city as hallowed. His line includes Gentile saints, but bars out of all Jerusalem everything profane, every worker of an abomination or a lie.

And he shewed me a river of water of life, clear as crystal, proceeding out of the throne of God and of the Lamb in the midst of the street thereof. And on either side of the river there was tree-of-life, bearing twelve fruitings, every month yielding its fruit, and the leaves of the tree for the healing of the nations; and there shall be no more anything accursed. And the throne of God and of the Lamb shall be in it, and his servants shall do him service, and shall

5 see his face; and his name shall be on their foreheads. And there shall be night no more; and they need no light of lamp, neither light of the sun; for the Lord God shall give them light; and they shall reign for ever and ever.

The river of water which according to Ezekiel xlvii. 1 comes out from under the temple threshold must issue from the throne; for the throne takes the place of the temple 'in the midst of the street'; whether that means 'in the middle of the square' or 'half-way down the High Street' one cannot say. The water 'flowing down the middle of the street' is not in St. John's Greek. Nor, surely, did St. John intend to say that *a* tree of life stood on either side of the water. 'Tree-of-life' without the article is to be taken as a collective, as we might say 'Both banks were planted with oak'. Ezekiel has 'trees in great number' on either side of the water. Ezekiel traces his river down from the city towards the Dead Sea; the trees are doubtless in the country beyond the walls. St. John's picture is indefinite; we go beyond the evidence in affirming that he plants his city with trees. In verse 14 below saints come to the tree of life (i.e. receive immortality) and so enter the gates.

The waters of Ezekiel are not called waters of life, but they act as such, healing the Dead Sea and making every live thing to abound. St. John takes 'water of life' from the parallel oracle of Zechariah (xiv. 8). The vital waters of Ezekiel carry 'every tree that is good for food' on their banks. The phrase echoes Paradise (Gen. ii. 9) and invites St. John to call the tree that 'tree of life' planted where a river went out of Eden to water the garden (ibid.). Is not this Paradise Regained? The leaves of the trees are for healing, simply, according to Ezekiel. The addition 'of the nations' results from an almost automatic symbolical development. The trees, says Ezekiel, bear fresh fruit every month—*twelve* fruitings, says St. John, underlining the appropriateness of such a yield to the nourishment of his twelvefold Israel: the fruit, then, to nourish Israel, the leaf to heal—the Gentiles! And they need healing, that is to say, purification, if they are to become pilgrims acceptable on Mt. Zion; cf. 2 Chron. xxx. 18–20. And so, as Zechariah says (xiv. 11) just after his prophecy of living waters, 'There shall be no thing accursed any more.'

'No death, no sorrow, crying or trouble' says the text St. John has been so vastly expanding (xxi. 3–5ᵃ); 'for the old has departed and he that sits upon the throne has said, I make all things new.' So now he passes back from the end of all things accursed to the enthroned presence which is the cause of all blessing and the heart of the vision here concluded. 'The throne of God and of the Lamb shall be there, and *his* servants shall worship *him*.' For the grammar of this, compare 'Measure the temple of God and the altar and the worshippers in *it*' (xi. 1). We must interpret 'The temple and the altar it contains, and the worshippers in it'. And so we must read here as though St. John had written 'The throne of God and of his Anointed shall be there, and his servants shall worship him'. That the worshipping of Christ is a worshipping of God, is a mystery set forth in xix. 10. 'Worship' here stands for a word which means 'do priestly service'. They are to be High Priests infinitely above Aaron, for they are to 'see God's face', as was true of him only in a figurative sense, when, wearing God's name upon his forehead, he appeared in the course of his priestly service yearly before the Mercy Seat of the Ark.

It was the privilege of Aaron and his brethren not only to wear the Name upon their foreheads, but also to 'put it upon the children of Israel, that God might bless them', using the well-known words: 'JHVH bless thee and keep thee, JHVH shine his face upon thee and be gracious to thee, JHVH lift his face upon thee and give thee peace' (Num. vi. 22–27).

It was but a foretaste of the day when his Name shall be on all their foreheads, and he shall so shine his face upon them that they need neither lamplight nor sunlight, but, by the imparted splendour of his royalty, they reign for ever and ever; not through lordship over other men, for all that are not lost are fellow-kings; but through union with the will by which all things are, and were created.

And he said unto me, These words are faithful and true; and the 6 Lord God of the spirits of the prophets hath sent his angel to shew his servants what things must shortly come to pass. And 7 behold, I come quickly. Blessed is he that keepeth the words of the prophecy of this book.

And I, John, am he that heard and saw these things. And when 8 I heard and saw, I fell down to worship at the feet of the angel that shewed me these things. And he saith unto me, See thou do it not; 9 I am a fellowservant with thee and with thy brethren the prophets, and with them which keep the words of this book; worship God.

In the last three verses of the previous paragraph a text which began with vision ran off into prediction, through a casual link. 'The leaves are for healing . . . and [so] there *shall be* nothing any more accursed; the throne of God *shall be* in her', &c. The change of presentation enables St. John to show the heavenly hope as what it essentially is—divine promise; he does not call on us to trust his visionary experiences, but the testimony of Christ which has taken visual form in his ecstasy. Through falling into the predictive form he falls into line also with what he had written at xxi. 3–5ª. He can now quite naturally take up xxi. 5ᵇ, 'Write that these *words* are trustworthy (faithful) and true.' That text is itself, as we saw, an echo of xix. 9–10 and St. John now sees back through the copy to the original. In xix the asseveration was associated with two striking features; a beatitude, and St. John's becoming aware of the angel who inspired him. Both these features now return, with a difference. St. John is bringing his book to a close; his revived consciousness of the angel becomes a reflection on the way in which his whole revelation has been given him, and the beatitude a blessing of those who receive it. When he turns back to add an afterthought-title or foreword to his book (i. 1–3) he will write it very largely out of this passage.

There is no reason to mark an end to the speech of the heavenly voice of 6, which speaks through the angel; not, for example, between the 'I come quickly' and the beatitude. The logic of the connexions can be appreciated from the following translation: '. . . has sent his angel to show his servants what must happen with speed—And indeed I come speedily!—Happy is the man who keeps the words of the prophecy of this book.' The beatitude appears once more to be the occasion of St. John's falling on his knees before the angel. As in the beginning of the book, he names himself as witness.

'The Lord God of the spirits of the prophets' echoes 'The testimony of Jesus is the spirit of prophecy' (xix. 10)—the spirit, or breath of inspiration, in any one prophet, and so the 'spirits' in them all. For this plural see 1 Corinthians xiv. 32, and the discussion on p. 61 above. In every act of prophetic inspiration we have to recognize (1) the God who speaks, (2) the Christ who is his living word, (3) the breath of spirit which passes to the prophet, and (4) the angel who communicates it.

As happened in xix the effect of the angel's refusal of worship is that he gives place to the *martyria*, the witness of Jesus. In xix Jesus came forward as the champion of all martyrs, leading them to a final victory; here he comes forward as the divine revealer, witnessing all prophecy: the sum and substance of it being the very thing which was there shown fulfilled—'Lo, I come quickly' (7 and 12).

10 And he saith unto me, Seal not up the words of the prophecy of
11 this book; for the time is at hand. He that is unrighteous, let him do unrighteousness still, and he that is filthy, let him grow filthy still; and he that is righteous, let him work righteousness still, and
12 he that is holy be hallowed still. Behold, I come quickly, and my

THE HEAVENLY MAN

reward is with me, to pay every man as his work is. I am the Alpha 13
and the Omega, the first and the last, the beginning and the end.
Blessed are they that wash their robes, that they may have right to 14
the tree of life, and enter by the gates into the city. Without are the 15
dogs and sorcerers, the whoremongers and murderers, the idolaters
and everyone that loveth or worketh a lie.

We must continue to refuse every temptation to distribute the text among several speakers. One inspired utterance runs on—it is John's, the angel's, Christ's—but fundamentally, Christ's.

The mention in verse 9 of those who keep the words of this book refers the speaker back to 7, where 'the words of the prophecy of this book' are connected with 'Lo, I come quickly'. The connexion is developed in 10-12. Because Christ comes quickly—because the time is near—the book is of immediate concern to St. John's contemporaries; it is not to be sealed up and put away for use in 'the times of the end', as Daniel's was (Dan. viii. 26, xii. 4 and 9). Indeed, these are the very days for which Daniel wrote, and St. John has been inspired to 'unseal' him.

After the last verse cited from Daniel (xii. 9) Daniel's angel goes on to predict that many shall purify themselves and be made white, but that the wicked shall do wickedly. The LXX Greek has it that the book is sealed *until* men shall have taken these diverse courses; and St. John's imperative verbs (verse 11) are to be taken in a corresponding sense. The culmination of iniquity in the kingdom of Antichrist and of righteousness in the testimony of the saints being the preconditions of Christ's advent, it is possible to wish for the fulfilment of the conditions, that the end may come. By praying that the world may come out black and white, so as to be ripe for judgement, we need not express the criminal desire that any soul capable of repentance should persist in sin.

Christ will come with recompense appropriate both to the sheep and to the goats—and so blessed are those who 'purify themselves and are made white' in Daniel's phrase—in St. John's, those who wash their robes. They eat the fruit of immortality and pass the gates of the city; the 'dogs' remain in outer darkness (14-15). i. 8 and xxi. 6 show other examples of 'I am the A and the O' supporting the promise of advent; he who began the page of history will finish it. The title was virtually transferred to Christ at i. 18. Here the transference is made explicit.

I Jesus have sent my angel to testify these things unto you for the 16
churches. I am the root and offspring of David, the bright and

17 morning star. And the Spirit and the bride say, Come. And let him that is athirst come. And whosoever will, let him take the water of life freely.

The inspired utterance runs on without a break. Jesus authenticates his words 'for the churches' with a self-description reminiscent of those which introduced the seven messages to churches, and all the more so, since it picks up one of the blessings those messages contained (ii. 28). The self-description is suggested by the promise just given—access to the tree of life. Surely Jesus is the reality for which the tree stands; to eat of the tree is to be fed with Christ's resurrection (John vi. 57). Yes, Jesus is the shoot from Jesse, i.e. from David (Isa. xi. 1), called branch by Jeremiah (xxiii. 5, xxxiii. 15) and Zechariah (iii. 8, vi. 12), a word which can just as well mean 'dayspring', and does so in Luke i. 78—but then the shoot from Jesse is certainly the same as the rod or star from Jacob (Num. xxiv. 17). So that star must be the star *of the dayspring*—the bright morning star.

The substance of Christ's speech has been 'Lo, I come quickly and my reward is with me'. Christ calls upon the hearer to join in the 'Maranatha'—'Come, Lord!'—with which the inspired Church greets the promise of his advent. The Spirit and the bride are one voice—what inspiration prompts, the body utters. Every single hearer of the book has but to add his prayer, and it is granted; he has free access to the fountain of immortality (Isa. lv. 1). The idea is expressed by an inversion of the 'Come'. He who prays that Christ should come, comes to Christ, and drinks the water of life. Compare the inversion in iii. 20–21. Is it simply a dramatic way of saying that his prayer brings the Christ who brings the living water at his coming? Or does the thirsty soul, by spiritual anticipation, drink living water now, with the Samaritaness of John iv. 14? The language suggests it, but the point is not developed.

18 I testify unto every man that heareth the words of the prophecy of this book, if any man addeth unto them, God shall add unto him
19 the plagues that are written in this book; and if any man taketh away from the words of the book of this prophecy, God shall take away his part in the tree of life and in the holy city, which are written in this book.
20 He which testifieth these things saith, Yea, I come quickly. Amen; come, Lord Jesus.
21 The grace of the Lord Jesus be with you all.

That the 'I' who testifies in 18 is still Jesus, is virtually stated in 20. Since the warning is addressed to *hearers*, it is not naturally to be taken as a warning against alteration of the text but as a warning against the impiety of comments, mental or spoken, which alter the word of God by omission or addition. To understand the word of God will commonly be to let it grow in one's mind—St. John's whole book is an example—but the genuine growth of the heavenly seed is something different from a fabrication of additions out of one's own head. St. John's text here combines the *prohibition* of any increasing or diminution of the words of God according to Deuteronomy iv. 2, xii. 32 with the *threat* contained in Deuteronomy xxix. 20 that the curses written in the book will fall on the head that defies its warnings.

St. John concludes with a repetition of the advent promise and with his own 'Amen, Maranatha!' Cf. v. 14–vi. 1.

Verse 21 is very variously transcribed in our manuscripts. Supposing that it is genuine, it is the conclusion not to the apocalypse as such, but to the epistle containing it; see i. 4–8. It is Pauline in style; see the endings of 1 Corinthians and of the Thessalonian Epistles. 1 Corinthians actually has 'Maranatha! The grace of the Lord Jesus Christ be with you.'

INDEX

Genesis i. 1, pp. 63, 82
i. 1–3, p. 197
i. 14, p. 68
ii. 9, p. 222
iii. 13–15, p. 153
iii. 15, p. 150
iv. 10, p. 102
xv. 5, p. 110
xix. 28, p. 163
xxii, p. 46
xxii. 13, p. 94
xxii. 16, p. 94
xxix–xxx, p. 107
xxxii. 28, p. 74
xxxv. 16–26, p. 107
xlix. 9–10, p. 93
xlix. 9–12, p. 111
xlix. 17, p. 108
Exodus iii. 14–15, p. 61
vii. 19, p. 114
viii. 5, p. 114
viii. 7, p. 177
viii. 16, p. 114
ix. 8, pp. 114, 119
ix. 10–11, p. 175
ix. 15–16, p. 119
ix. 22, p. 114
ix–x, p. 100
x. 6, p. 119
x. 12, p. 114
x. 14, p. 119
x. 21, p. 114
xv, pp. 171, 192
xix. 4, p. 148
xix. 6, p. 62
xix. 13, pp. 65, 87
xix. 16, p. 90
xix. 19, pp. 65, 87
xxii. 1, p. 157
xxv. 40, p. 214
xxviii. 17, 29, p. 219
xxxii. 32–33, p. 209
Leviticus xxiii. 9, p. 165
xxiv. 10–11, p. 108
xxv. 9, p. 112
Numbers x. 2, p. 112
xiv. 33, p. 168
xvi. 28–33, p. 201
xvi. 32, p. 148
xxii–xxiv, p. 74
xxv, p. 74
xxi. 8, p. 74
Deuteronomy iv. 2, p. 227
x. 17, p. 186

xii. 32, p. 227
xiii. 1–5, p. 136
xvii. 6, p. 132
xix. 15, p. 132
xxv. 3, p. 168
xxix. 20, p. 227
xxxii. 33, p. 163
xxxii. 44, pp. 171 f.
Joshua vi, pp. 137–38
Judges v. 19–21, p. 178
2 Samuel xxii. 5, p. 148
xxiv. 8–9, p. 106
1 Kings v. 17, p. 218
vi. 20, p. 218
vii. 21, p. 81
x. 18, p. 208
xii. 26, p. 157
xii. 28–30, p. 108
xvii. 2–4, 8–9, p. 149
xviii. 20, p. 178
xxii, p. 178
2 Kings i. 4, p. 77
vii. 1, p. 100
ix. 22, p. 77
xiii. 15–17, p. 99
1 Chron. xxiv. 4–6, p. 89
xxix. 11, p. 96
2 Chron. iv. 6–7, p. 90
xxx. 18–20, p. 222
xxxv. 20–25, p. 178
Esther i ff., p. 117
ix. 22, p. 135
Job iii. 21, p. 119
xxvi. 6, p. 119
xxviii. 22, p. 119
xl. 15–xli. 34, p. 143
Psalm ii, pp. 57, 76, 137 ff.
vi. 3, p. 101
xviii. 4, p. 148
xxxiii. 3, p. 96
xlv. 3, p. 119
lv. 6–7, p. 148
lxix. 28, p. 209
lxxii. 17, p. 82
lxxiv. 9–10, p. 101
lxxiv. 14, p. 144
lxxix. 1–3, p. 135
lxxx. 4, p. 101
lxxxviii. 11, p. 119
lxxxix. 27, p. 61
lxxxix. 37, pp. 61, 82
xc. 4, p. 204
cv. 30, p. 177
cxv. 5, 7, p. 156

Psalms (cont.):
cxv. 13, p. 192
cxviii. 24, p. 192
cxviii. 25, 27, p. 111
cxxx. 16–17, p. 156
cxli. 2, p. 96
cxliv. 9, p. 96
Proverbs viii. 22, p. 82
xxx. 27, p. 119
Isaiah i. 8–10, p. 135
ii. 10, p. 104
vi. 1–3, p. 88
viii. 8, p. 212
ix. 1–2, pp. 82, 94
xi. 2, pp. 61, 76, 226
xi. 4, p. 68
xi. 15, p. 176
xxi. 6–9, p. 163
xxi. 8–9, p. 190
xxi. 9–10, p. 165
xxii. 22, pp. 69, 80
xxiii. 15, p. 187
xxiii. 17, p. 183
xxiv. 23, pp. 88–89
xxvi. 16–xxvii. 1, p. 143
xxvii. 1, p. 202
xxviii. 13, p. 112
xxix. 11–12, p. 93
xxx. 33, p. 201
xxxiv. 4, pp. 103, 201
xxxiv. 9–10, p. 164
xxxiv. 10, p. 189
xliv. 6, p. 63
xlviii. 12, p. 63
xlix. 16, p. 214
liii. 7–9, p. 161
liv. 11–12, p. 218
lv. 1, p. 226
lx. 3–20, p. 221
lxi. 3, pp. 212, 218
lxi. 10, pp. 212, 218
lxii. 1, p. 221
lxii. 1–2, p. 75
lxiii. 1–6, pp. 197 f.
lxv. 13–22, p. 212
lxv. 15, p. 75
lxvi. 7–8, p. 144
lxvi. 24, p. 201
Jeremiah i. 9–10, p. 127
iv. 15, p. 108
iv. 31, p. 143
viii. 16, p. 108
xv. 2, p. 154
xxiii. 5, pp. 76, 226
xxiii. 15, p. 226
xxiv, p. 83
xxv. 10, p. 191
xxxiii. 11, p. 191
xxxiii. 14–26, p. 133
xxxiii. 15, p. 76

xliii. 8–13, p. 190
l. 38, p. 176
li. 6–9, p. 189
li. 7, p. 183
li. 7–8, p. 163
li. 13, pp. 183, 189
li. 45, 48, p. 189
li. 59–64, p. 190
Ezekiel i. 4–28, p. 88
i. 7, p. 68
i. 10, p. 99
i. 12–13, p. 90
i. 26, p. 66
i–iii, p. 129
ii. 9–10, p. 93
ii–iii, p. 19
iv. 10, p. 100
vi. 11, p. 98
ix, p. 105
x. 1–7, p. 173
x. 14, p. 99
xlv. 12–23, p. 100
xiv. 21, p. 99
xvi, p. 187
xxiii, p. 187
xxvi–xxvii, p. 189
xxxv–xlviii, p. 204
xxxvii. 27, p. 212
xxxix. 17–20, p. 201
xl. 3, p. 217
xl–xlviii, p. 129
xli. 4, p. 218
xliii, p. 66
xlvii, p. 167
xlvii. 1, p. 222
xlviii. 35, p. 81
Daniel i. 12, 14, p. 73
ii, p. 20
ii. 1–24, p. 93
ii. 46, p. 194
ii. 47, p. 186
iii. 25, pp. 67, 76
iv. 4–8, p. 93
iv. 13, p. 123
iv. 13–14, p. 93
iv. 30, p. 163
v. 5–17, p. 93
vi. 17, p. 202
vi. 24, p. 202
vii, pp. 20, 53, 58
vii. 2–21, p. 135
vii. 8, p. 153
vii. 9, p. 66
vii. 9–14, pp. 88–89
vii. 10, p. 209
vii. 12, p. 202
vii. 13, p. 95
vii. 13–14, pp. 62, 66
viii, p. 20
viii. 3, p. 155

INDEX 231

Daniel (cont.):
viii. 10, p. 144
viii. 16, p. 123
viii. 17-18, p. 69
viii. 26, p. 225
ix, pp. 7, 8, 20
ix. 21, p. 123
x, p. 66
x, 5-6, pp. 67-68
x. 8-10, p. 69
x. 13, 21, p. 147
x-xii, p. 20
xi. 1, p. 147
xi. 30, p. 147
xi. 35, pp. 79, 110
xii, p. 123
xii. 1, pp. 79, 209
xii. 1-3, p. 110
xii. 2, p. 206
xii. 4, 9, pp. 124, 225
Hosea ii, 23, p. 212
x. 8, p. 104
oel i. 6, p. 119
ii. 2, p. 119
ii. 4-5, p. 119
ii. 10-11, p. 119
ii. 30, p. 114
ii. 31, p. 103
iii. 13, p. 166
Amos i. 2, p. 124
iii. 4-8, p. 124
iv. 10-11, p. 135
Micah iv. 9-10, p. 143
vii. 1-2, p. 83
Zephaniah iii. 13, p. 161
Zechariah i, p. 101
i. 7-17, p. 99
iii. 2, p. 67
iii. 8, pp. 76, 226
iii. 8-10, p. 95
iii-iv, p. 99
iv. 1-2, p. 65
iv. 4-10, p. 95
iv. 14, p. 133
vi. 12, pp. 76, 95, 226
xii. 8-14, p. 178
xii. 10-14, p. 62
xiv. 2-4, p. 201
xiv. 3-5, p. 179
xiv. 8, p. 222
xiv. 11, p. 222
Tobit viii. 3, p. 202
Wisdom xvi-xix, p. 43
xviii. 15-16, pp. 30, 198
xviii. 18, p. 68
Ecclesiasticus xlviii. 1, p. 133
1 Enoch xlviii. 2-3, p. 82
lxvi, p. 105
Mishna Aboth ii. 19-20, p. 165
Menahoth x, p. 165

Sibyllina v. 1-50, p. 34
Matthew i. 23-ii. 23, p. 31
i. 25, p. 144
ii, p. 76
ii. 13, p. 144
iv. 15-16, p. 82
vii. 15, p. 155
vii. 27, p. 186
x. 34, p. 98
xiii. 18-23, p. 166
xiii. 37-42, p. 166
xiii. 46, p. 219
xvi. 18, p. 216
xvi. 19, p. 80
xviii. 18, p. 216
xix. 28, pp. 206, 216
xx. 2, p. 100
xxiii. 4, p. 77
xxiii. 29-36, pp. 102, 116
xxiii. 39, p. 43
xxiv. 6-14, p. 98
xxiv. 14, p. 105
xxiv-15, p. 32
xxiv. 15-22, p. 136
xxiv. 16-18, p. 134
xxiv. 18, p. 178
xxiv. 24, pp. 32, 74
xxiv. 28, p. 116
xxiv. 30, pp. 31, 62
xxiv. 31, p. 112
xxiv. 41, p. 191
xxv. 1-13, p. 89
xxv. 10, p. 161
xxvi. 52, p. 155
xxvii. 51, p. 179
Mark iv. 29, pp. 47, 166
ix. 4, p. 139
ix. 42, p. 191
xiii, p. 10
xiii. 14-15, p. 149
xiii. 22, pp. 74, 155
Luke i. 11, p. 139
i. 78, pp. 76, 226
iv. 25, p. 132
x. 18, p. 146
xx. 36, p. 218
xxi. 20-24, p. 136
xxi. 24, p. 32
xxii. 43, p. 139
xxiv. 34, p. 139
John i-xx, p. 41
i. 1-3, pp. 45, 197
i. 4-9, p. 66
i. 15, p. 45
i. 18, pp. 45, 88
i. 29, pp. 45, 94
i. 32-33, p. 45
i. 36, p. 94
i. 47-48, p. 45
ii. 1-11, p. 45

232   INDEX

John (cont.):
  ii. 6, p. 45.
  ii. 20, p. 45
  ii. 24–25, p. 45
  iii. 8, p. 78
  iii. 12–13, p. 88
  iii. 13, p. 125
  iii. 29, p. 45
  iv. 14, p. 226
  iv. 17–18, p. 45
  iv. 20–24, p. 160
  iv. 29, p. 45
  iv. 33, p. 47
  iv. 34–38, p. 165
  v. 2, 5, p. 45
  v. 31–39, p. 133
  v. 33–35, p. 66
  vi, p. 44
  vi. 7, 9, 13, p. 45
  vi. 27–29, p. 165
  vi. 30–63, p. 75
  vi. 31, p. 45
  vi. 57, p. 226
  vii. 30–36, p. 145
  vii. 32–36, p. 47
  vii. 37–38, p. 48
  vii. 44–46, p. 47
  vii. 52–53, p. 82
  viii. 12, p. 48
  viii. 12–14, p. 66
  viii. 14, p. 145
  viii. 17–18, p. 132
  viii. 21–23, p. 47
  viii. 21–24, p. 145
  viii. 34–44, p. 45
  viii. 57, p. 45
  ix. 4, p. 165
  ix. 35–x. 9, p. 80
  x. 1–9, p. 45
  x. 29–30, p. 46
  xii. 1, p. 43
  xii. 28, p. 46
  xii. 35–36, p. 145
  xii. 36–50, p. 43
  xiii–xvi, p. 49
  xiii–xvii, p. 48
  xiii–xx, p. 43
  xiii. 33, p. 47
  xiv. 1–6, p. 145
  xiv. 7–9, p. 88
  xiv. 23, p. 47
  xiv. 30–31, pp. 47, 145
  xv. 27, p. 45
  xvi. 1–3, p. 45
  xvi. 10–11, p. 47
  xvi. 19–22, p. 47
  xvi. 20, p. 136
  xvi. 33, p. 45

  xvii. 11–12, p. 46
  xix. 14–18, p. 46
  xix. 26–27, p. 47
  xix. 31–36, p. 46
  xix. 37, pp. 63, 136
  xx. 16, p. 65
  xxi, p. 41
  xxi. 11, p. 45
  xxi. 24, p. 41
Acts xi. 28, p. 29
  xv. 10, p. 77
  xv. 28, pp. 31, 77
  xv. 39–40, p. 132
  xxi. 10–11, p. 29
Romans iv. 11, p. 105
  viii. 31–39, p. 146
  viii. 32, p. 94
1 Cor. v–x, pp. 74, 77
  vi. 2, p. 205
  vi. 2–3, p. 89
  vi. 15–20, p. 161
  x. 1–2, p. 171
  xiv. 32, p. 61
  xv. 22–28, p. 203
  xv. 26, p. 210
  xvi. 22–23, p. 227
2 Cor. i. 21–22, p. 105
  iii, p. 134
  vi. 15, p. 148
  xi. 2, p. 161
  xii, p. 38
  xii. 2–4, p. 4
Galatians i. 1–5, pp. 60–62
Ephesians ii. 20, p. 216
Philippians ii. 17, p. 174
  iv. 3, p. 209
Colossians i. 16, p. 89
  i. 18, p. 61
  ii. 15, p. 197
  ii. 20–23, p. 77
  ii. 23, p. 38
1 Thessalonians iv. 16–17, pp. 112, 136
2 Thessalonians ii. 6–7, p. 105
1 Timothy v. 17, p. 93
Hebrews vii. 11–14, p. 108
  xi. 19, p. 94
  xii. 18–22, p. 221
James i. 18, p. 161
  iv. 13, p. 154
  v. 17, p. 132
1 Peter iii. 20–21, p. 158
2 Peter ii. 5, p. 158
  iii. 5–7, p. 213
  iii. 8, p. 204
1 John v. 7–9, p. 132
  v. 20–21, p. 195
Revelation[1] i, p. 14
  i–iii, pp. 10, 18

[1] Only the citations in the Introduction are indexed here.

Revelation (cont.):
i. 3, p. 28
i. 7, p. 31
i. 12–iii. 22, p. 45
i. 14, p. 37
i. 19–20, p. 27
ii–iii, pp. 9, 14, 49
ii. 1, p. 27
ii. 8, p. 27
ii. 12, p. 27
ii. 14, p. 38
ii. 18, p. 27
ii. 20, p. 38
iii. 1, p. 27
iii. 7, p. 27
iii. 14, p. 27
iii. 24, p. 31
iv, pp. 10, 14
iv–vii, p. 58
iv–xi, p. 18
v, pp. 14, 30, 45
vi. 1–11, p. 21
vi–vii, pp. 9, 10, 14
viii ff., p. 10
viii–xi, p. 14
viii–xiv, pp. 8, 9, 18, 43
viii. 2–xi. 18, p. 15
viii. 13, p. 17
x, pp. 17, 19
xi, pp. 10, 33, 46
xi. 15–19, pp. 17, 57
xii, pp. 20, 31
xii–xiii, pp. 10, 16, 17
xii–xiv, pp. 14, 57
xii. 1 ff., p. 56
xii. 1–6, p. 45
xii. 2, p. 32
xii. 10–12, p. 46
xii. 12, p. 17
xiii, p. 33
xiii. 1, pp. 52, 53
xiv, pp. 17, 20
xiv. 1–5, pp. 22, 45–46, 57
xiv. 6, p. 16
xiv. 6–20, p. 22
xiv. 13, p. 27
xiv. 14–16, pp. 45, 47
xiv. 20, p. 9
xv, p. 14
xv. 1, p. 21
xv–xxii, p. 18
xvi, pp. 14–15
xvi ff., p. 9
xvi. 15, p. 29
xvii, p. 18
xvii–xxii, p. 14
xvii. 10–11, pp. 32–34, 37
xviii. 1–xix. 5, p. 18
xix ff., p. 12
xix. 7–16, p. 45
xix. 9, p. 27
xix. 10, pp. 28, 38
xix. 11–15, p. 30
xix. 11–16, p. 22
xix. 15 ff., p. 56
xx. 1–10, p. 4
xxi–xxii, p. 48
xxi. 9 ff., p. 18
xxii. 6–20, p. 29
xxii. 8, p. 38
xxii. 9, p. 28
xxii. 18, p. 28

www.ingramcontent.com/pod-product-compliance
Lightning Source LLC
Chambersburg PA
CBHW070311230426
43663CB00011B/2087